Vincent C. Peloso

PEASANTS ON PLANTATIONS

Subaltern Strategies of Labor and Resistance

in the Pisco Valley, Peru

Duke University Press   Durham & London   1999

© 1999 Duke University Press

All rights reserved Printed in the United States

of America on acid-free paper ∞

Typeset in Sabon with Frutiger display by

Keystone Typesetting, Inc.

Library of Congress Cataloging-in-Publication

Data appear on the last printed page of

this book.

For Matteo Calzanera and

Antonio Núñez Pazos,

in memoriam

lo zio e lo zio politico

tutto due dedicati a la lotta del popolo,

eroi da giovane

CONTENTS

List of Maps, Tables, and Figures   ix

Preface   xi

Acknowledgments   xix

Introduction: *Peasants, Plantations, and Resistance*   1

1: *Planters, Managers, and Consent*   17

2: *Indenture, Wages, and Dominance*   34

3: *Stagnation, Recovery, and Peasant Opportunities*   55

4: *Plantation Growth and Peasant Choices*   81

5: *Yanaconas, Mechanization, and Migrant Labor*   109

6: *Yanaconas, Migrants, and Political Consciousness*   133

Conclusion: *Plantation Society and Peruvian Culture*   154

Notes   169

Glossary   209

Bibliography   215

Index   247

MAPS, TABLES, AND FIGURES

Maps
1. Peru   2
2. Department of Ica   3
3. Pisco River Basin   4
4. Land and Labor Use, Hacienda Palto, 1925   140–41

Tables
1.1 Administrators of Hacienda Palto, 1867–1940   19
3.1 Dominant Plantation Labor and Major Crops, Hacienda Palto, 1878–1908   57
3.2 Expansion of Rented Land, Hacienda Palto, 1886–89   61
3.3 "Dos de Mayo" Rent Increases, Hacienda Palto, 1893–94   68
4.1 Changes in Landholdings, Fixed Rent Tenants, Hacienda Palto, 1893–1913   106
4.2 Tenant Loans, Hacienda Palto, First Quarter (September), 1917–18   108
5.1 Cost of Producing 2.9 Hectares (1 Fanegada) of Cotton, Hacienda Palto, 1927   129
5.2 Per Tenant Cost of Producing 2.9 Hectares (1 Fanegada) of Cotton, Hacienda Palto, 1927   130
6.1 Total Land Planted in Cotton, Peru, 1930–40   135
6.2 Volume of Cotton Production, Ica Department, 1929–40   142
6.3 Cotton Prices and Wages, 1930–41   144

Figures
6.1 Cultivation Wages, Hacienda Palto, 1915–34   147
6.2 Total Raw Cotton Harvested, Hacienda Palto, 1915–34   152

PREFACE

A single two-lane road meanders through the Pisco valley along a river that flows from the Andes to the port of Pisco, about 220 kilometers south of Lima, Peru. The river's alluvial fan tilts northward, as if resisting its rush to the sea, and makes a broad arc twenty kilometers north and south of the main channel. Within these alluvial soils lie a series of vineyards and cotton and sugar plantations that in the century after independence were among the most important locales in the formation of Peruvian culture. Cotton plantations dominated the valley, and within their borders thousands of peasants annually cultivated and harvested cotton crops that returned large profits to the powerful landowners while the peasants remained destitute and powerless.[1]

Through the generosity of the office of the Tribunal of Agrarian Reform I had an opportunity in 1975 to visit some of the Pisco valley plantations. Two officers of the Fifth Agrarian Reform Zone office accompanied me in a Volkswagen Beetle, and on our approach to Hacienda Palto they summarized recent local events. Earlier that day agricultural workers had seized control of the plantation and notified the local agrarian reform office of their action. Now the workers were awaiting directions. Would they be paid if they went to work in the fields? How much, and who would pay them? The agrarian reform officers and I were visiting Hacienda Palto coincidentally with the takeover; we could not provide answers to those anxious queries.

The plantation house and the broad fields sweeping down toward the river below it caught my eye. With its long, low, pastel green ranch-style structure, red-tiled roof, lead-lined windows, porticoed patio, and pool, the mansion, both the color and style of it, appeared similar to the architecture commonly seen in the suburban southwestern United States. But the illusion of familiarity quickly ended. The roadside facade of the house contrasted sharply with its riverward side. Three floors deep, the plantation house featured a wide veranda along the entire second floor and dominated the landscape before it. This grandiloquent deteriorated plantation house once served as an idyllic *palmar,* as a nineteenth-century observer expressed it, an oasis in the country for its owners, the Aspíllaga family, one of the two or three dozen richest families in mid-twentieth-century Peru.

Deterioration was a visible testament to the end of the rule of great landowners — or so it seemed. Although the agrarian reform had ushered in a new stage in the modern history of Peru, the reform was bothersome in that it had been announced and executed not by a democratic reform government but rather by an authoritarian military regime. It was an unusual military dictatorship, pledged to carry out social reforms that weak democratic governments had not cared — much less dared — to support. But its agrarian reform was foundering on an authoritarian handling of land distribution. Few peasant leaders and organizations had been consulted prior to the pronouncement of the agrarian reform, and peasants were divided on its worth. Some were said to broadly support the plan spelled out by the military populist government of General Juan Velasco Alvarado; others claimed that it left much to be desired.[2]

By seizing control of the planation, then waiting for the government's imprimatur, the Pisco farmworkers evinced a deep-seated ambivalence toward authority. The sources of this social tradition have not been well studied by Peruvianists. Notably, the peasants had not mounted a serious challenge on the land question until some time after the planters had begun to lose their grip on power. Now alternately revealing defiance and humility, the fieldworkers displayed considerable ambivalence about their own actions.

Ambivalence and uncertainty were in keeping with the long history of struggle by peasants with plantations in the coastal valleys of the country. Indeed, the negotiation of power in the countryside of Peru seemed to have been a key to the successful growth of plantations. To explain this paradox, I had first to pass through a number of intervening hoops. It seemed important that I turn my attention less to the export orientation of commercial plantations than to the social order that had evolved within them. I found it puzzling that scholars had readily designated the field hands on the plantations — especially the cotton plantations — generally as labor. I suspected that this generalization missed the mark, and I speculated that a large literature thus had been overlooked, a literature that would characterize this social order as something more complex and subtle than a massive wage gang. As I studied it further, plantation society appeared to be made up of a number of different social segments whose association with cotton growing varied from one group to another. Rather than speak of wage labor, I would have to study the means available to peasants for coaxing a livelihood from plantation fields. But this led to further confusion. It appeared as I read that wage laborers and peasants shared the same tasks and worked the same fields. Yet there seemed to be differences between them. Were these distinctions important? Were there further segmentations within rural society, even within the peasantry? If different interest groups existed within the peasantry, what were the sources of those interests? What social dynamics propelled this world?

Prevailing conventions about the peasantry spanned a number of issues. Debt was one of them. Debt had been seen as an instrument of landowner power, a means for holding peasants in bondage. But how debt worked its ways within a segmented peasantry was not clear. Did some peasants feel the weight of debt less drastically, for example, and if so what mitigated the effects? The scant evidence suggested that little was known about how the peasants viewed debt. But mid-nineteenth-century social relations led me to assume that a modest pyramid of wealth and power had already existed in the countryside, permitting some peasants to avoid debt while leaving others mired in its intricacies and social stigmata.

Which peasants avoided debt and how they made such calculations were not clear. At first, shortly after the abolition of slavery (1854) and then of indenture (1874) in Peru, they apparently refused tenant contracts that might have meant their reconfinement within the intolerable plantations. After the War of the Pacific (1879–83) the peasants became more self-confident, their attitudes toward debt changed, and many now sought out contracts to rent land. There was more to the history of peasants on plantations than first met the eye.

In order to improve my grasp of peasant economic behavior on the cotton plantations, it was necessary to learn why contracts looked attractive. Peasants who rented land had taken a great risk in subordinating themselves to the landowners, but by this point it had become clear that subordination to the landowners did not mean reenslavement. Tenants began to realize that tenantry was a flexible condition and, more important, that it would allow them to make many of their own farming decisions. Ironically, the plantations may have provided the peasants with choices not previously available.[3] Joseph D. Reid Jr. and José María Caballero have suggested that in these circumstances peasants almost always were faced with a range of farming choices, and that choice was fundamental to successful tenantry.[4] But it seemed that the landowners also deliberately left many decisions to be made by those who worked the land. Thus a critical part of my task would be to explain the context in which peasants took up the challenge of farming. If I linked context and choice I might illuminate the formative role of the plantations in the evolution of Peruvian culture.

Another problem I faced was the question of violence and repression. Was it not obvious that the planters dictated and the peasants obeyed? It disturbed me to learn that the answer to this question was not easy to come by. For the most part, peasants stepped warily through social life on the plantations. They engaged the owners and managers in dialogue through the well-known conventions of countryside social behavior. Such conventions, often small rituals, eased the tensions that arose periodically on the plantations and provided outlets for the worn tempers, deep hatreds, and resentments that otherwise might disrupt the pursuit of commercial farming.

Polite public exchanges and the rites of *compadrazgo*—informal kinship—were two of the rural institutions that accompanied plantation growth, limiting its worst excesses and lending an air of dignity to a process that otherwise generated great social traumas.[5] Whether in casual conversation, contract negotiations, or haggling over rent, correct manners ruled over the discourse of plantation life. Most of the time this was true of the correspondence between owners and managers, and it even appeared to hold for the rare conversations that occurred between owners and the subordinate peasant population. Managers for the most part (save when they lost their composure) also addressed the peasants with respectful language and heard the same in return.

Tension between the need to control labor and its nearly constant scarcity could become unbearable. Sometimes managers used physical violence to enforce the cotton plantation rules. Although owners tried to hold such incidents to a minimum, the palpable contempt in which managers held the tenants led, unsurprisingly, to abuses of authority. What forms did these abuses take? Was it simple physical force? Or were more subtle measures involved? If they took verbal forms, might they also involve deception, exaggeration, and falsification, as some prominent studies suggest, and if so how did the peasants respond? Did they act "rationally" on false information, or did they respond in kind?[6]

What we have learned about landowners is that they preferred to rule with courtesy and benevolence rather than with force; to reward as much as they punished; to instill the idea in the daily routine of the fieldworker that the landowner was aware of his burden and sympathized with his plight. Many planters sought to project the image that a good landowner was like a good father, kind but stern; predictably insistent that the rules of production be enforced but willing to be lenient in exceptional circumstances. Planters cultivated the aura of fatherhood as an appropriate metaphor; it fit with the idea that peasants were like children: unruly, petulant, unpredictable, easily distracted, and slothful if the planter did not constantly remind them of their duties. Students of plantation society will recognize immediately that this description is longhand for conventional "patron-client relations." Although I do not deny the usefulness of the patron-client trope for understanding planter attitudes, I found during research that the literature's identification of it did little to reveal the daily negotiations of power that coursed through plantation society.

At one end of the spectrum of social conventions on the plantations stood daily owner and manager courtesy toward tenants; at the other end one encountered daily brutality. As a stark reminder of the limits of polite discourse, at Hacienda Palto managers and tenants discussed contract terms in the shadow of the plantation stocks, which remained in use until well into the twentieth century.[7]

In most studies the conviction prevails that the plantation was a trap into which peasants fell in ignorance or in the realization that they had no choice: it was either work at the planter's rate or starve. But this view presupposes a number of conditions that will receive close scrutiny here. For one, the absence of serious choices is thought to have encouraged a fatalistic attitude toward plantation field labor. But even if the peasants were not fatalistic, the convention yet holds that they had few means to resist the authoritarian mandates of plantation owners and managers, and that, in fact, the consent of peasants was irrelevant to the mode of farming on plantations. Finally, most studies assume a virtually limitless supply of cheap peasant labor.

A focus on labor alone would not provide an adequate response to these assumptions; nor would it do justice to the myriad of activities peasants might engage in while they cultivated cotton. As tenants, they would have to be flexible, playing by the rules of the market. To pursue this idea, I would have to watch for peasant risk taking, for instance, when peasants made a choice to search for credit, and also activities that signaled a careful husbandry of resources. I would have to be alert for opportunities when peasants might have saved or accumulated wealth. In short, I would be looking at tenants or sharecroppers whose actions closely resembled those of farmers.[8]

To demonstrate that peasants as tenants took initiatives and made choices would require careful examination of their farming behavior, especially of the context in which farming decisions were made. To argue further that such initiatives constituted resistance to the plantation regime would demand that I show how peasant activities might be at odds with the measures adopted by the plantation to reach the same end; that is, how and when they refused to consent to rules of the plantation regime. The meaning of "resistance" is an object of study here. The resistance peasants offered to the plantation regime was not always the kind to which James C. Scott called attention. Scott's view of resistance was as a counterforce to coercion. As Alan Knight aptly pointed out, however, sometimes peasants resisted in ways that were not so obvious; nor were they always struggling against open force.[9] At times the term "resistance" has not always fully captured the intent of peasant actions. Peasants sometimes seem to have been engaged in a twofold struggle. In one sense they sought greater power. But in another sense they also sought to secure something more tangible: a set of rights. This latter objective fit clearly within the capitalist world economy that shaped the hegemonic order governed by plantation owners. That is why a phrase employed by Ranajit Guha resonates well in the Peruvian countryside. By dubbing peasant indignation as "rightful dissent," he associated dissent with the moral posture that seeks redress of rights. Guha thus broadened the concept of dissent beyond resistance to resistance within the rules of hegemony.[10] Potentially more dangerous than resistance, "rightful dissent" recognizes the need of peasants to occupy the high moral ground while they struggle for power. It also opens the door to subversion of the hegemonic position of the planters. To put the matter more clearly, by insisting that the position was morally correct, peasants were not simply challenging the rules of land leasing but were calling into question the legality of planter ownership of the land.[11]

Having reached this point in my thinking, many years and several detours after I first visited Hacienda Palto, I turned to writing. In the pages that follow I examine in more detail the many questions that arose while reading the records of cotton plantations. The setting was the farming economy of Hacienda San Francisco Solano de Palto and its neighbors in the south coast Pisco valley, where landowners, managers, and tenants engaged in a prolonged struggle for power.

ACKNOWLEDGMENTS

Many people helped me through the various stages of this study. The staff of the former Archivo del Fuero Agrario (AFA) helped in collecting the data; Elena Calle organized a team of Lima university students who called themselves "El Equipo Palto" and read and discussed the documents with me under stimulating, seminar-like conditions. Prolonged conversations with Humberto ("Tito") Rodríguez Pastor, erstwhile director of the AFA, deeply influenced this study. Tito became a lifelong friend and his entire family, especially his wife, Adriana, graciously has allowed me to disrupt their lives whenever I arrive in Lima. The Communidad Atahualpa — Enrique Mayer, Martin and María Scurrah, Mike Twomey, David Gow, Susan Ramírez, Richard Smith, and Helaine Silverman — contributed profoundly to my education in *lo Peruano*. Peruvians with whom I held conversations, long and short, serious and light, on buses; in bars; in fishing villages; in private homes; in plantation houses; in government, cooperative, and commercial offices; in fields and on beaches, sometimes in great privacy and at others encircled by observers and commentators, provided me with innumerable insights into their angle of vision on Peru. Often they were served up over plates of ceviche, or *cuy,* bowls of *parihuela,* or glasses of *pisco puro,* in the Lima *galpón,* on the peaks of the Andes, and in the deserts of Ica and Sechura. The kaleidoscope of ideas I took from those conversations helped to sharpen my understanding of Peruvian cultural history.

Several social scientists in Lima helped to advance this study. I especially treasure my conversations with Pablo Macera, whose remarkable insights and tireless exploration of ideas were infectious. Heraclio Bonilla introduced me to families in several parts of the central highlands of Peru I might otherwise not have had the privilege to meet. Julio Cotler drew my attention to the energetic group of social scientists forming in the early 1970s at the AFA. I was privileged to gain some knowledge early in the project from the late Jorge

Basadre. Dr. Félix Denegri Luna, Peru's master bibliophile, generously placed his personal library at my disposal as he has done for so many others.

A number of colleagues made valuable suggestions as the project evolved. Herman Belz, the late Clifton Brown, Bill Albert, Rob Wright, Bill Elkins, Tom Davies, Lou Pérez, Barbara Tenenbaum, Jim Riley, and Paul Gootenberg read and dissected early versions of the opening chapters. Tom Orum provided bibliographical and archival suggestions. Murdo Macleod applied his acid wit to my cruder formulations, summing them up as "a little bit of fluff." While the project was in its critical stages, Enrique Mayer and David Gow — who carefully read the penultimate draft — lit fires in my mind while we "confessed" at "Father Eagan's," and I am forever in their intellectual debt. Valuable advice also came from Joanne Rappoport, Fiona Wilson, Denys Cuche, and Colin and Maggie Harding.

Others read all or parts of the manuscript as the work neared completion. I especially benefited from Sidney Mintz's counsel. His guidance provided me with an excellent teaching model, and I took shameless advantage of his generosity, badgering him into allowing the completed text to interrupt an incredibly demanding, unenviable workload. I do not regret it, however, for the finished product would not have been the same without his review. Tom Wright gave the work a close, carefully, reading, as did my colleague at Howard University, Joe Reidy. I suspect it could not have become a book without the gentle but unyielding criticism of John J. Tepaske, to whom I am grateful for insisting that I clarify the central meaning of the story.

Fortunately for historians of Latin America, numerous public institutions are staffed with dedicated professionals ready to aid our work. The personnel of the Biblioteca Nacional del Perú, Sala de Investigaciones, were always helpful and supportive, as was the overworked, harried staff of the Sección de Historia of the Archivo General de la Nación in Lima. The staffs of the United States National Archives, the United States National Agricultural Library, and the Library of Congress, especially the Hispanic Division, were helpful at all times. The Howard University–Sponsored Faculty Research Program in the Social Sciences, Humanities, and Education, then directed by Michael Winston, funded portions of the research. The American Philosophical Society contributed to the completion of the study, and I thank the Commission for the International Exchange of

Scholars (better known as the Fulbright Commission) for a research grant that permitted an extended stay in Peru. The Family History Library of the Church of Jesus Christ of Latter-day Saints (Silver Spring, Maryland, office) and the staff of the Sterling Library of Yale University were also helpful. The unwavering faith shown in me by Dolores Martin and Georgette Dorn, respectively editor of the Handbook of Latin American Studies and Chief of the Hispanic Division, have proven to be invaluable. At Howard University, I drew upon the help of several graduate assistants, including Aubrey Thompson, Sally Schwartz, Keith Look-loy, and Linda Aminah Batta. Caroline, Michelle, and Andrew were patient and constantly supportive over the years as they lived with the germination of the ideas, the tiresome delays, and an unholy number of broken promises. I offer this story in partial repayment of the theft of their time.

INTRODUCTION

Peasants, Plantations, and Resistance

Plantations and Peasants

Plantations conjure up time-worn images in Latin American history: vast undulating fields of grass and scrub trees overrun with cattle herded by wild-eyed, weather-beaten ranch hands; or flat stretches of hot lands choked with sugarcane overseen by domineering landlords who force brutal, backbreaking labor on cowering canecutters under a hot sun. Thanks to the writings of Gilberto Freyre and his epigones, we associate plantations most often with slave society. After abolition, however, plantations assumed a new role in most of Latin America.

During the independence wars (1808–25) plantations underwent heavy depredations. The fields were trampled in battle, and slave labor forces were raided to fill military ranks. Ownership of plantations changed hands when aristocratic families fled or could not adjust to the new economies. Plantations fell into the hands of the state or were swooped up by eager new owners, and fresh blood meant other changes. New markets stimulated changes in crops as well as owners; the new planters were often part-time merchants who spent more time making deals in the city. Absentee ownership became a common feature of export plantations.

The new-style landowners hired managers to direct field operations on a daily basis in their absence. They expected the hired administrators to bring to the plantation a sense of continuity; they would be the voice of the owner. Despite the changes, in other words, the new owners wanted everything to remain on a smooth course without disruption. Indeed, the transition seems to have been easy. Black slaves continued to bend their backs to field labor. It is not unlikely that free peasants might be found alongside them from time to time, a curious — perhaps new — but not unusual phenomenon. On the whole, plantations and laborers abetted the perception that plantation society underwent little change with the end of Spanish colonial rule.

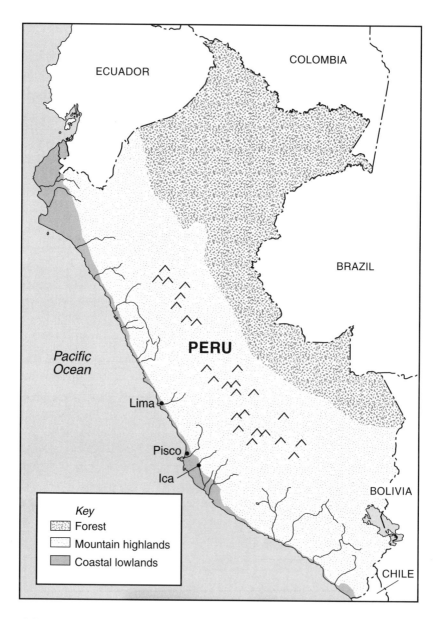

Map 1   Peru

Map 2   Department of Ica

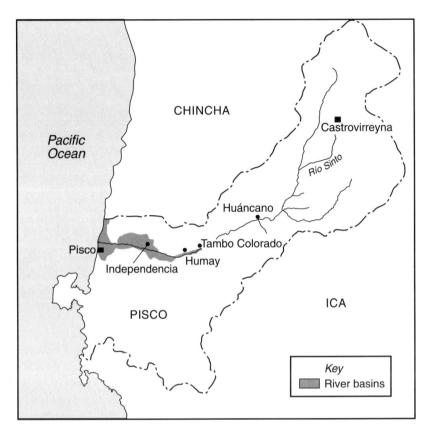

Map 3   Pisco River Basin

A closer look reveals that in some ways the new landowners scarcely resembled the old. Among the new owners were ambitious caudillos and merchants who laid claim to fields abandoned after the wars. The revived plantations succored internal markets and provided a growing portion of Peru's export earnings in wine, sugar, wheat, cotton, and more exotic products. Highland estates, the counterparts to the plantations of the coastal valleys, served as springboards to local political power for the new landowners.[1]

The place of large landholdings in the formation of rural society in Peru has not been clear. Wild swings in growth and stagnation, so typical of the history of agricultural capitalism, undoubtedly made a strong impact on plantation labor. Economic fluctuations forced the landowners to focus on the best way to replace slave labor and to contemplate further technological change thereafter. Yet it is not fully clear if the cycles of capitalism alone convinced the big planters to rid themselves of an inefficient form of labor or if the slaves themselves took the lead in breaking the tie between slavery and the large, commercial plantations.[2]

After abolition, Peruvian planters followed one of two paths left open to them. Some sold the land to new owners. Others avoided the high cost of importing machinery by searching for alternative forms of cheap labor. One source they considered was the free population settled in coastal villages and on the edges of the great estates. Made up largely of free people of mixed ancestry — mainly Indians and free Africans, in the early nineteenth century this population presumably survived in the settlements at the fringes of the plantations.

In some cases the rural population inhabited villages whose fragile legality was soon swept away by the avaricious new planters.[3] Others subsisted as squatters on lands overlooked or ignored in poor economic times; still others survived, briefly, as bandits. Plantations usually hired these campesinos as harvest temporaries to supplement the slave labor force. As slavery waned, the planters hired the squatters more frequently and watched forlornly as the cost of keeping them around became prohibitive. The coastal planters quickly turned elsewhere in search of cheap, permanent field hands.[4]

Knowledge of this preabolition, preindenture labor force admittedly rests on some guesswork and comparisons with studies done in other locales. All indications are that the impact of commercial agriculture on Peruvian campesinos was similar to the experience of their counterparts throughout the world.[5] In periods of high population growth and plenty of labor, demand for plantation labor left campesinos at a disadvantage. Wages fell, sharecropping became disadvantageous, and campesinos usually suffered inversely with the vigor of agrarian markets. Their conditions — especially their treatment at the hands of plantation management — usually descended in such periods to inhumane levels. But in periods of agricultural growth, population decline, and labor scarcity, farmhands found field conditions attractive, and despite the contempt in which they were held by planters and managers, they sought out labor on the big estates.[6]

The atmosphere on plantations seems not to have been constantly oppressive. Recent studies have noted that campesinos sometimes enjoyed relief from authoritarian control at moments when it might least be expected, particularly when the owners were in distress. Periods of economic stagnation, for example, seem to have provided opportunities to make claims against owners who needed the cooperation of the field hands in order to survive. In such moments, campesinos often turned the disadvantages of subordinate status into an advantage, to successfully resist landlord demands and thus to win occasional small victories against the dominant landowners. Granted, those instances came after long intervals marked by survival under abject conditions without hope of improvement.[7] Longer periods of advantage, I will argue, occurred when campesino labor was scarce.

The meaning of rural labor on the plantations is not fully understood. Current research does not offer sufficient detail on the daily or seasonal activities of these field hands, and consequently stereotypes of the following sort dominate our thinking: landowners governed the process of production, hiring campesinos to gather the harvest and — once the crop was in — held them through debt, soothing their anguish with benevolence. Periodic spontaneous rebellions are believed to have occurred anyway, unleashing reprisals by the landowners, one more vicious than the next, in a cycle that has grimly repeated itself without end. Landowners are seen as forever in control and the campesinos by turns submissive and explosive.[8] The routine economic behavior of rural labor — and the legitimacy of campesino resistance — are obscured in this scenario.

The perception holds that after slavery, plantations remained in the shadow of economic sloth and backwardness until the final decades of the nineteenth century. Sometime in those years, our understanding continues, international markets stirred plantation owners by demanding their raw goods — principally sugar, cotton, and coffee. The next step was critical: in a complex process that concentrated power in a few hands, planters expanded the amount of land cultivated while they reached overseas for new sources of controllable labor and/or lured greater numbers of villagers out of the highlands with high wages and settled them onto the plantations. The newly entrapped peons worked incessantly to meet the demands of the international market while plantation owners reaped huge profits from their indebted labor. Rarely did the workers find the means to dissent, and when they did it was usually explosive. But the enclaving of plantations kept campesinos from becoming aware of their potential as a group and as individuals.[9]

At this juncture it is important to dwell for a moment on the meaning of the words "rural folk," "field hand," "campesino," "rural labor," "fieldworker," "peon," and the like. For many who study agrarian history, these have been uncomfortable substitutes for the elusive term "peasant."[10] It has seemed clear to earlier scholars that rural dwellers carried out the activities ordinarily associated with the freehold farmers who were central to the economies of early modern Europe and precolonial Asia and Africa. Yet their varied legal and social positions made a poor fit with the classic peasant model. Hence it was difficult to claim that a peasantry existed in Latin America.

Studies of rural society have relied upon the general term "campesino" (literally country dweller) and by doing so have elided the question of whether a classic peasantry ever emerged in Latin America. Perhaps it has been taken for granted that country dwellers were not freeholders, but even so, no other term seems to fit the need to describe this broad sector of society. Another means of handling the problem has been to describe the many activities of campesinos in context, suggesting the varied roles played by peasants. There may be several reasons scholars have been reluctant to define a peasantry with more precision, perhaps most prominent among them being a sense that the classic freehold peasant never existed in the region. Many scholars associate the emergence of a freehold peasantry with the earliest stages of a capitalist economy; in Latin America that association may not be as strong as elsewhere. In Peru, the early years of capitalist growth in the nineteenth century are marked by a strong link between the availability of credit, the beginnings of commerce on a world scale, and — among other things — the reorganization of large plantations. Precisely in that era, when slavery ended in many countries, specifically in Peru, a classic peasantry might conventionally have been expected to take center stage. That did not happen.

We are left, then, with two choices. Either we sever the tie between freehold farmers and the beginnings of a capitalist economy, or we take a broader view of the peasantry. We leave for others the problem of defining the broader picture of capitalist expansion in Peru, associated with metal mining, banks, and establishment of urban factories. Our task is to clarify how rural dwellers responded as peasants to the economic changes that brought about alternating waves of stagnation and expansion on the cotton plantations over the late nineteenth and early twentieth centuries. Our working definition of peasants will include those rural dwellers who pursued a commitment to subsistence on the land and secondarily to the production of a surplus, taking into account the many detours along the path. In short, as was the case for classic peasants, to be a peasant in the coastal valleys of Peru meant carrying out many activities peripherally associated with subsistence farming without losing sight of the primary objective: to control production on the land and to market the product with an eye toward savings. When the offer of rental contracts on the cotton plantations appeared to open a door toward fulfillment of that objective, the peasants, cautious but determined, took up the challenge. A major purpose of this study is to track the strategies employed by peasants in pursuit of their central dream. By sharpening our focus in this manner, we may also be able to learn some things about what it means in Peru — and perhaps all of Spanish America — to be a peasant.[11]

Plantation correspondence and reports provide access to a healthy antidote to the core thread of the conventional image of peasants. The documentation contains a wealth of detail on daily routines, revealing that the peasants gained intimate knowledge of the land and a degree of control over their use of it. It is likely that the mix of routine intimacy and experience shaped peasant ideas. Over time peasants came to focus on two closely linked ideas: resistance to an unjustified labor regime that threatened their livelihood and — less coherently — the emergence of a sense of legitimized ownership of the land. Peasant resistance may have depended for its moral tone on the perceived legality of tenure on the plantation. The longer the peasants remained on the land, the more they may have felt they had a stake in it. Early studies by E. P. Thompson and George Rudé draw attention to the existence of a strong sense of righteousness among the peasantry, and they provide examples to guide other studies along this path of inquiry.[12]

Past research has cleared some of the rubble from my path by linking peasant society to the plantations. Pablo Macera carried out some of the earliest work on nineteenth-century plantations and raised important methodological questions, as did Shane Hunt. A preliminary assessment by Douglas Horton, a sociological analysis by a group of Peruvian scholars, and a study of the origins of the Peruvian Aprista party by Peter Klaren provide clues to further research.[13] Although helpful, these works focus on the tensions between capitalist agriculture and broad social changes but not specifically on social relations within the plantations. Early studies of the ties between peasants and plantations reflect interest in land use as a marker of Latin America's place in the history of mercantilism and capitalism. Magnus Mörner and his cohorts clarified the evolution of colonial land tenure and land use, and scholars thereafter debated whether haciendas and plantations illustrated a social order governed by prestige or by commerce.[14] In those discussions, the authors viewed labor as an instrument — rather than a core vehicle — in the evolution of land use. The effect of wages and debt on plantation society remain unclear.

Debt was understood to be the principle means by which plantations legally detained peasants against their will, but the context for its use was not well developed. Pablo Macera and Eric Hobsbawm concurred that debt peonage emerged under conditions of labor scarcity, but they were somewhat at odds about why landlords resorted to it. Hobsbawm viewed peonage as a form of retrenchment in hard times: debt permitted landowners to reduce costs without going through the trouble of throwing the peasants off the plantation. Macera agreed but saw debt peonage as an instrument of competition for European markets.[15] Other works look beyond these leads to more specific variables impelling landowners to control labor with debt. These studies share with Hobsbawm's, Macera's, and the others' the view that debt and wages formed part of a continuum, with various kinds of debt following one another until they all ended with the adoption of wage labor. Few studies assume that debt and wages might coexist in close harmony on the plantations, and fewer still look upon them as weapons in the hands of the peasants.[16]

Other assumptions have clouded the study of peasants on plantations in Peru. Many works adopt questionable ideas about the mechanics of labor indebtedness, leaving the impression that debt peonage was universally a "lifetime" condition. Nor has the problem of labor migration come up in calculations of debt peonage. Clearly planters sought to restrict the movement of peasants when the harvest demanded many hands. But what happened to the peasants when the harvest ended? What became of a peon's debt when he or she was idle and earning barely enough to subsist? When, if ever, did planters dismiss debt peons? Other works emphasize the migratory character of rural labor, particularly as twentieth-century plantations demanded massive labor mobilizations. What did debt peonage mean if peasants lived with both entrapment in debt and ejection from the fields?

Much about peasants on the plantations remains unknown. A clearer understanding of the relationship between scarcity of labor, wages, and debt seems critical for explaining the fit between peasants and plantation society in Peru.

Domination and Resistance

One key to understanding the importance of peasants on plantations involves a simple transaction. When cotton planters turned from wages to contracts, they also surrendered a certain amount of control over the land. In return for this seductive whiff of power, peasants became tenants, taking the risk that they could meet contract terms and avoid the heavy burdens of debt. Questions arise here. When did the landowners find it necessary to offer the peasants small amounts of power over the land? Did the transfer of power weaken planter domination of land and labor? If peasants gained some power, why did they then protest and resist the arrangement?

In this study two assumptions are made about the links between peasant power and resistance. One is that a complex hegemonic order guided planter strategies for overcoming the problem of scarce peasant labor. The hegemonic character of the social order is exemplified by the planters' use of numerous enticements to persuade peasants that they could become tenants on the plantations without harming their freedom. Related to that argument was an implied exchange — of subordination for trust. Peasants who accepted subaltern rank on the plantations would be entrusted with stewardship of a parcel of land.

But the exchange of trust for land was only implied, not stated, in the tenant contract. For that reason, owners gave plantation administrators responsibility for oversight of plantation operations. As representatives of absentee owners, managers relied on authoritarian measures to secure peasant labor. They found independent land management by tenants a threat to successful farm management. To make their situation worse, managers received ambiguous signals from the landowners, to rule "tactfully" on the one hand but to maximize output on the other. Unable to properly decipher these ambiguities, the managers found themselves seeking to contain and direct the farming behavior of a free peasantry by gaining its consent to authoritarian management. For their part, the peasants contested the manager's authority at every opportunity.

A second assumption that guides this study is that the growth of commercial cotton agriculture relied for success upon a divided plantation social order. Social segments arose from assignment by the landlords, who named different groups of tenants by type of contract. As land use and forms of labor changed, the owners identified the field workers by various labels. The labels were not capricious; they were a product of the needs of landowners to secure greater control of labor and to keep pace with changes in the market. More specific labor categories might also be a product of the wish to establish labor hierarchies in which such items as the most productive lands, water, credit, and other essentials of tenantry would be seen as badges of good tenant husbandry.

Following Hobsbawm and Macera, plantation studies have found distinctions arising within the labor force as planters sought access to world markets in the nineteenth century. Several studies in the volume by Kenneth Duncan and Ian Rutledge note that nineteenth-century commerce uprooted peasants from villages and funneled them toward the plantations. Several of the studies question the convention that on the plantations peasants lived not as members of distinct groups but rather universally as a cheap labor force without internal distinctions.

A few of the studies speculate that not all peasants suffered equally from debt peonage, and all of them agree in the end that a one-dimensional view of plantation labor can no longer be sustained.[17]

The links between social divisions, resistance, and debt on the plantation have been suggested in a number of widely read works. Charles Gibson and Edith Couturier, for example, drew attention to the idea that colonial Mexican villagers found debt to be not an oppressive instrument of landlord domination but rather a weapon of resistance. Both scholars argued audaciously that colonial peasants episodically used debt to fend off total estate domination of their lives.[18] Eric Van Young pointed to labor's surprising fluidity in the evolution of Guadalajara haciendas due to low numbers. Richard Salvucci explored the flexibility of personal debt in Mexican *obrajes* (primitive textile factories) and questioned the standard view of colonial peonage. Similar inquiries came from Arnold Bauer, Mario Góngora, and Jan Bazant when they examined nineteenth-century estates in Chile and Mexico.[19]

In Peru the abolition of slavery was a necessary step in the process of rural social differentiation. Peter Klaren and Henri Favre suggested the loosening of ties between communal villages and haciendas, and a shift in peasant economic activities toward the satisfaction of family and individual needs, as signs of a deterioration of communalism. Peasant resistance to the expansion of large landholdings in the sierra as well as in the coastal valleys may provide the earliest conditions for the study of those important changes.[20]

William Roseberry provided a critical advance in the effort to assign weight to social differentiation in the study of peasant resistance. In "Rent, Differentiation and the Development of Capitalism among Peasants," Roseberry surveyed the arguments of Marx and Lenin that specialization and segmentation of the labor force signaled the arrival of capitalism. After Marx's application of the idea to the rise of industrial capitalism, Lenin, in *The Development of Capitalism in Russia* (1905), used it to better understand Russian agriculture. Lenin concluded that in addition to foreshadowing industrial capitalism, labor segmentation also signaled the arrival of capitalism in Russian agriculture. Roseberry speculated that the same process also occurred elsewhere when capitalism broke through a traditional economy.[21]

Recent studies of Andean society support Roseberry's analysis, demonstrating the impact of market forces on particular localities.

Florencia Mallon and Gavin Smith examined the introduction of capitalism into peasant society in the central Peruvian highlands. Mallon found that the rhythm of capitalist penetration of the Yanamarca valley in the early twentieth century drove one sector of rural society, who became known as *gamonales* (bosses), to dominate other sectors. While the gamonales' neighbors retained a communal outlook, resisting petty capitalist intrusions into the community, the gamonales became avaricious. Increasingly the need for cash drove a fissure between community segments. In a similar work Gavin Smith studied the shepherding community of Huasicancha. The *Huasicanchinos* felt the effects of capital penetration perhaps a bit more slowly than did the villagers of Yanamarca but to no less effect. After World War I they were swept into a commercial and commodity-producing economy that depended increasingly on cash in mining and brokerage. Many migrated to a variety of other centers, including Lima.[22]

The highlands studies reveal how cash and labor discipline cracked village unity, bringing divisive forces to the forefront. The driving forces behind segmentation on the coastal plantations were similar, although the contours of the social segments might differ. Highland ethnic differences, as Smith and Mallon observed, featured cultural distance between mestizos and Indians. Although highlanders came from both camps, coastal peasants were a mixture of indigenous villagers and descendants of Africans, to which Asians recently had been added. As the twin processes of plantation expansion and social differentiation occurred, cultural differences may have played a more prominent role on the coastal plantations.

An unspoken element in the creation of peasant resistance was labor scarcity. Lack of reliable census data for long periods in the nineteenth and twentieth centuries make it difficult to accurately state population growth rates and settlement patterns. But it is clear that the coastal cotton plantations experienced labor scarcity from the end of Asian indenture (1874) to the close of World War I. Several factors, existing alone or in combination, might account for scarcity on the coast: indications of low population growth, competition among several economic sectors, poor communication, and an adequate village economy of subsistence. There is little agreement on the weight of these factors, but this study gives preeminence to labor scarcity as a primordial issue on the coastal cotton plantations.

As the book proceeds, it will identify patterns of peasant economic

behavior on export cotton plantations in the Pisco valley. It will examine how hegemonic landowners sought to dominate and divide the
peasantry. Subsequent chapters will recount how peasants emerged
as various kinds of tenants on the plantations and how their farming
activities evolved into resistance against authority. A discussion of
this complex agrarian drama will illuminate how the economic inter-
actions of peasants, managers, and landowners formed plantation
society and, in turn, Peruvian culture. As the study reaches the post–
World War I era, it will examine the limits of peasant resistance and
the counterattack on peasants that was undertaken as labor scarcity
diminished and plantation mechanization became feasible. Finally, it
will review the impact of internal migration from the highlands,
which created a surplus of labor, and the penetration of modern era
politics into the cotton plantation regions.

Systematic, detailed study of plantation society under growth in
Peru began with the work of Shane Hunt. Hunt thoughtfully dissected hoary arguments about plantation "enclavement" and isola-
tion from the national economy, and he set plantations within the
body of tasks that begged for greater attention.[23] Rosemary Thorp
and Geoffrey Bertram found that especially in the 1890s and the
1930s the domestic agrarian market benefited immensely from heavy
investments by Peruvian merchants, which spurred the domestic
economy, including cotton production, in ways that were not previously recognized.[24] Further studies of nineteenth-century Peru by
Alberto Flores Galindo, Paul Gootenberg, Nelson Manrique, Alfonso Quiroz, and Rory Miller, among others, question the dominance of foreigners in commercial agriculture. These scholars viewed
the nineteenth-century Peruvian oligarchy increasingly as a home-
grown force that relied on national financiers to underwrite agrarian
expansion and who forged advantageous alliances with foreign commercial houses to market their products.[25]

A handful of the most powerful families in Peru have been sub-
jected to close examination, among them the Boza, Beltrán, and
Aspíllaga clans, whose business dealings are best known in their
twentieth-century manifestation in the writings of Dennis Gilbert
and Michael Gonzales, while Manuel Burga examined those owners
of the Jequetepeque valley properties who successfully adjusted to
economic change after independence.[26] These landowning-merchant-
banking families and others like them held key positions of power in

Peru after 1870. They ruled from bank boards of directors or merchant house boards; many held public office or positions in clubs and organizations, where they influenced those who wielded military and political power.[27]

This study will devote only brief attention to the activities of the dominant social sector. The Aspíllaga family receives most of the attention because its detailed records yielded the best information on cotton plantation agriculture. The Aspíllagas are fairly representative of their fellow Pisco valley cotton planters and generally of their class. Emigrants from Chile in the 1820s, they rose steadily to power in Peruvian society, propelled by astute social behavior, opportunism and commercial success. An association emerged in the nineteenth century between aggressive entrepreneurship and coastal plantations. The association became evident in the late 1830s cotton boomlet, again in the second great cotton boom of the mid-1860s, and in the other major waves of expansion in raw cotton commerce that appeared more frequently in the cotton-growing valleys of the central and south coast during the twentieth century. The Aspíllagas missed the earliest of those booms, but they profited from all the others until World War II.

Planters such as the Aspíllagas expected to dominate the land and shape the field of play simply by announcing the plantation rules. But as we shall see, they learned that plantation management was not so simple when free peasants did the work. The appearance of tenants on the coastal cotton plantations in the late nineteenth century went unrecognized as a social phenomenon for a quarter-century, and contemporary social analysts then made often unwarranted assumptions about repression and submissiveness, leading to the first assertions about debt peonage that unquestionably influenced our later views.[28]

To try to answer the questions that have come up in the course of this introduction, the story picks up the theme of labor, peasants, and cotton in Peru in the second half of the nineteenth century. By that point the cotton planters already had stocked their fields with gangs of indentured Chinese workers. They left the indentured Asians in the hands of plantation managers and mailed often vague and sometimes contradictory instructions to the plantations on how to care for labor and increase production. The labor problems encountered in this administrative organization, and efforts to overcome them, are the subject of the early chapters.

After indenture ended, the cotton planters and rural workers together faced the very problem both had assiduously avoided ever since the abolition of slavery. Owners and peasants had to come to terms with demand for scarce labor; peasants became a factor in calculating the success of cotton plantations. How to entice the peasants onto the plantation fields at the lowest possible cost without discouraging them became the greatest challenge the cotton planters faced. Race played a subterranean but undeniable part in the process, and in this study we shall try to gauge the weight of race as a measure of attitudes, including trust, that figured in the calculations of peasants, managers, and owners. For the peasants it was a matter of convincing the planters of the *sur chico* that they could manage the land and produce a high volume of cotton.[29] The subtext of this struggle was a future expectation that prolonged use of the land by the peasants might form a claim to ownership.

The degree of independence peasants exercised on land owned by someone else should not be exaggerated. To argue that free peasants were not coerced to work is not to say that they were free and independent farmers in an open market. They rented land — they did not own it — and the market gave the greatest attention to landowners who produced cotton in large volume. Most of the other factors of production also were beyond the grasp of the peasants (thought not necessarily of their cognizance). But questions of labor and land use were not. By identifying peasants who recognized opportunities to manage land (and responded accordingly) not as farm laborers but as contract-holding tenant farmers, we can develop some estimates of the extent and nature of peasant society and resistance to landowner dominance in the Pisco valley of Peru. Perhaps we can even contribute to an understanding of how the peasants helped to define the culture, and by extension the nation.

CHAPTER 1

Planters, Managers, and Consent

[I]t's not the same as when the owner is present.
— *lament expressed by one of the Aspíllaga brothers, 1884*

An obscure, unpretentious plantation in the Pisco valley became a setting in the middle of the nineteenth century for profound social change in Peru. A pioneering agrarian entrepreneur, Ramón Aspíllaga, purchased Hacienda San Francisco Solano de Palto, adding to his already extensive holdings in sugar on the north coast. His family's wealth and power grew steadily throughout the late nineteenth century. Later his sons would expand the Aspíllaga holdings in the region, acquiring a warehouse, offices, and a dock in the port town of Pisco.[1] Aspíllaga aspired to the kind of high social standing that successful commercial agriculture might provide in nineteenth-century Peru. He worked the financial maze of the country with great skill, and eventually he rode cotton and sugar to virtually aristocratic social standing.

The family owed its power to the social acumen and political persistence of its leading figures. At the outset of his investment in cotton, Ramón Aspíllaga had taken a number of steps to increase his chances of success. He acquired choice, well-located properties, established an impeccable credit rating, obtained the cheapest available labor to work the fields, and carefully supervised operations. After he died his sons labored on in their father's footsteps. They expanded the fields in use, increasing the volume of production, and converted the profits from cotton and sugar exports into levels of power their father could only have looked upon with admiration.[2]

Yet in one area the accomplishments of the Aspíllagas and other coastal planters fell short of their goals; despite their power and prestige, they failed to convince the cotton field hands that they were in control. The field hands too often seemed to pay lip service to the commands barked at them by plantation managers, offering excuses for not carrying out an assigned task. Almost from the first moment that free peasants entered the cotton plantations, they apparently intuited that their labor was in great demand and could command a high price. They also detected a breach between the wishes of the landowners and the efforts of plantation managers to carry those wishes out. In short, the cotton planters failed to fully extend their hegemonic position into the rural coastal valleys of the country. Many of the actions taken by the planters to do so had the opposite effect: undermining their authority. This chapter examines one aspect of a mystifying gap: the difference between the social and political display of power by the landowners and its dilution when it was applied to the plantations.

The case of Hacienda Palto illustrates the problem that bothered landowners. To some extent, the lack of conviction among the peasants was a by-product of owner neglect. Unlike their father, the Aspíllaga sons felt little emotional attachment to the Pisco valley or to Hacienda Palto. Indeed, Ramón Aspíllaga's nostalgic attraction to the valley translated poorly in business terms. He had provided an exemplary model for his sons by directly managing the first plantation he had bought, Hacienda Cayaltí in the north coast Lambayeque region. But the contrast between his attention to Cayaltí and his neglect of Hacienda Palto was unmistakable. Ramón barely set foot on the cotton plantation after he bought it. Instead, he sent his younger brother, Antonio, to manage the operation with the help of Ramón's sons, Ramón the younger and Ismael. After the father died, the brothers removed themselves even farther from the cotton plantation by leaving it in the hands of a succession of administrators. To the extent that they too hired managers, the following generations of Aspíllagas in turn adopted the practices of their forebears.

Hacienda Palto clearly was important in the scheme of things as viewed by the Aspíllagas. When they discussed their financial status and future plans, Ramón's sons spoke of Palto as an integral part of their assets. After their father died in 1875 the brothers inventoried their father's legacy. One of them remarked that he had left them with S/44,382 ("S/" represents the *sol*, the currency of Peru) in disposable capital, a result of the "foresight of our unforgettable father who rests in peace." But they could not rest on this windfall, for he also had burdened them with an enormous set of debts, albeit in the form of long-term loans. Thus to keep their obligations under control they would count heavily "on the contingency of the Palto harvest."[3]

Table 1.1 Administrators of Hacienda Palto, 1867–1940

Name	Previous Position	Term (Approx.)
Ramón Aspíllaga F.	Second son of owner	[?]1867–[?]1873[?]
Ismael Aspíllaga	Fourth son of owner	[?]1873[?]–[?]1874[?]
Juan Casanova	Unknown	[?]1875[?]–[?]1875[?]
Eugenio Angosto	Unknown	[?]1876–Feb. 1877
Francisco Pérez y Céspedes	Brother-in-law	Mar. 1877–Oct. 1878
José Pérez y Albela	Unknown	Oct. 1878–Dec. 1884
Manuel F. Brihuega	Unknown	Dec. 1884–Dec. 1888
José B. Velarde	Tenant, Hacienda Palto	Jan. 1889–[?]1890
Nestor Cerdeña	Tenant, Hacienda Palto	[?]1890–Feb. 1901
Tomás Acevedo	Tenant, Hacienda Palto	Feb. 1901–[?]1918
Maximiliano M. Alcántara	Tenant, Hacienda San José	[?]1918–[?]1947[?]

Sources: AFA, Hacienda Palto, *Accounts and Letterbooks, 1867–1940*; Pablo Macera, *Palto: hacendados y yanaconas del algodonal peruano (documentos, 1877–1943)* (Lima, 1976).

Note: [?] = family records do not reveal exact dates of employment or termination

This theme, the expectation that returns from Hacienda Palto would contribute significantly to the family's wealth, suggests that the modest cotton plantation in the Pisco valley held strategic importance in their commercial plans. Perhaps hoping to gain greater control of the Pisco valley property, in the early twentieth century the brothers detached Hacienda Palto from their other business operations. They left oversight of the cotton *fundo* (plantation or hacienda) to Ismael, the youngest of the brothers. Yet Ismael had no more inclination to live on the plantation than did his older siblings, and like them he left Palto in the hands of an administrator. Although periodic visits in the twentieth century grew more fruitful for the gathering of information, later Aspíllaga generations continued to provide oversight from the family business offices far off in Lima.

This left the owners of Hacienda Palto with the difficult but extremely important task of hiring a trustworthy, skilled manager. As table 1.1 suggests, their early efforts failed; they found a succession of individuals who could not handle the job, and they quickly dismissed them. Juan Casanova, a man of uncertain origins, did not last a year. Reliance upon family members as managers, whatever the merits, also exposed potential hazards. How, after all, did one dismiss an incompetent cousin or an in-law without creating ill will in the family? After several years of poor guesswork and repeated failures, the Aspíllagas began to rely for plantation managers on experienced, trustworthy former farmhands. Administrators thus came to be chosen from within the peasantry of the Pisco valley, a strategy that — while apparently successful — as we shall see also was fraught with hazards.

It was not unusual for a plantation owner to seek public office in late nineteenth-century Peru. Although there is no readily available count, the occupations of numerous public officeholders in the executive and legislative branches of national government were similar to those of Ramón Aspíllaga and his sons. Ownership and management of plantations was but one of their enterprises. Many of them were merchant-planters, and they spent a large amount of time in conversation with fellow merchants, buying, selling, and keeping track of their merchandise, the paperwork of commerce. Price fluctuations of sugar and cotton on world markets no doubt riveted their thoughts. This and other kinds of information vital to merchants could best be obtained by remaining in close touch with fellow merchants, lenders, lawyers, exporters, and others in Lima. But by leaving the plantation in the hands of a competent surrogate, the planter left a major source of livelihood at risk. Managers did not necessarily command the plantation with the same aura of authority as landowners.

Managers

For the first few years the Aspíllagas owned Hacienda Palto they devoted a great amount of time to its fields. In those early years they evidently felt they could trust no one to run the operation, and in any case they probably wanted to learn firsthand what the plantation was like — the character of its soil, the extent of the space it occupied, the irrigation network, and other potentially troublesome elements of the operation. For the first few years they owned Hacienda Palto, one of the brothers or their uncle Antonio remained in residence at the plantation. Thus they avoided the problem of delegating authority. Eventually, however, the moment came when someone aside from the brothers had to be entrusted with the cotton fundo. Ideally this person was a close family member, one who knew his employers well, their business methods, their style of communicating important information and making decisions. Above all, he should know their inclinations regarding how the plantation should be managed to meet the owners' commercial objectives. The shrewd plantation owner sought out the administrator who could readily make his meaning clear to the plantation minions hired to oversee the activities of the labor force, especially of the indentured Asians, but with equal concern for the labor of a free peasantry. In effect, the hiring of an administrator tested the ability of a landowner to exercise authority through a second party.

Hiring an administrator proved to be far more difficult than the Aspíllagas had expected. The owners soon realized, as the quotation at the outset of this chapter reveals, that no stranger could be expected to view the plantation with quite the same intensity and care as the owners, but they used every means available to solve this problem. They surveyed family members and sought the counsel of friends in the Pisco valley, especially the local family accountant. At first they chose administrators from among men who were distantly related to the owners: cousins or cousins by marriage. But such choices proved to be a miscalculation. The owners concluded that distant family members, however well supported by appeals to kinship, did not approach the task with the rigor expected by the owners. And they often lacked the skills necessary to manage the delicate task of getting the best results from an often truculent labor force. The Aspíllagas quickly rid the cotton plantation of family appointees.

As table 1.1 shows, the longest-lasting plantation administrators at Hacienda Palto came from within the ranks of the tenants. Men who exhibited good farming skills and leadership among the peasants soon gained the attention of the owners. Such men also were prized for their long, trouble-free association with the plantation. They had rented land from the Aspíllagas for many years and on the whole had maintained good relations with the owners, paying their debts and demonstrating a high degree of loyalty to managers who preceded them. The planters chose these individuals for their productivity, reliability, and steadfastness. In the eyes of the owners, those qualities were as important as a knowledge of commercial farming, if not more so. In any case, the owners became convinced that men with experience farming the fields of Hacienda Palto would find it easy to command the labor of fellow peasants.

This thinking did not directly address the problem of a transfer of

authority to the plantation administrator. There was no easy solution
to this matter. Collaboration with the owners did not always endear a
tenant to his neighbors. Cotton planters in the Pisco valley varied
widely in how they chose to govern the plantations. At Hacienda San
Jacinto, for instance, owner Vicente del Solar presided over cotton
farming himself and regularly attended the valley meetings, where
many cotton plantations were represented by administrators.[4]

But personal preference weighed far less in such decisions than did
the need for oversight. When an owner could rely on the hired administrator, he or she felt greater freedom to attend to other business
interests as well as to the political aspects of ownership. That freedom might be linked to the social rank of the administrator. In the
early twentieth century, the owner of Hacienda Urrutia leased the
property to Fermín Tangüis, a scientific cotton breeder, who resided
on the estate and conducted his experiments there. When management or leasehold was not effective, planters found it necessary to
visit the site often. They became irritated at having to concentrate
attention on the farming side of their affairs and discreetly expressed
dissatisfaction to the managers.[5]

Great distances and lengthy travel times between city residences
and plantations encouraged demonstrations of loyalty by the manager. There were several ways such attachment could be expressed.
On the practical side, the owners' need to hear such sentiments voiced
could be satisfied by frequent reports of a constantly growing rate of
production and a trouble-free work regimen. But these were not possible in an imperfect world, and owners had to make do with other
proofs. Chief among those was constancy. It was extremely important
to the Aspíllagas that the manager of Palto send them highly detailed
reports of his administrative activities on a weekly basis. They acknowledged such missives and further responded with answers to
questions on a wide array of subjects along with instructions for
executing other activities. In times of stress — disputes between manager and workers, between the plantation and government authorities,
or between neighboring plantations — administrators found themselves dealing with matters that went far beyond questions of proper
field cultivation. In these instances the social skills of former peasants,
skills for which their upbringing presumably had prepared them,
would be severely tested. Coursing through the exchanges between
owners and managers in these moments was a question that lay at the
heart of order and dominance by the landowners: Did the manager

command the respect of his adversaries, be they the authorities, other managers, or the peasants who worked the land?

Distance undoubtedly exaggerated the views of owners toward conditions in the far-off plantation areas. Typical of their group, the Aspíllagas were bored by the slow pace of country life yet they were strongly attracted to its idyllic qualities. An "oasis," or a "garden," is how they liked to depict Hacienda Palto when the stress of life in Lima overwhelmed them. But they lived under no illusions about the business purpose of the enterprise.

Among the management activities the owners monitored to determine how well the manager represented their interests were the accounting of the harvest; accuracy in maintaining an operating budget; the safekeeping of tools and equipment; the proper care and upkeep of animals, fields, and irrigation facilities; and above all control of the labor force. That only nine managers oversaw Hacienda Palto on behalf of the Aspíllaga clan between 1875 and World War II attests to their ability to judge character. Nevertheless, the absent owners never fully trusted anyone with their source of livelihood.

The weekly correspondence between owners and managers mainly addressed questions of expenditure and labor, demanding careful explanations of requests for funds. Illustrating how attentive they were to the balance of cotton accounts and the realities of absenteeism, the owners admonished managers to stay focused on the task at hand. They complained bitterly when machinery broke down or when the manager reported that tools had worn out or disappeared. "Good management," they intoned at every opportunity, "consists of efficiency and high production."[6]

Instructions to managers reveal that the landowners sought to make up for their absence by imposing assembly line discipline on the fieldwork of indentured Asians.[7] Its application was left entirely to the administrator, who was given sweeping powers. He was to brook no nonsense, an admonition broadly defined. The men were fed poorly; and Palto was no different from Hacienda Cayaltí, where, Michael Gonzales reported, a similar niggardliness prevailed. Indeed, these examples and others suggest that many indentured Chinese workers in Peru fell ill from meager rations and overwork. Each man received one and one-half pounds of rice a day, apportioned carefully by the manager overseeing the distribution, and on weekends and holidays the ration included a bit of meat or meat broth. Feigning illness and not showing up for work meant deductions from the

weekly wages. Whipping and mistreatment were absolutely pro-
hibited, but again vague meanings gave the manager broad leeway:
"only in grave cases, for disobedience, lack of respect, in case of flight
or fights between them" could physical punishment be used, to be
"not . . . greater than six lashes upon the underwear." And then the
ominous qualifier: "you will exhaust all measures of persuasion to
make them understand [when] they have made a mistake."[8]

Rather than inspire confidence in the owners and workers, managers predictably sank to the level of their task: they provoked and tol-
erated brutality against the Asians by plantation minions. Tensions
between managers and indentured workers grew accordingly, with
murderous results. When indenture ended, managers had to be more
circumspect in dealing with former indentured Asian field hands as
well as with peasants who came to the fields as day laborers. The
peasants had limited obligations to the plantation. At that point conflict between management and labor took new forms.

The immediate presence of the administrator made him the most
visible symbol of oppression and deceit. The venom of angered workers was directed at him, not at the distant plantation owners. The task
required the tactfulness and foresight of a diplomat and the iron will
of a military officer. It seems that few men were successful at it for
very long. Plantation owners rapidly dismissed those men who lost
control of the labor force. Only gradually and with great reluctance
did they release successful administrators, even when their abilities
had deteriorated with infirmity or age.[9]

Further suggesting the high rank they held in Pisco valley society,
plantation administrators served in several public offices by turns.
The *subdelegado de aguas* (water commissioner) and the *juez de primera instancia* (justice of the peace) supplemented the *comisario* (police commissioner) and his deputies. When the landowners needed
someone to mediate a dispute between them, they often sought out
these local officials. In the 1870s several administrators in the Palto
neighborhood acted briefly as the subdelegado de aguas, and in 1886
valley authorities prevailed upon the Palto administrator to serve as
juez de primera instancia for one year after his neighbors adamantly
refused to do so.[10] It was not a routine duty. Justices and commis-
sioners were called upon to settle disputes among owners, and as can
be imagined they found the task almost impossible. Accusations
against owners could lead to shooting wars, as happened in the Pisco

valley in 1896 when one owner perceived that the weight of the law had tipped against him. The most severe tests of loyalty and sense of duty the plantation managers had to pass came when the planters challenged one another — not in the courts but in conflicts that burst out in local warfare.

Challenges to Planter Hegemony

A brief depression in the early 1870s badly affected Peruvian exports at levels unknown since the era of silver in the early years of the republic.[11] Part of the strain that accompanied agricultural growth and technological change during a surge in European industrialization, the depression was a sign of Peru's increasing connections with world commerce as a provider of raw materials, especially wool, guano, sugar, and cotton. The fall in world prices crippled world industrial production and shrank the budding overseas markets for sugar, wool, and cotton. Numbers of coastal cotton export enterprises collapsed, as throughout the Pisco valley cotton fields gave way to grasses, grains, vegetables, and cattle.[12] Yet where the Aspíllagas were concerned, cotton remained an export item. Soon afterward, production of cotton in the coastal valleys showed strong signs of revival. Scientist Aurelio García y García's shipboard comment of an earlier era, that wherever he went the most obvious product of the valleys when viewed from offshore was cotton, later would seem prescient.[13] By the end of the century the Aspíllagas, second-generation cotton entrepreneurs, had made the transition successfully from pseudoaristocrats to oligarchs with the full social acceptability their parents desired for them.

WARTIME PARALYSIS

War and plantation authority did not mix well. The War of the Pacific (1879–83), precipitated by economic competition for control of south coast nitrate fields and by diplomatic miscalculation, severely jeopardized the structure of authority on Pisco valley cotton plantations.[14] Aspíllaga family commerce in the north coast Saña valley suffered severe war damage. On the south coast, enemy troops disembarked at the Bay of Paracas, south of the Pisco River in November 1880 and marched northward. Inexperienced local militiamen, poorly funded and quickly pressed into service by the coastal land-owners, were no match for the well-trained invaders, who easily overpowered them and organized a rudimentary occupation govern-ment.[15] The Chileans sought war taxes to supply their army, demand-ing that they be paid "in metal or in species, such as sugar, cotton, rice, alcohol, etc." They authorized destruction of property "to com-pel individuals and the [local] authorities to cover the quantities de-manded." All those who resisted payment "should be made to feel all the rigor of the laws of war."[16]

Thus a confrontation developed between the occupation army and the planters of the Pisco valley that was observed carefully by the Chinese indentured laborers. At Hacienda Palto, the contractees wit-nessed the humiliation of the manager at the hands of Chilean sol-diers more than once. The Aspíllagas had instructed the Palto man-ager to guard their most valuable possessions and to keep the labor force intact. Owners sought to hide cattle and field hands on planta-tions farther inland. But owner resistance quickly collapsed and within a month of the invasion, Palto lost twenty-four head of cattle and several horses to the Chileans.[17]

The disastrous effects of the war spread throughout the valley. Managers reported widespread flight by Chinese contractees, thiev-ery, banditry on the roads, uprisings everywhere, racial conflict on the plantations, and other signs of total social breakdown. Fleeing Chinese contractees returned in bands to steal at night from hacienda *tambos* (plantation stores) and barns, making off with tools and dry goods. Travelers found the roads hazardous even in broad daylight. In every corner could be found "bandits, or better said, assassins," while the workers were in a state of "constant alarm and agitation." Estates had been abandoned save for those whose administrators had remained on duty, "running the risk of their lives from holding on at the forefront of the interests entrusted to their care." Workers at Palto had attacked the manager physically, and it had required the forfei-ture of an entire day's labor to put down the uprising. The situation, he concluded, "had demoralized the Chinese contractees."[18]

After many complaints, Chilean occupation officials finally admit-ted the need for a rural guard, but they refused to allow soldiers to act as police. Pisco landowners pleaded that only the trained Chileans could perform such a difficult assignment. The matter was resolved when the Chileans agreed to police the valley for a fee, thus shifting financial responsibility to the plantations. Valley owners and administrators quickly fell to wrangling over the form and manner of its payment, then decided to split among themselves a *predio rural* (real estate tax) of thirty head of cattle. The owners viewed the tax as a necessity for recovering a labor force, and by 1883 regional occupation officials had collected an estimated annual average of S/1 million through a series of taxes.[19] But the patrols returned few of the missing Chinese laborers, and the landowners began to lose hope. Surprisingly, the landowners had viewed Chinese flight not as a rejection of contract labor but rather as a product of encouragement by the Chileans. They were in the midst of experimenting uneasily with sharecropping and wage contracting to revive the plantation labor force when in 1883 cotton production nearly came to a dead halt.[20]

At the close of the war the Aspíllagas felt that their Pisco valley plantation was defenseless and vulnerable to attack. It had been sacked, the fields had been trampled, and the workers had run off. With a final swagger of contempt, late in 1882 a knot of drunken Chilean soldiers rode up to Hacienda Palto brandishing guns and demanded horses and S/500. They threatened that if the manager refused, they would set fire to the plantation house. The manager gave them what he could. Between runaway contractees, bandits, and occupying soldiers, the Palto manager was at his wit's end, and he bemoaned his fate: "this valley shortly will become another Calabria and no one will be able to remain here unless he holds his purse open to all."[21]

For years afterward, valley owners sought help from the central government in Lima to restore order in the Pisco basin. Their analysis of the problem convinced no one in Lima and failed to get results. Faced with petty theft and assault by drifting Asians and others in the countryside who preyed on the plantations at night, the owners conveniently lumped criminals and hungry fieldworkers together as "bandits." No doubt the demand for funds without conditions, and the argument that Lima authorities should leave the organization and control of a police force in the hands of the valley landowners, caused the planters' argument to fall on deaf ears.[22]

FACTIONAL STRUGGLES

Local control was only one issue in the struggle over valley security. Another was factional jealousy among the landowners. In late 1884 the reconstruction-minded Andrés Cáceres government in Lima was in no mood to cater to contrary Pisco cotton growers. By announcing the formation of a national police whose regional duties would be centered in the departmental capital, Ica (a town located in the Ica valley; it governed the towns from Chincha Alta in the north to Nazca in the south after 1856 [see map 2]), Cáceres lumped Pisco's problems with those of other valleys nearby. A tax collector soon arrived in Pisco to remind the cotton owners that in the previous year their taxes had paid for "liberating" the valley from the terrors of over 200 "bandits," as he called them, "who were shot where they were caught."[23]

Nonetheless, Pisco owners and managers emphatically rejected a new police tax. They preferred to organize among themselves a local rural guard to be headed by a manager selected from the valley plantations every three months. The first comisario of police chosen was the administrator of Hacienda Caucato.[24] By January 1885 the plantation owners already were complaining about the inequity of the self-imposed Pisco valley levy, and some refused to pay their designated share. Further meetings were needed before the valley cotton planters found a way to compromise their mutual jealousies with a common need to control plantation labor. Finally, the owners agreed to collect from one another a monthly fee to be used to support a small mounted security force.[25]

Occasional outbreaks of unrest and banditry between 1890 and 1894 allowed no respite from the security issue. Several new plans were put forth by valley owners to equalize payments for support of the mounted police. None of the plans surmounted the jealousies that prevailed among the landowners, who constantly suspected one another of failing to contribute a fair share. Much of the rancor had sources in other issues. The cost of irrigation, for example, was related to the security question and divided the owners with equal stubbornness. Tempers flared when water questions joined security issues on the agenda of owner discussions.

A dispute over distribution of Pisco River water became part of the political conflict over presidential succession in 1894 to 1895 that ended in a civil war. The two sides in the conflict were led by Nicolás de Piérola and Andrés Cáceres. Nicolás de Piérola viewed the threat of a return to power by war hero Andrés Cáceres as among other things an unwarranted continuation of military rule, in which the Partido Civilista (Civilian Party) had acquiesced.[26] Such opposition as the powerful Partido Civilista once had voiced against military rule now gave way to the party's collaboration with it in the face of the humiliating loss to the Chileans and the internal threats posed by Indian uprisings in the Andean highlands. The proper handling of these questions divided the party into competing factions as the century drew to a close.[27] The Aspíllagas and Piérolas, the latter joined by the del Solars, lined up on opposing sides on many issues.

The uprising of 1894 to 1895 entwined the paths of Pisco landowners with those of national political leaders.[28] As minister of finance before the War of the Pacific and dictator of an emergency wartime government, Piérola had earned the mistrust of the Aspíllaga family and its friends. But Piérola had built a loyal following among urban intellectuals and Andean oligarchs. Nicolás de Piérola represented the powerful Arequipa regional faction of the Andean oligarchy, who, seeking control of wool exports and local agrarian policy, stoutly maintained its independence from Lima. Arequipa regional interests had nurtured a tradition of closer ties between oligarchs and urban middle sectors than could be found most elsewhere in Peru.[29] In the Pisco valley, meanwhile, Vicente del Solar, a brother of the 1894 vice-president Pedro Alejandrino del Solar, was the contentious owner of Hacienda San Jacinto and neighbor with whom the Aspíllagas had quarreled repeatedly since 1867. Most recently they had fought over the sharing of common river water and riverbank maintenance. Del Solar was a loyal *pierolista*.

The complaints of the Pierolistas in part focused on reconstruction programs that had benefited large coastal financial and export interests and did little to help the middle sectors in Lima and in the growing cities of the outlying regions of the country, especially the southern Andean highlands. In formulating a recovery plan, Deputy Antero Aspíllaga had not paid attention to these increasingly articulate groups, now represented in the national Chamber of Deputies by such men as sociologist Joaquín Capelo and an artisan, Pedro Vidaurre.[30] The outbreak of warfare in the Pisco valley between the owners of Hacienda Palto and Vicente del Solar of Hacienda San Jacinto coincided with the return of Piérola from Chile to lead the dissidents.[31]

The simmering Pisco water dispute overheated at the most inopportune moment. At Hacienda San Jacinto, Vicente del Solar needed extra river water because his seasonal requirements exceeded the normal allotment. The prolonged dispute already under way between the two plantations led the Palto owners to deny del Solar the usual courtesies. Del Solar then decided to construct a dike, forming a new channel from the river that would in turn weaken the regular river flow into the Condor aqueduct that served the surrounding plantations. The building of a dike meant that a factional conflict among oligarchs would involve the peasants.[32]

Peasants renting land near the dike especially felt threatened, and they appealed for help from the landowners. Upon learning of the San Jacinto project, Antero Aspíllaga made a few desultory appeals to del Solar for a meeting and then ordered the manager of Hacienda Palto to destroy the new dike. By the time the authorities arrived, the damage had been done. The tenants of neighboring San José haciendo, also owned by the Aspíllagas, were satisfied with well-watered fields, but the die of war had been cast.[33]

In mid-October 1894, government forces attacked and burned Hacienda San Jacinto. Vicente del Solar fled, and the government unsuccessfully hunted for him. A few days later 200 men arrived from Cañete Province (north toward Lima) and seized horses from Hacienda Palto and other plantations. The Palto manager feared that field hands throughout the valley were fleeing "willfully" to the forces of del Solar, remarking "it is like when the Chileans came."[34] Del Solar made off with all the local horses and pack animals, an act facilitated by the fact that his "guerrilleros" knew "every corner" of the nearby plantations. His audacity led the local subprefect to remark that "the planters and the peons together are *montoneras* [peasant militia] in this valley."[35] Before the war ended, government forces and rebels alike had ravaged the fields. Early in 1895, the government occupied Hacienda Palto, arresting the manager; Antero Aspíllaga also spent two weeks in jail. The Palto owners paid more war taxes, lost cattle, and fended off threats of kidnapping. Both sides soon realized how much was at stake if they could not resolve their differences, and they backed away from further hostilities. The political compromise that ended the war ushered in the *república aristocrática*.[36]

Conclusions

The changes wrought in the landowning elite of Peru as represented by the Aspíllaga clan and their Pisco valley neighbors in the eighty years after they purchased Hacienda Palto are truly remarkable. Ramón Aspíllaga, the original entrepreneur of the clan, operated in an era when relative peace marked the ruling elite, a time when the rivalries that had erupted in the first decade after independence were resolved with the advent of Ramón Castilla. The avarice and opportunism that dominated the guano boom, and the successful establishment of an export plantation sector of the national economy based on sugar and cotton in the coastal valleys of the country, helped to reshape the national ruling elite. Of course, all was not smooth and free of tension. Regional jealousies lay just beneath the surface of the calm imposed by Castilla, and urban forces awoke toward the end of that era to challenge the dominance of the military-planter coalition. Other forces the oligarchs could not control intervened in the 1870s in the form of the world depression and bank failures, the campaign to end Asian indenture, the War of the Pacific, and the long period of labor scarcity that followed.

But on the whole competition between the different sectors of the national elite was not keen. Bankers, merchants, miners, and landowners—domestic entrepreneurs as well as exporters—had worked out a modus vivendi based on the availability of agricultural and mining credit that by 1860 left all of these interests with very little to fight over. What remained were the identification of a national elite and the articulation of a national purpose convincing and inclusive enough to involve subordinate sectors of the population. If the urban and rural middle sectors could ever point to the existence of an inclusive "Peruvian" national purpose, it conceivably would foster hegemony, and the coercive aspects of the state would be replaced by instruments for the nurturing of consent—a strong, politically neutral military; vigorous media of communication; schools; and other such secondary structures that might peacefully usher in an oligarchic civil society.

After 1875 the elites were preoccupied with the disastrous Chilean invasion that threatened the foundation of their world. One important consequence of their inability to step back and see the whole picture was a continued explosion of social rivalries into civil war. Mark Thurner's research provides incisive analysis of the ethnic foundations of those rivalries and their potential for destroying the national project in the late nineteenth century. An incidental example of the parallels between personal jealousies and potentially ruinous civil strife was the del Solar–Aspíllaga dispute over the proper division of river water. Its resolution by gunfire was closely linked with the failure to resolve similar oligarchic rivalries, including the mistrust that ran between Piérola and the Aspíllagas.

The social and political power of the Aspíllaga clan peaked between the death of the father, Ramón Aspíllaga Ferrebú, in 1875 and the death of his son Antero Aspíllaga Anderson in 1927. Its trajectory was paralleled by the claim to hegemonic rule by the commercial agrarian oligarchy and its industrial counterparts. Yet though the landowners dominated the valleys, their word was not cast in stone. On the contrary, it was challenged by the growing consciousness of an opposition centered in the cities and the highlands. As Thurner made abundantly clear, a struggle took shape whose stakes were higher than simple control of available resources. More at issue was the character of hegemony, whether it would be creole or Andean.[37]

Relations between the dominant and subordinate sectors of society in the late nineteenth century also were characterized by the nearly total absence of a strong opposition to the Asian indenture traffic. Heated argument occurred within elite circles over the extent to which greatly expanded production based on this cheap form of labor would do irreparable damage to Peru's culture. But too many elements of the national elite benefited socially from Chinese indenture to expect agrarian entrepreneurs to tolerate high labor costs. For the most part, the era of Ramón Aspíllaga and his sons was a time of transition from a weak aristocratic order to domination by an oligarchy uncertain of its mandate.

No sector of the Peruvian elite could easily argue in favor of sacrificing the potential for great national wealth on the altar of cultural or racial harmony, much less continued scarcity of labor. Cotton planters and their cohorts in other sectors of the export economy remained dominant over their respective spheres, leaving the oligarchy as a whole in a position to delude itself with visions of a hegemonic order sufficient to repel an enemy in a major war, an illusion that would result in a disastrous defeat by Chile in the War of the Pacific. The illusion did not persist much beyond the war, but the confrontation with reality came too late for the landowners to take the lead in forming a hegemonic order.

A system of water regulation was not part of the peace agreement that gave the presidency to Nicolás de Piérola in 1896, but the reform water law of 1902 was part of the general accommodation that ushered in the *república aristocrática* of 1895 to 1919. A further sign of new class solidarity within the Peruvian oligarchy was the choice of presidential candidates that suited the Partido Civilista leadership irrespective of the needs of voters. The practice that reached its apogee in 1903 when Manuel Candamo, virtually unknown to the wider electorate but familiar to the oligarchs as the heir of a wealthy merchant and banking family that symbolized the links between aristocrats and entrepreneurs, became president.[38] In the Pisco valley, the planters agreed on an arrangement that called for the dominant parties, the *civilistas* and the newly formed *demócratas,* to alternate in choosing the subdelegado de aguas and the juez de primera instancia at all times. A simple compromise, it left the water issue unresolved, meaning in effect that the owners had abdicated one of their most important management responsibilities.[39] This was not inconsistent with the steady erosion of planter authority over local matters in the early twentieth century.

The peace of 1895 between the Piérola and the Lima oligarchy established the outlines of a civil order in Peru. It also invited the expression of consent by the antioligarchic sectors of society. On the cotton plantations that opportunity fell most clearly to peasants who held fixed rent contracts. After the landowners had rejected a system of wage labor with the close of indenture, these cautious tenant-farmers had emerged as a key social sector on the cotton plantations of the sur chico. What convinced the planters to rely on tenantry in cotton agriculture will be examined in the following chapter.

CHAPTER 2

Indenture, Wages, and Dominance

[a landowner] is forced to bear the title of slave to all these bastards.
— *Ismael Aspíllaga to the plantation's Lima office, ca. 1886*

By the measure of cotton output and value, the sur chico fared well at the end of the nineteenth century. In part the price of local cotton on the world market signaled the success of the region. Cotton prices stagnated briefly after the War of the Pacific, then rose gradually until the end of the century. Volume statistics also provided a general measure of regional well-being. In 1892 exports from Peru to Great Britain alone reached an all-time high of 4.97 million pounds. South coastal ports exported 6.85 million pounds to all markets, a figure exceeded only by the widely reputed fecundity of the northern Piura River valleys.[1] Despite the surge in output and prices, Pisco valley planters were not happy with the results. They complained that cotton agriculture was stagnant and no longer appeared profitable. Reports from Pisco held that although plantations produced more, cotton cost more to produce, and from every direction planters complained that labor remained scarce and truculent.

Rising production seems inconsistent with scarce agricultural labor. As we will see in this chapter, the cost of labor was the key to the discrepancy. As indenture ended and planters failed to control the rural labor force of former indentured Asians, Afro-Peruvian peasants, and other villagers, the cost of labor rose steeply. In testimony to the growing importance of free labor in plantation agriculture, cotton planters moved into a market-driven wage structure in the Pisco River countryside. Through a painful process of wage bargaining, cotton planters learned that they could not hope to control wages until they found a way to reconstitute a resident labor force. Landowners were anxious and ambivalent about the best means to settle labor into place on the plantations. They assumed that they had available only a slothful peasantry that did not respond to incentives, and they were not eager to sacrifice the expansion of cotton to achieve labor stability.

The size of the workforce often determined the number of fields in production, and when labor contracting failed to yield the requisite gangs of formerly indentured Asians, the owners adopted different measures. In lieu of other alternatives, they offered the men wages. Rural laborers responded positively to this turn of affairs; Afro-Peruvian peasants as well as Asians now sought farmwork during the harvest season. An interesting side effect occurred. Wage payments seemed to blur distinctions that managers once had maintained between groups who were thought to be hostile to one another because they were racially different. Landowners had previously stressed the importance of separatism by race for maintaining a harmonious work environment. Now it was no longer necessary to keep workers of different races engaged in separate tasks. But despite the new blurring, the peasants retained their low status in the eyes of plantation managers, and the former indentured Asians now came to be called "contractees."

Wage labor did not solve the deep structural problems that beset the plantations under change. Although the planters worked out a complicated formula for paying wages, it was so complex that it encouraged cheating by managers. This reinforced the mistrust in which peasants and contractees already held plantation authorities. Devaluation of the Peruvian sol also hurt the fieldworkers. When another worldwide depression deepened these financial problems, plantation society took a momentous turn. Peasants and contractees, although shedding the uncertainties of indenture for a wage economy, abruptly were faced with the elusive world of credit. In this chapter, we will examine the effects of the passage from wages to credit on plantation society.

Contractees and Peasants

Planters sought desperately to keep indentured Chinese workers from leaving the cotton fields, realizing that once they left only high wages would lure them back. The landowners intuited that cotton export agriculture could not support free wage labor, and a brief glance at population growth favors that argument. Indeed, from the era of slavery until after World War I the rural Peruvian labor force did not increase sufficiently to meet demand in the cotton valleys of the Peruvian coast.[2]

Labor scarcity after abolition has been the subject of much speculation. It is often suggested, for example, that the slaves left the plantations and headed for the towns, never to return to agriculture. But there is little evidence to support this assertion as it stands, and a more nuanced argument would take gender into account. Recent studies indicate that those who were pressured to remain for some time on the plantations of Lima Department (which at that time included the sur chico) were the best fieldworkers, often hardy young men. Their wives and mothers had not been able to arrange for their manumission.[3]

Without adequate studies it is safe to say that most of the young men (and surely women as well) freed in 1854 remained in rural areas, taking one of several precarious paths to survival. Although craftsmen often ventured into nearby towns to market their skills, most of them used land informally ("squatted") on the edges of the plantations, in the interstitial areas neglected by the big landowners. In these patches of turf they cultivated foodstuffs, raised families, and occasionally worked for cash on the fields of nearby plantations, especially during harvests. In bad years some of them joined together in banditry and preyed upon the traveling population or raided the major estates. But even if the 17,000 former slaves freed in 1854 had remained in place, their labor would not have met the needs of all the coastal landowners who were in search of expansion and higher production.[4]

Indenture, a labor practice associated in Peru exclusively with imported Asian men, was introduced in the sur chico when rising world demand for cotton led landowners to open wide swaths of uncultivated rich land to planting, and the practice further increased the demand for fieldworkers.[5] Within a year after they bought Hacienda Palto, for example, the Aspíllagas reopened cotton cultivation with forty newly indentured Asians. The cost of additional labor climbed predictably as demand increased. Indenture contracts that had cost 172 pesos in 1859 nearly tripled in cost by 1874 to 450 pesos. By 1870 the Aspíllagas had sent an additional 179 indentured men to the Pisco valley, and it appears that — given the amount of land in use — Hacienda Palto had reached its maximum indentured labor population.[6] After cotton prices slumped, the Aspíllagas pulled back on labor, and thereafter the numbers at Palto declined steadily. When the traffic in Chinese indenture halted in the 1870s, the number of field hands had fallen to ninety-nine men.[7]

The labor shortage that followed the War of the Pacific (1879–83) was a product of a seemingly inevitable conjuncture of events. In addition to the Treaty of Tientsin signed with the government of China that had halted the renewal of Chinese indenture (1874), the owners had experienced further losses during the war.[8] To reduce the impact of the treaty and later the war on their prized lands, Pisco valley landowners employed tactics designed to prevent the Asians from leaving and to draw those who had already fled back to the fields. Some of the methods they pursued were intended to strictly enforce the original indenture contracts, a step sanctioned by the treaty. Owners began to give precise attention to the timely payment of wages, and they balanced them scrupulously against plantation receipts. They also began to offer the men advances in the form of personal loans. A set of terms came to signify various kinds of labor contract. Limited contractees, "free" contractees, *jornaleros* (day laborers), tenants, and sharecroppers were descriptive terms signifying labor arrangements that followed the elimination of indenture. To ensure a large and continuous labor force, planters often combined several of these arrangements within the same time period on the plantation. Free day laborers worked in the fields at various times in the agricultural cycle during the indenture era at Hacienda Palto. It is hence necessary to examine the strategy of using labor contracts and their reception on the part of laborers. It should be kept in mind that the first era of free wage labor represented an effort on the part of the landowners to buy time in the hope that they might weaken the effects of sharing their plantation fields with peasant lessees.

Postindenture Labor Strategy

STAGGERED CONTRACTS

Before the war with Chile Pisco planters had devised a number of means for retaining the indentured Chinese. These devices followed an impasse in the treaty negotiations that occurred when representatives of the Chinese government demanded an immediate end to indenture and the landowners pressed for compensation. But the Chilean invasion presented a new threat. As we saw in the previous chapter, the Chilean occupation gave Chinese workers an opportunity to escape the remainder of their debts. Not all of them fled, it must be said, despite what the moaning and breast-beating of the landowners would indicate.

Meanwhile, labor retention plans had been drawn up at numerous plantations, and owners served notice to the remaining indentured hands that they could not leave until they had satisfied the debts and other obligations accumulated over the years of the contract. Planters cited debts for the purchase of goods not covered by contracts including medicines and off-plantation medical care, recreational goods, broken tools, and missed days of labor. The evidence was recorded in the records the planters kept for each indentured worker. Freedom from indenture could thus be delayed for an added two or three years and sometimes more.[9]

What might come after that was more difficult to foresee. Means for handling this problem were drawn up at a number of plantations in the Pisco valley on the eve of the War of the Pacific, but they could not be implemented until the occupation ended. A widely followed example was that of Hacienda Caucato, where the owners tried to renew contracts with former indentured Chinese on a descending scale of inducements. They had offered the men without a contract up to S/100 for immediate renewal of an eight-year term. Men with six months left on a contract were offered S/80, one year S/70, and those with three years or more S/60 to S/70.[10]

At Hacienda Palto, two groups of Asian laborers could be found before the war. One was composed of men who already had broken free of indenture, worked for wages, and resided on the plantation for varied periods of time. The other group consisted of the few remaining but fast disappearing indentured laborers. The latter were working off their debts. By mixing the two groups, Antero Aspíllaga sought to create a block of resident laborers. He planned to award contracts to individuals by taking into account a man's length of service, debts, youth, and health. In 1877, some contractees nearing completion of their indenture debts were badgered and threatened until they signed contracts for an additional three and a half years of indenture. Others continued at Palto from a few months to two years.[11]

Beginning in 1880 the owners of Hacienda Palto instructed the manager to offer the men contracts that promised an annual salary of 250 pesos, plus housing and two pounds of rice a day. The contracts proved not to be attractive enough to prevent wholesale flight during the Chilean invasion. Indentured men and contractees fled in equal numbers, and by the end of 1881 forty-nine workers were missing at Palto. Seven had joined the Chileans, seven had been pressed into Peruvian battalions, two had been jailed, and the remaining thirty-three could not be accounted for. The following September only thirty-four contractees remained on the plantation.[12]

When the occupation ended the planters resumed their efforts to control field labor. Although not generous, contracts that held out the possibility of earning nearly five pesos a week drew numbers of free Chinese agricultural workers back to the cotton plantations. Thus soon after the end of the War of the Pacific, two distinct groups of men worked the fields on many cotton plantations. One group consisted of Chinese men who could be called "residents." Their original indenture obligations had begun in 1874 before the Treaty of Tientsin and had been prolonged through the war. These men had not taken the opportunity to flee when the Chileans invaded the valley. The second group was composed of "returnees." The motives of the returnees can only be guessed at, but they may have been impelled by a combination of terror and lack of alternative options for earning a living. A few studies have suggested that those men with craft or business skills quickly established themselves in Lima and coastal towns. The problem of terrorized Chinese contractees made itself felt after an angry populace rejected the wandering farmhands and a general sense of ill will and hostility to them led to the feeling that they were vulnerable to physical attack without recourse. The plantations at least offered a refuge from the hostility shown them for years by the local peasantry. Failure to secure help in finding a way to return to China was no doubt also a source of disillusionment for some of the former indentured Chinese who returned to the plantations.[13]

But the numbers were inadequate. Scarcity of labor continued to plague the valley plantations despite the contracts offered to returnees and residents. The emergence of a bargaining process must have wounded the fragile pride of landowners and managers. Yet labor contracting seemed to offer the only approach to solving the labor problem, and plantation owners continued to rely upon it.

Competition for many kinds of labor, not only among planters in the sur chico but in other regions of Peru, revealed the promise as well as the limits of this practice. New mines that opened in the highlands in the 1880s drew villagers from the nearby Andahuaylas region, successfully competing for labor with coastal valley cotton plantations. Meanwhile, their relations with contractees running into difficulties, the owners of Palto looked once more to the local peasant population whom they sought out for a stable contractual relationship beyond day labor.[14] The owners hoped to avoid giving special consideration to the labor arrangements they made with peasants, and they prodded manager Manuel Brihuega to order their most active labor contractor to "find other people besides Chinese who could carry out the same duties under the same conditions."[15]

CONTRACTEES AND DAY LABOR

The search for stable labor incessantly bedeviled the cotton planters. Owners expressed discontent with a number of seemingly insoluble aspects of a scarce labor market, high cost being merely one of them. Problems they cited indicate clearly that they were not adjusting well to a new labor force. Race continued for some time to divide the workers in the field. Each group, Asian and Afro-Peruvian, voiced jealousy and hatred of the other, expressing their feelings in the form of complaints that the other group enjoyed better pay and working conditions. The contractees could not mistake the fact that the peasants, now working as jornaleros paid by the week, moved with ease from plantation to plantation.

Owners placed great importance in the differences between the two types of labor. Because contractees could be signed on at a periodic rate, wage fluctuations could be held to a minimum. Problems came up only when conditions of labor scarcity might suddenly coincide with the period set aside for contract renewals. Because labor scarcity was more likely to occur than not, landowners preferred contractees as a resident labor force. But the owners realized there were limits to this practice. Contractees saw no reason for working quickly and efficiently. In contrast, the wages of jornaleros fluctuated somewhat unpredictably, in close relation to the number of workers available at any time and the demand for labor throughout the valley.

The scramble for free farmhands (former Chinese contractees,

Afro-Peruvian peasants, and others) sometimes became intense because of the nature of cotton cultivation. In the Pisco valley, demand
rose in May or June with the beginning of the harvest, and peaks also
came at key points in the cultivation and irrigation cycles. Plantations
desperately sought jornaleros, who paid for their own upkeep, during
the harvest, but then their daily wage demands in slack time seemed
exorbitant compared to the low cost of upkeep for contractees. The
worst scenario for the owners combined high cotton prices, a cotton
harvest ripe for plucking, and only a few contractees available to
haul it in.

The search for rural labor might have remained a purely economic
problem had it not been for a racial distinction the owners made that
became more problematic as plantation fields became more crowded.
Although contractees were Chinese, nearly all jornaleros were Afro-
Peruvians or Afro-mestizos, descendants of the former slave population of the coastal valleys, who subsisted on the peripheral lands at
the margins of the plantations.

Since abolition in 1854 these peasants understandably had feared
entrapment on the plantations and had shunned such labor if they
could. Occasionally, as when wage rates rose the way they had during
the cotton boom of the 1860s, they found plantation day labor unavoidable. After 1874, and especially after the war with Chile, labor
scarcity drove wages to new heights. As the prospect of good pay
brightened, Afro-Peruvian peasants worked the plantation fields
more frequently. They shunned contracts like those given to the former indentured Asians, however, preferring daily pay meted out at
the end of the six-day week. In the war and postwar years, those who
avoided the army could be found migrating from valley to valley
throughout the sur chico as jornaleros in search of farmwork for
wages.[16]

Distrustful of the planters and disdainful of the Chinese, the Afro-
Peruvians may have felt hostility toward the Asian contractees on
several grounds. Competition for jobs no doubt created some ill feelings between the groups, particularly because the owners usually
doled out work along racial lines. The owners divided plantation
labor tasks that way during the indenture era for the sake of convenience as well as to intensify the differences between the races. It became common practice on many plantations to hire Afro-Peruvians
as field *caporales* (foremen) and guards to prevent flight among the

Asians. When indenture ended, nothing happened to change this practice. Other sources of racial hostility were rooted in the unknown. Afro-Peruvians feared that social mixing with non-Christians would be culturally ruinous. Repeated clashes had occurred between the two groups on almost every plantation where both could be found in the fields. The confrontations too often led to mob beatings, shootings, and much spillage of blood. On occasion, mass racial uprisings followed such clashes, and one planter later claimed that on at least one occasion in 1881 Afro-Peruvian peasants attacked Chinese of all classes en masse.[17] Such incidents convinced the landowners and plantation managers to fulfill their own prophecy, keeping the two groups away from one another.

ISMAEL ASPÍLLAGA

Landowners acknowledged the racial conflicts but seemed to take them in stride as if they were expected. Indeed, some landowners were prepared to take advantage of the mutual hostilities. Ismael Aspíllaga made several visits to Hacienda Palto near the end of the War of the Pacific, and on every trip he reported at length on the state of labor. Although his conclusions contained much foresight, and much later were adopted by the planters throughout the region, Ismael's presentation was often incoherent, his comments impetuous and scatological. He relied heavily on his immediate observations of the racial and cultural distinctions in the labor population and on his discussions with the Palto manager and neighboring landowners and managers. His anecdotal, unconfirmed reports offered the family an analysis of the present condition and future prospects of Pisco cotton plantation agriculture that though difficult to penetrate was the best information available.

In essence, Ismael Aspíllaga thought that all three problems — contracting, race, and labor mobility — were intimately connected. He thought that the scarcity problem could be solved by broadening the planters' approach to *enganche* (labor contracting with an advance on future wages, literally a hook) beyond the current practice of offering contracts only to Asians. Additionally, where others saw labor contracting as an essential tool for separating the volatile racial groups in the fields, Ismael would view contracting only as a temporary expedient for maintaining a labor force. He deemed enganche to be a tool in the search for a stable resident labor force no matter what its racial character.

Ismael Aspíllaga's thinking was formed in large part by the issue of labor scarcity after slavery. The endless efforts of the owners to organize labor after 1874, when the dimensions of the crisis grew steadily more apparent, had not borne fruit. Owners had not yet awakened to the fact that an intense competition for labor was under way across several sectors of the national economy of Peru. Nor had they anticipated that the contractees would be so quick to manipulate the Chilean occupation. In this the owners had underestimated the former indentured Chinese workers and had become unduly arrogant in their handling of labor. Observing the consequences of wartime flight from contracts by Asians in the Pisco valley, Ismael Aspíllaga remarked: "there are no workers and those that are here are so poorly disciplined that they do what they want to, not what they should, busy doing nothing but asking for higher pay for only four hours of work and . . . if one says something to them, they go elsewhere."[18]

For Ismael and other planters heavily engaged in labor contracting in the sur chico valleys, the question at this point was how to regain control of the field hands. Ironically enough, Ismael advocated that the owners begin by recognizing the differences among the agricultural labor groups available in the cotton regions. Race served Ismael as a useful instrument for judging the workforce. Distinguishing between Chinese contractees and Afro-Peruvian peasants, Ismael viewed the former as exhausted and sickly, the latter as fresh and vigorous. Yet their relative youth and vigor compared with the Asians did not necessarily make the peasants of African descent more attractive as field hands. In fact, Ismael judged that the two groups were racially similar in their deceitfulness: although the Chinese were the more available of the two, "these same are so old, so spent and so full of the same tricks as the blacks" that they could not serve as a reliable basis for rebuilding a stable labor force.[19] Essentially, he denied that one group might be preferable to the other. Both races, he argued, had learned from one another only the worst habits of slothful fieldwork. With a population of Asians and Afro-Peruvians whose skills were deeply suspect, Ismael continued, the plantation owners had little choice but to extend enganche to both.

Labor contracting accentuated the problems cotton growers associated with wages. Before the war Pisco valley owners had developed the practice of using scrip for coin of the realm when paying the field hands. But as the Chilean occupation ended, contractees and jornaleros found plantation scrip to be useless. Scrip from one plantation was not negotiable at another, and that made it difficult for mobile field hands to pay off personal debts and purchase goods at neighboring plantation stores. Merchants in Pisco and the surrounding villages refused to accept scrip from any of the plantations, demanding silver instead. Free contractees and jornaleros began to feel a noose tightening around their necks, and they took their complaint back to the plantations. At Palto, violent confrontations erupted between workers and field captains on this question, prompting the exasperated manager to rant in reference to the Afro-Peruvians: "not only do we have to fear the Chileans but all these bastards as well[,] who since time out of mind have had all the citizens of the province in check."[20]

SCRIP

It proved to be difficult to abandon scrip in payment of wages. The return of coin would mean the price of goods at the plantation store (except for items on which the landowners had a local monopoly such as opium) would be subject to market forces, inevitably driving down their cost. In short order, lower prices on the plantation would undermine enganche. As landowners realized, the discrepancy between wages and prices at the tambo helped to keep resident contractees in debt to the plantation and also discouraged jornaleros from moving about too much. Scrip on the cotton plantations thus had become a critical ingredient in the success of labor contracting. To overcome peasant hostility to the use of scrip at Palto, the Aspíllagas ordered the manager to amplify the list of goods sold in the tambos.[21]

Scrip was a key instrument in the tactics undertaken by the *enganchador* (labor contractor or agent) in search of field hands for the cotton plantations. Labor agents normally roved the countryside, surrounding up men in the taverns found in surrounding villages and settlements. Such contractors became quintessential entrepreneurs on the plantations during and after the war with Chile. Agents carried scrip with them and offered it to men who accepted a contract that obligated them to appear at the plantation within a short time. The scrip was an advance on wages, and though it placed the field-worker in debt (from which the cotton planters hoped he could not recover) it also established his credit at the plantation tambo. *Tamberos* (storekeepers) expected to recover the advance with interest.

The connections among labor contracts, scrip, and the tambo were obvious to all parties. Initially cotton planters selected as enganchadores those free contractees who had remained on the plantation. A more convenient employee to carry out the duties of enganchador was the tambero, who had won the privilege of selling necessities and minor luxuries to the fieldworkers. Labor agents thus had a strong interest in making enganche succeed. The success of labor agents was critical if the planters expected to derive any advantage from contracts and tambos. Citing debts accumulated at the tambo, cotton planters might legally restrain contractees from leaving the plantation. Likewise, a debt that had been incurred at the tambo by a fugitive licensed his recapture, a task in which the tambero joined with enthusiasm. An institution that attracted and potentially held labor from near and far, the tambo quickly became a permanent feature of plantation life.[22]

ENGANCHE

As a means for controlling day labor contractees as well as jornaleros, enganche had its limits. It depended too heavily on the skills of the enganchadores. Managers and owners grew impatient with the labor agents, finding them difficult to control despite the link to the tambo. The experiences of one enterprising enganchador provide an example of the problems that arose. An Asian labor agent named Ayate clashed repeatedly with a plantation manager and drew some attention for his efforts on behalf of the Chinese contractees. He held a tambo concession at Hacienda Palto during the Chilean occupation of the Pisco valley. A trustee and a barracks overseer before the Chilean war, Ayate was a clever man. Despite admonitions that Ayate broaden his searches, the plantation manager complained that Ayate only sought men in villages where he knew the leading Chinese settlers, and he only hired those who could present *fiadores* (guarantors). Using advances of scrip, he promised potential contractees easy access to low-cost favored goods such as salted fish, *aguardiente* (sugar cane whiskey), opium, and coca.[23] Sometimes he disappeared for weeks at a time, then billed the plantation for his train travels. When he began defending the field hands in pay negotiations, the exasperated Palto manager complained, "this is the worst enemy we have here, he always comes to ask for a higher daily wage and less labor for the peons," and the manager repeated this charge almost ceaselessly for a year. But the only indication of the owners' view of all this was a threatening rejoinder: "About the Asiatic Ayate, demand that he comply with his promise [to bring more peons to Palto], and if he reacts badly, point out to him that this is the reason that he is allowed to rent the tambo."[24]

Eventually the manager confronted Ayate with these breaches of promise and he was forced to leave his lucrative post, but not without a final enterprising gesture of independence. Months earlier the manager had loaned Ayate a sack of rice, but in response to demands for payment Ayate stalled and made excuses. Later an employee returning from the town of Pisco with provisions was set upon by thieves. Ayate learned of the attack and immediately informed the manager of Palto that one of the returning sacks of stolen rice was, lo and behold, the very one he had sent back in payment to the owners of Hacienda Palto: "Which is a lie," retorted the manager. "He wants to take advantage of this incident to avoid paying [his debt]."[25]

Restricting enganche to the Asian farmhands did nothing to deepen the pool of available plantation labor or to hold down its cost. Its racial boundaries, wherein agents and contractees usually were acquainted, probably made it more useful to the farmhands than to the planters. Asian enganche also was of limited use to planters because the previous indenture experiences of the contractees were too vivid in the memory. The labor contracts offered to the freely roving Asian farmworkers may have differed substantially from indenture and the staggered contracts designed to prolong bonded labor, but the men dismissed the nuances. So long as the use of scrip restricted access only to the tambos of a single plantation, Chinese field hands saw in the contracts a revival of the demons that incarcerated them on the plantation. No doubt for those reasons free contractees rebelled against unjust contracts by striking, work stoppages, and other actions. When pay stagnated and all protests failed to achieve any changes, contractees simply fled the premises.

From Scrip to Currency

The terms of the struggle to control farm labor entered a new stage when central government fiscal policy forced cotton planters to stop paying fieldworkers with scrip and return to hard currency. Scrip first had been used when planters agreed to issue wages as part of the conditions set forth in indenture contracts. Wages came to be seen as an important measure of the size of an indentured hand's debt to the landowner. The wage tally also permitted owners to ascertain the labor costs that went into each stage of agriculture — field preparation, planting, cultivation, harvest, and rejuvenation. Plantations charged the indentured Chinese for every item not specified in the contract — and contracts were written very vaguely. Indentured men paid for many medicines and hospital services; they paid for broken tools, religious and holiday celebration goods (candles and firecrackers), and missed days of work. Sick days were subtracted from wages, as were days missed when a person had fled from the plantation. In the final accounting of indenture, owners rarely found it necessary to invent upkeep statistics. Many men found themselves unable to refuse demands for extension of the indenture contract beyond the promised date of expiration.[26]

Planters sought to continue these practices after the end of indenture. Staggered contractees who remained on the plantations after the Treaty of Tientsin also received wages in the form of scrip, as did the free contractees who in the late 1870s roamed the valley in labor gangs. Plantation personnel receiving cash wages in the years surrounding the War of the Pacific included only managerial employees and seasonal jornaleros. Together the managerial group totaled less than 10 percent of the plantation population, while at harvest time the number of jornaleros could rise to make up half the labor force. During the war, seasonal jornaleros were fearful of wartime economic chaos, and they had begun to demand payment in hard currency. Such a demand posed significant problems for the Pisco cotton planters. Banditry was rampant in the valley, and planters tried to avoid the cost of protecting the wagon that would carry the cash from Pisco to the fundo. Authorities in Pisco had given scant attention to the appearance of illegal tender during the war; plantation scrip had seemed harmless, whereas the "Inca" bills issued by the emergency wartime government did not command much respect. Cotton planters were forced to deal with the problem on their own. Sometimes they paid jornaleros in kind and made other concessions to overcome the currency drought.[27]

With the peons, a politico-legal problem emerged. The postwar central government disapproved of using plantation scrip that threatened the already devalued Inca. Pressured from two directions, cotton planters abandoned the use of scrip to pay farm labor wages not long after the end of the War of the Pacific. The change in plantation pay had immediate social effects in one respect: Racial conflict between Asians and Afro-Peruvians became less noticeable as hard currency reduced the differences between these racially distinct farm labor gangs.

Predictably, the return of currency wages alarmed cotton planters and managers. Hard currency had to be kept on hand in amounts that demanded increased security. The larger investment of cash in current operations also encouraged owners to view plantation decisions within the wider context of other business concerns. National economic forces would make a greater impact on the cotton plantations. Under the regime of scrip, the value of wages could only be tested against cotton prices; but hard currency wages encouraged comparisons between cotton wages and wage rates in other economic sectors, potentially drawing labor away from the cotton fields.

Labor demands grew more strident with the advent of hard currency. Having contracted with an agent, gangs of up to a dozen farmhands of increasingly multiracial composition appeared at the plantation gate armed with questions. Primary concerns raised by the men were the type of labor to be performed, the time it might take, and the wage to be paid. The outlines of the contract had been agreed upon when the agent made an advance to the group and, citing specifics, managers reassured the men that the terms would be upheld. Principal among the questions asked by jornaleros before going into the fields was the means used to calculate the wage. Would pay be based on the *tarea* (task, or piecework) or the *jornal* (a day's labor)?

The two scales were the source of much bargaining. Planters clearly preferred piecework. A task varied widely in character from day to day and from place to place, making it difficult for the migrant workers to compare wages across plantations. Jornaleros and contractees fought against piecework. They felt less cheating could go on if they were paid for a day's labor. Nevertheless, though managers insisted on piecework, there were limits to how much they could abuse its vague meaning. When the Palto manager tried to redefine piecework as the equivalent of a workday, sunup to sundown, labor gangs rejected his standard. He soon found himself in the worrisome position of competing for hands with other plantations, and he ordered the *mayordomo de campo* (field captain) to give "the peons a comfortable amount of time for tarea" to encourage them to finish the work.[28]

The definition of piecework stimulated fierce labor competition among the plantations and led to a speedy reduction in the amount of labor and a rise in the wage. News of the changes spread quickly throughout the valley. In 1881 Hacienda Manrique had defined as piecework the weeding of three overgrown rows in a field, with a *lampa* (hoe) provided at no charge to the worker, and paid S/3 for completing the job. Hacienda Urrutia paid S/4 for uprooting a like amount of grapevines, but discounted weekly rice rations from the wages earned. The Palto manager reported disconsolately that he could find no more than twenty men who would work for less than S/4 per job. He would have to keep pace with the neighbors, and soon he was forced to offer labor gangs two jobs a day.[29] Earning S/8 a day "they find very alluring," reported the agitated Palto manager: "[Neighboring Hacienda] Urrutia has upset the whole valley . . . whereas before all the haciendas paid the same for piecework, day labor or harvest, now I fear the competition: just when the timing is bad for cotton, all the neighbors will pay more."[30]

Disadvantageous labor conditions forced the plantation owners to meet more frequently in the hope of setting wage standards. Day-long sessions held periodically among planters in the Condor aqueduct district of the valley in 1882 and 1883 sometimes ended in verbal agreements to hold down wages, prompting guarded optimism by some skeptics. "God grant that there might be shown in this good accord the faith it is due," prayed one of the Aspíllagas after such a meeting, and a week later he repeated, "God grant that it endures."[31] No one listened, least of all the owners of the Pisco plantations, who, as the Chilean occupation drew to a close, hoped to make up for lost harvests by relying more heavily on enganchadores.

RESISTANCE

Landowner collusion spurred the day laborers and contractees to greater resistance. At times they walked away from the plantation in anger, and at other moments they demonstrated directly in the field. On May 9, 1882, a payday, Hacienda Palto experienced its first notable labor demonstration. The contractees complained that the manager had improperly recorded their work, shorting the total number of the week's jobs by S/20. Caught cheating, the manager offered to split the difference. An hour later, he reported, ten of the men, "led by [a man named] Aona," dropped their tools. The following Monday they demanded a raise and refused to go to work. The manager quickly offered them the S/20, and when the men gave in he personally ushered all of them to the fields, "except Aona, who was expelled from the hacienda."[32]

As the war dragged on, scarcity of labor led to other problems in the south coastal valleys. Sudden peaks in daily wages doubled pay rates on a number of occasions between 1882 and 1884, raising concerns about currency. In early 1883 jornaleros were threatening to carry out another strike at Hacienda Palto, demanding pay in something other than "torn bills." Field hand complaints about pay had reached yet another level of complexity. Just when scrip was being exchanged with some success for government Incas, confidence in the national currency declined. In the countryside the Incas were in short supply. Popular distrust spread quickly, and one Pisco valley peasant voiced a common opinion on the well-used Incas: "the rich buy them at half the value in order to give them to the poor at their face value."[33] However valid, the popular lack of confidence promoted widespread farm labor unrest. Planters and managers were at a loss how to contain it and spread the blame where they thought it might do the most good. Ismael Aspíllaga fumed that the haciendas were "subject to the *hijos del país* [native peons], who are a calamity for how insolent and bad they are," and the manager of Palto blamed the problem on Pisco merchants who refused to accept the torn bills.[34]

Suspect currency, labor scarcity, and labor unrest had prompted drastic reductions in the amount of land planted in cotton in 1883, and for the next three years cotton planters undertook what appeared to be an emergency expedient. They rented parcels of plantation land not to the free contractees in whom they had expressed a degree of trust but to the formally untrustworthy Afro-Peruvian day laborers, known generally as hijos del país, who received sharecropping terms.[35] The new tenants were permitted to grow grains and vegetables — potatoes, maize, and *pallar* (pulses) — that could be marketed locally, paying half the crop in rent. This restriction (as seen by the landowners) proved to be the main attraction to the Afro-Peruvians, who now sought tenant contracts where they earlier had been suspicious of accepting long-term rental agreements. Foodstuffs became plentiful almost immediately as landowners converted half the fields of the valley into vegetable plots.[36]

The cycle of foodstuffs endured for three years when once again food prices stagnated and cotton prices reclaimed earlier levels. At that juncture, planters sought to force the sharecroppers to switch from grains and vegetables to cotton. The sharecroppers fought re-conversion. They registered complaints about the rising cost of main-taining share contracts, pointing out to the manager at Hacienda Palto that the fault lay with cotton for the "heavy expenses that its cultivation and harvest require."[37] Ismael disparaged the black peas-ants as he had the Chinese for exhibiting much the same sort of independence of mind. Combining hyperbole with bitter irony, he bemoaned the effect of resistance to reconversion on the owners, who were left in such a hapless condition that "one must bear the title of slave to all these bastards."[38]

In fact, landowners sought to pass on to the sharecroppers the burden of reconversion from foodstuffs back to cotton, and many peasants responded to the pressure by simply abandoning rental agreements. Cotton planters had no choice but to turn once more to wage labor to bring in the cotton, and the results were predictable. Between 1886 and 1890 the cost to the plantations of fieldwork in cotton climbed steadily, and in just a few years wages for field labor had doubled.

Lest this development appear once again to contribute to the stag-nation of cotton, it should be noted that the owners did not protest too strongly the abandonment of rental contracts. The most likely reason for this relative calm was a change in the financial condition of Peru that made wage labor more attractive than it was earlier in the decade. Provincial merchants continued to reject the Inca, and they were forced to watch helplessly while the silver sol, Peru's hard cur-rency, also fell victim to inflation. In 1888 the government devalued once again, and the effect on plantation wages, already dropping, was unmistakable. Wages in the countryside fell from S/8 to .30 centavos a day for harvest labor, strongly supporting the reconver-sion to export cotton.[39]

At the end of the 1889 harvest, reports coming out of the Pisco valley suggested that landowners viewed the future with some ambivalence. At Hacienda Palto, where labor seemed plentiful and the plants healthy, the prospects appeared bright. In the next few months the manager would boast that he expected the next harvest to increase sevenfold.[40] But other planters continued to find cotton unpredictable, and some had been forced to shrink the number of fields in cotton when market prices fell sharply at the end of the year.[41] Even the owners of Hacienda Palto speculated that the status of cotton was "not entirely resolved," and they gave some thought to converting their fields entirely to the "raising and pasturage of cattle."[42] That speculation died when two years later they rejoiced in the largest cotton crop of the recovery decade.[43]

Conclusions: Contractees, Jornaleros, and Tenants

Agricultural stagnation blanketed the south coast valleys after the War of the Pacific, nudging landowners and laborers reluctantly closer to one another. Landowners searched for cost-cutting measures that would mean they had reasserted control of the cotton fields. By placing their collective bet on finding a solution that would provide steady labor in an aimless economy, they bowed to the inevitable. They needed to work with the labor force at hand, scarce, suspicious, and truculent as it might be.

The fields had for all intents and purposes been abandoned. Near the end of the 1880s the international mixed commission investigating complaints of abuses against Asians inevitably found some. The commission also found that the numbers of Chinese men living on the plantations had dropped by two-thirds from the 1876 census. Part of the reduction no doubt was due to premature death from overwork.[44] Some migrated to coastal towns and Lima where they pursued petty commerce. But if the Chinese had left the plantations, for the most part they had not left the valleys.[45] Chinese contractees simply sought a reliable means of livelihood without compromising their freedom to roam. Many, lured by tenant contracts, joined the resident labor force on the cotton fundos. They often married locally and some even remained on a single plantation, where they raised families for the rest of their lives.

Early Chinese indenture had provided the cheap labor for successful commercial plantation entrepreneurship. While Peruvian society struggled through the transitional tumult brought on by guano and Asian indenture, the face of the south coast countryside changed dramatically. Plantation owners soon recognized that the adjustments made by black slaves who arranged for a manumission price, as described by Aguirre and Hünefeldt, did not apply to Chinese indenture.[46] Asians in the barracks lacked access to family life. Their existence, no less than that of the slaves who remained on the plantations, was constantly tense, violent, chaotic, and doomed to brevity.

The Chilean war allowed the planters to put off the end of indenture, despite the 1874 treaty, and after the war many concluded that the only way to stabilize the plantation economy was to re-create a resident labor force. Frightened by the project, which was to be undertaken with ostensibly free peasants, the owners sought a way to combine resident labor with legal restrictions on the workers. Enganche, or indebted labor contracting, appeared to be the first step in the creation of a web of legal entanglements for farm labor. Thus the contract began to play a more prominent place in cotton plantation agriculture. For the Afro-Peruvian peasants and Chinese contractees, on the other hand, the contract at least established a basis for agreeing to work on the plantation. It surrounded the coercive elements of plantation labor with legal limits, and it left plenty of room for escape.

For the workers, labor contracting acted as a weapon in the struggle to stabilize wages. Wages paid by the season were inherently more stable than those paid by the day or the week. Yet the rural valleys could not be kept isolated from national fiscal difficulties, and a labor problem that seemed near solution slipped out of control once more. At the end of the postwar decade, landowners were feeling market pressures to increase production and new fields had to be opened. It seemed that the only question left unresolved was the form of an agreement that would induce peasants to rent land.

Peasants and contractees remained leery of the plantations. When managers brought pressure to bear on them, used threats, intimidation, cheating, and lies to manipulate them, they simply abandoned the contract. Indeed, given scarce labor a strategy of intimidation and deceit undermined the ability of managers to fully dominate labor on the cotton plantations of Peru. Potential farmworkers viewed the plantations merely as a hostile work environment, not as a place to whose commercial success they felt committed.

As gang laborers, free contractees successfully challenged the authority of the owners to set wages and conditions that would have created a resident labor force to undermine rising field wages. The contractees refused to work for a wage that did not allow them to live independently of the plantation tambo, and the jornaleros readily joined in their protest. To secure their interests, plantation managers did all they could to keep the roving postindenture laborers from cooperating across racial lines.

Scholars are basically in agreement that planters nurtured interracial conflict in the hope of weakening resistance to planter domination.[47] But postindenture Chinese contractees and local peasants alike refused to give in to racial hatred for very long, and the adoption of hard currency for plantation wages, despite its instability, in part overcame racial hostility. It is notable that the intense racial battles fought in the cotton regions before 1883 dissipated soon thereafter. When fieldworkers fought for wages in the remainder of the decade, they vented their wrath on the plantations, not upon fellow laborers or other subaltern groups. A shift in the way the laboring population beheld fieldwork had weakened the shell of planter domination.[48]

The groundwork had been laid for the peasants and migrant laborers of the cotton valleys to challenge landowner domination of the prime bottom lands in the lower Pisco valley. Lacking the formal education that would have prepared them to compete in a growing commercial economy, including a knowledge of their legal rights and some sense of the possibilities for support from other sectors of society, the peasants would employ little more than their traditional knowledge and their recollected experiences as weapons in this struggle. Efforts to understand and assert their rights would be part of a long and often twisted itinerary. The pathway was strewn with seemingly incomprehensible obstacles, and the end point, to say the least, rarely was articulated in the public sphere.

Having been bold enough to reenter the plantations after their parents and grandparents had left, the peasants revived their recollections of the social dynamics of the plantation world. This time, however, law and custom aside, they learned that the rules of the game had changed and that an opportunity had presented itself. Their presence would swell the ranks of labor on cotton plantations and further stimulate the expansion of cotton. An intense, protracted struggle precipitated the formation of resident labor forces and the creation of permanent tenants in Peru's coastal valleys.

CHAPTER 3

Stagnation, Recovery, and Peasant Opportunities

[T]oday I am given 20 centavos less an *arroba* [approx. twenty-five pounds]
by discount on the money surrendered to me for the harvest of my crop. . . .
[I]f I went elsewhere I would find myself free of interest. I beg you to be
aware that it would not go unnoticed if you did what in justice I ask of you.
— *Luis Ferreira to Aspíllaga brothers, 1897*

Despite the importance of subsistence farming in a stagnant economy, during the Chilean occupation Pisco valley peasants abandoned
smallholdings. In the next decade they entered the plantations in
large numbers to labor in the fields. At issue in evaluating this remarkable change in peasant behavior is the importance of coercion
and choice. Did the plantations coerce the peasants onto the commercial fields, or did the peasants choose to enter those forbidding plantation gates? One new tenant at Hacienda Palto provides us with a
case study of the difficulties we may encounter trying to answer
this question.

In 1883 the owners hired a new mayordomo de campo named
Silverio Rosas, an Afro-Peruvian former gang captain from neighboring Hacienda San Juan. Rosas requested a contract from Palto on his
own initiative, not through a labor contractor. Described as humble
and "very well behaved," Rosas refused bonuses and other emolu-
ments in favor of a lifetime position as field steward and tenant. The
manager personally awarded him possession of a piece of land on
which Rosas paid half the harvest in rent. The agreement included
other important items — his portion of the harvest must be offered to
the owners who could choose to buy it at a price below the market,
and he was obligated to provide labor to the plantation when needed.
Although the contract weighed heavily on Rosas, he kept most of the
proceeds of half his crop and the position of mayordomo gave him
authority and prestige.

The owners hoped this step might cause other peasants to notice the "favorable conditions" at Hacienda Palto.[1] In fact, it seems that the tactic was successful, although the results were not immediately obvious. In the next few years numbers of peasants who had been earning wages as day laborers stopped roaming the valley and entered the plantations, taking up contracts to rent land for a stipulated period of time, usually one to three years. This chapter will examine the inducements and deterrents that explain why peasants overcame their fears and returned to the cotton fields.[2]

At the close of the Chilean war, two problems drew the incessant attention of landowners and peasants, forming their attitudes toward free plantation labor. One was the stagnant market in cotton and the other was a persistent scarcity of labor. Important differences appeared in the views of the dominant and subaltern groups toward these problems. Landowners viewed stagnation and scarcity as major obstacles to the success of the plantations. From this angle, cotton plantations could not regain their position in the market without a massive increase in cheap labor.

Peasants viewed the situation somewhat differently. Attempting to vary their sources of income when the national currency deteriorated, peasants shied away from gang labor. Independent subsistence remained attractive, especially after the national paper currency came under suspicion, but subsistence farming grew difficult after plantations expanded the lands under commercial use. Subsistence gradually was reduced, and the plantations became a major employer. Only the terms of labor were open to question.

Peasants initially resisted this subtle change in the local economy, but when the plantations varied the terms of labor, resistance turned to negotiation. Changes in the major forms of plantation labor occurred throughout the postwar decade. The changes are registered in table 3.1. Wage labor carried out by gangs of men predominated from the 1870s through roughly mid-decade. For the next few years high-risk sharecropping, known as *compañía* in the Pisco region, held favor. Compañía fell into disuse as cotton revived, and it was replaced by a more stable variation of sharecropping that lasted until the mid-1890s. At that point fixed rent tenantry, referred to as *arrendamiento,* became the dominant form of labor in the Pisco valley.

The table allows two further observations. The time frame for the move from wage labor to tenantry is noticeable. Although gang labor persisted through much of the decade, its usefulness dwindled as the

Table 3.1 Dominant Plantation Labor and Major Crops, Hacienda Palto, 1878–1908

Years	Labor	Length of Contract	Crop
1878–88	"gangs"	Daily/weekly wages	Cotton
1884–94	*Compañía*	1–3 harvests (1½ years)	Foods/grains
1886–95	*Compañía*	3 years	Foods/cotton
1895–1908	*Arrendamiento*	3 years	Cotton

Source: AFA, Hacienda Palto, *Letterbooks,* volume years indicated.

peasants and planters sorted out the implications of tenantry. Labor forms were mixed much of the time. A relationship also appears between the forms of labor used and the dominant crop grown in each period. Cash labor for cotton gave way to sharecropping for foodstuffs, which in turn gave way to fixed rent tenantry. Fixed rent accompanied the return of cotton.

During the Chilean occupation and the postwar years, peasants agreed to short-term leaseholds of one to three years that endangered the freedom of movement they formerly enjoyed as subsistence farmers and day laborers. Scholars long have charged that tenants entered into contracts under coercion and manipulation, and there is some merit to this view although the war no doubt pushed many peasants onto the plantations. In the closing years of Chilean occupation, valley roads were hazardous and any movement on them entailed the risk of attack by occupation soldiers. After the occupation a rise in banditry kept local travel hazardous. Both conditions threatened small local markets and made plantations seem more like safe havens.[3]

Despite its brevity of tenure, the early compañía rental contract stipulated that a tenant must work the plantation-run fields a certain number of days each season, earning cash for his labor, but it also provided the opportunity to plant subsistence crops. Tenants should bear the expense of removing the *espinos* (thorn bushes) which "ought not to cost them anything."[4] Part of the crop would be taken by the owners in payment of rent, irrigation, and field oxen. Migrant former Asian contractees and local black peasants, gambling that the stipulations were straightforward and the conditions tolerable, accepted sharecropper contracts.

To the planters, a sharecropping contract was a means of spreading risk in a stagnant market. For the most part a verbal agreement, the contract sometimes was written down to aid a new plantation administrator. Occasionally model contracts might be drawn up to illustrate a change in labor or land use practices.

At the end of January 1882, Pisco valley planters were discussing labor recruitment strategies, and some planned to step up labor recruitment among valley peasants. The Aspíllagas admonished the Palto manager to "offer a bonus to whoever is charged with bringing in more people," and they directed him to set aside a *gramadal* (fallow area) of Hacienda Palto for the labor recruiter. Recruiters were instructed to offer a contract to rent land to anyone who wanted it and to let the contractee know that credit would be available.

Peasants cooperated with this regime when it seemed just; that is, when the tenant contract seemed to meet the condition of fairness. It might be argued that such a condition was not demonstrable, yet fairness did not mean perfection; a plantation had only to state a few attainable goals. The contract ought to balance opportunities against pitfalls. Its length should allow for the condition of the land: a longer time frame for land long untilled. The agreement should make the rights and responsibilities of the tenant clear, at the same time providing some flexibility. Too rigid a calendar for the payment of rent, for example, might not allow for the caprices of nature that could slow a harvest. If these standards were met, other things being equal, peasants were prone to accept tenant contracts over weekly wages.[5]

Compañía Contracts

Peasants were skeptical about the brevity of tenure in the early rent arrangements. At Hacienda Palto the contract was limited to one harvest, and though it might be renewable, that was not enough time to clear debris from a long-neglected field, sow it, and produce a marketable crop. There were no takers, and in the next few months the owners adjusted their offering to cover three harvests (about one and one-half years) in return for a rental payment of one-third of the resulting vegetable or grains. Peasants now found sharecropping somewhat more attractive. New sharecroppers planted *sementeras* (food or fodder grains), with satisfactory results.[6]

Landowners feeling the losses of the Chilean occupation were uneasy about using tenants to grow cotton, and some spoke of abandoning cotton altogether in favor of cattle. Others declared they would rent the pastures to the peasants, who had already planted foodstuffs and grains. But these declarations proved to be fanciful; the landowners could not abandon the potential rewards of cotton, and the conversion of the fields to foodstuffs and grains was merely a temporary cushion. In the end, to sustain the neglected and bedraggled cotton fields, plantation owners supplemented the compañía food growers with day labor.[7]

In 1884 owners conceded further sharecropping incentives. New contracts offered the peasants land, water, field animals, tools, and seed free of charge. At Palto the owners agreed to contribute "the value [labor costs] of a third part of the harvest." If the sharecroppers hired field hands, the planters would build *posadas* (huts) for them from the plantation woodlands. With concessions came more explicit restrictions and obligations: *compañero* responsibilities included transporting crops to the plantation warehouse at one's own expense. The agreement mandated schedules for planting and harvesting, and the owners claimed all seed, for return of which sharecroppers mortgaged one-third of the anticipated harvest. Agreements continued to be limited to only three harvests.[8]

Now committed to sharecropping vegetables and working for wages in the cotton sections, peasants would have to monitor prices carefully to avoid excessive debt. Such concerns were justified. The ample foodstuffs markets of early 1885 shrank by the end of the year. Planters began dumping foods, and in the following year they resorted to bartering among themselves. The stagnant vegetable market worked against a quick return to cotton planting. Expressing a short-sighted pessimism. Palto's manager bemoaned the fate of the plantations: "the days of cotton in this valley have passed."[9]

The supplementary harvest wages of sharecroppers also fell, and the rent payers thereupon sought ways to resist the trap of debt. Using one plantation as a home base, many migrated temporarily to nearby plantations. This added to the meager earnings available at the home base, and in the declining agricultural economy it constituted a form of resistance. In response to increasing migratory activity, the manager of Palto complained long and loudly to the owners, and he called for greater control of the resident workers. He wondered aloud if fixed rent tenants would not yield a more reliable income "and one not so *eventual* [temporary] as that of the compañero."[10]

But migration was of limited value as a form of resistance. More seriously, managers accused sharecroppers of illegal activities: theft, carelessness, and willful obstruction. At Palto, foodstuffs came in severely bruised, and croppers brought the grain in late each day, thus preventing the manager from making advantageous decisions about selling price. But this proved nothing about intent. Willful obstruction could only harm the peasants, who bore the cost of transport and who found it necessary to abbreviate the harvest day to arrive on time. By speeding up the harvest they might bridge the difference in transport costs, but haste undoubtedly caused damage. Quality and speed were contradictory goals, and tenants were faced with fearsome loss of control of the crops. The Palto manager provided no evidence to support the accusation that peasants engaged in willful crop destruction.

A decade of tactical maneuvering between cotton planters and peasants failed to provide stable farming residence for Pisco valley peasants. As sharecroppers they moved warily between vegetable contracts and cotton wage labor, satisfied with neither. Meanwhile, along with migrant workers they provided sufficient labor in the cotton fields to sustain the landowners in their plans to open new cotton fields when market conditions improved. But before peasant protests against bad conditions could spread beyond the level of personal complaints, the owners found new tenants.

One could conclude that the subalterns who are the subject of this study had chosen poorly. By sharecropping under misleading pressures and inducements, they seemingly lost the advantage of scarce labor, especially when foodstuff prices fell. But this dismal scenario ignores the gains peasants made in a particularly difficult time. By seeking income outside the resident plantation, the peasants avoided unbearable debt, and when planters did not object to temporary migration, the peasants continued the practice — small reward, indeed, yet a haven that bridged those difficult postwar years.

Cotton began a gradual recovery that put an end to short-term sharecropping. The space available to peasants for sharecropping, which had been temporarily constricted, widened as the plantations proved unable to meet the rising demand for cotton without further additions of labor. Along with the fall in foodstuff prices, in 1886 owners opened new cotton fields. For the first time in over a decade, additional swatches of land were readied for commercial use.[11] As illustration, the increases in land use at Hacienda Palto shown in table 3.2 occurred simultaneously with increases in the number of

Table 3.2 Expansion of Rented Land, Hacienda Palto, 1886–89

Year	Fields Rented	Fanegadas	Hectares	Crop
1886	5[a]	16.14	46.8	vegetables/grains
1888	17[b]	18.67	54.1	vegetables/grains
1889	16[c]	42.3	122.7	vegetables/grains

[a] Fields indentified as "Torrico detrás de la casa, al lado de Arriva" and "Torrico de la calle" later were combined into one section.
[b] Four of the seven "quarters" of the "Chirimoyo" fields were rented to a single large family of tenants.
[c] Three separate pastures were combined into a single rental in three cases.
Source: AFA, Hacienda Palto, *Letterbooks,* 1886–89.

tenant contracts in foodstuffs and grains. The pattern continued for the next decade. Of more than 33 *fanegadas* (2.9 hectares per fanegada) under cultivation in 1886, 16.14 were planted in foodstuffs and grains and 16.86 in cotton, with 6 set aside for pastures. In two years land planted in foodstuffs increased only 16 percent (to 18.67 fanegadas) whereas that sown in cotton rose by 38 percent (to 23.29 fanegadas) and pastures increased by 400 percent (to 24 fanegadas). In 1886 there were 39 fanegadas in use at Hacienda Palto, and three years later land in cultivation and pastures totaled 65.96 fanegadas, a 69 percent increase.[12] The owners of Hacienda Palto had committed themselves to cultivating over three times the amount of land in use a few years before.

Further preparations included the purchase of new teams of oxen, bringing the total at Palto to thirteen pair in 1889. By the end of 1893 Palto could boast thirty-eight field oxen, some of which were used on unrented fields, employing *gañanes* (hired plowmen). Tenants were placed in many newly opened sections, including fifteen tenants from highland Castrovirreyna province and six hijos del país and their families. Together these teams produced 5,000 arrobas of cotton, the largest Palto harvest since the Chilean occupation.

Arrendatario Defiance

Opportunity and choice do not always imply purely economic responses. James C. Scott suggested that peasant resistance to the constriction of choices led to behavior that he depicted as occurring in two forms: "symbolic" and "real."[13] Whenever peasants judged that confrontation with the landowners had little chance of success, direct opposition to landowner policy ceased and symbolic opposition took over. Peasants began to "act out," such action taking any number of forms. At this point, however, Pisco valley peasants found little need for acting out, and resistance to the plantation was undercut by increases in the resident labor population.[14] But symbolic behavior was carried out during other times when tenants felt isolated from their neighbors and it left tenants at great risk. Such individual acts might induce counterresponses by the plantation authorities. Anyone who acted out had to be prepared to suffer short-term losses in the slim hope of a long-term gain.[15]

The knowledge that justice has not been well served traditionally has galvanized peasant resistance. Holding owners and managers to a standard of justice was a paramount goal of the tenants at Hacienda Palto. Although it was rarely stated, the desire to see justice done was a virtual constant in the lives of the rent payers. Without such a claim to justice, the peasants were lost, bereft of any way to demand that the manager adhere to the contract or listen to their pleas for leniency. Unable to appeal a disadvantageous decision on the grounds of injustice, a tenant had little room to further argue the case. A tenant who could not argue the righteousness of a grievance was in serious danger. To lodge a complaint merely out of self-interest conveyed the impression of greed. That person would quickly become the object of managerial disrespect and perhaps might also lose tenant rights and standing in society.[16] Undermining one's respect was tantamount to alienating oneself from one's neighbors. On the other hand, a tenant wise enough to express his or her loss in terms of the absence of justice commanded the respect and support of other tenants.[17]

In effect, insistence on justice was a weapon that made up for the disadvantages peasants faced as tenants. By insisting on justice as the litmus test of a rental contract, tenants took the highest moral ground on the plantations. Such moral ground might gain a tenant the space to make many decisions affecting daily life. This psychological space was significant for its limits as well as its breadth. The space was created strictly within the confines of the plantation and, as Scott noted was the case among Malay peasants, it was not carried in from the outside world. His conclusion encourages a search for a sense of justice within the architecture of plantation society.

In this environment, a fixed rent contract that called for minimal supervision by plantation authorities gave tenants a degree of personal responsibility for farming decisions. Indeed, tenants had opportunities to make many decisions without the constant consultation and supervision of the plantation manager: the right to sell "unmarketable" surplus, the right to keep garden lands and commercial fields free of pasturing animals, and the responsibility to provide workers for lengthy tasks undertaken by the manager. These were yardsticks of a tenant's skills, and they helped to define the possibilities and limits of fixed rent tenantry. Justice demanded that given a contract, a tenant ought to have the opportunity to execute it by carrying out such responsibilities.

A plantation standard of justice also had a less palpable dimension. When arrendatarios behaved deferentially toward the manager, and he returned their deference with exaggerated politeness of his own, the tenants received this message and gave it a meaning that the owners fully intended, one that suited their own needs. An important exchange had taken place, an exchange of politeness for deference. Not easy to measure, the exchange nevertheless contributed significantly to the rural definition of justice. In this case the concept came not from the owners or the manager but from the peasants, who in part measured their welcome on the plantation by it.

Peasants also measured the presence of an acceptable concept of justice by the extent to which a tenant commanded the respect of his fellow tenants and other farmworkers. One test of respect at this level was one's ability to gain access to the labor of his or her neighbors. Justice meant opportunity; it did not necessarily mean equality between tenants and planters. No self-respecting tenant would argue that extraordinary labor should go unrewarded or that sloth should be respected. Farming acumen and constant labor earned a tenant praise from his and her peers. The owners at times sanctioned the judgment of the peasants, often inadvertently. By offering a tenant the right of first refusal on rental of a field, the owners extended him or her the ultimate sign of respect.[18]

Contract negotiations reflected the stature gained by fixed renters. Unlike the sharecroppers who preceded them, *arrendatarios* (fixed rent tenants) made agreements to farm the land directly with the landowner. By giving this economic agreement contractual status, the owners and tenants entered into a relationship that contained clear elements of social reciprocity. As the owners feared, by focusing on the land the contract implied an almost imperceptible shift in social power. It reduced the control exercised by the owner and somewhat narrowed a large social gap in Peruvian culture. Fixed rent tenants had the right to bypass the manager and correspond directly with the landowner. Their status significantly blunted the cruder coercive measures available to plantation managers and gave unforeseen weapons to fixed rent tenants. The first group to gain this status and to grapple with its risks were arrendatario families who farmed three-fanegada (8.7 hectares) plots of cotton land on Pisco valley plantations.

LAND USE

World market collapse in 1893 nearly destroyed cotton on Peru's south coast. The following year, however, the cotton market recovered much of what it had lost. Encouraged by this turnabout, landowners sought fixed rent tenants to farm cotton and provide occasional field labor to the plantation.[19] As Hacienda Palto exemplifies, the search for fixed renters proved to be more difficult than the owners expected. Of the twelve new *chacareros* (smallholders) who had rented land at Palto in 1886, only Adrián García, who rented four fanegadas (the largest single plot of land rented by any pre-1900 tenant) remained to become an arrendatario.

In 1893 another dozen new tenants joined García, several of whom would remain on the land for a very long time. Nicanor Islas moved from fixed rent tenant to compañero and back several times in the twenty years he was associated with Palto, settling finally in 1913 as an arrendatario of a small parcel. Several others, such as Pedro Otoya (who entered Palto in the 1880s). Gustavo Buteler (who entered in 1890 and left before 1898), and Polo Rosas (whose father, Silverio, was the model mayordomo-tenant contracted in 1882) led an especially busy life. Rosas worked several other haciendas in the 1890s before returning to Palto at the turn of the century, and even at that he moved back and forth between tenantry and sharecropping, often renting small parcels of a fanegada or less at several plantations. By the end of October 1893, fifty-two fanegadas of Hacienda Palto had been rented to twenty arrendatarios, men and women, and the plantation manager was seeking candidates for twenty-three more contracts. Several fields in the Dos de Mayo section, the wettest lands, where "the weeds are so old [even] the goats will not eat them" remained unrented.[20]

As arrendamiento blossomed, owners hoped to employ two technical changes to foster the return of cotton. They moved to compress the harvest cycle, and they poured large amounts of capital into the conversion of fallows. Puzzled by a poor crop response in the first two years of the conversion, the Aspíllagas solicited the advice of the new manager, a former Palto arrendatario. The new manager viewed the difficulty as a tactical problem, and he replied that three-year tenant contracts would serve as a corrective. Three-year tenants would make more efficient use of field animals and, he went on, with its fields fully rented "Palto [will give] no less a return than at least 8,000 net soles."[21] The employment of arrendatarios, the manager noted, would allow the Aspíllagas to finesse the entire cost of opening the fallows.

Experience also taught the manager to avoid forced increases in planting that might encourage disease, undernourished soil, lack of water, and related ills. He buttressed his advice: "This I have experimented with much, and the experience I have in cultivating [cotton] I have acquired cultivating it personally, leaving my sweat on the land."[22] Impressed, the owners of Palto forestalled further alterations in the traditional planting and harvesting rhythm. Very soon thereafter several former compañeros and newly arriving peasant families received arrendatario contracts.

The 1894 fixed rent contracts at Hacienda Palto contained sixteen clauses, specifying the apportionment of land use and labor responsibilities. Vaguely similar to the contracts drawn up in the 1880s, the latest rental agreements spelled out the obligations on both sides in greater detail. Owners surrendered a plot of land of a specific size for three years, with appropriate irrigation gates, cattle and pasturage, cotton storage, and tools. Trees and stumps had to be cleared; preexisting roads, bridges, and pathways within the allotted fields had to be maintained. Tenants were encouraged to supply their own field animals, a decision the landowners later rued when the animals competed for pastures with the main plantation herd. Whenever a tenant's workers were not occupied in tenant fields, they became fair game to the plantation manager for "whatever labor might be necessary on the hacienda," at the current daily wage. Similarly, a tenant's labor and animals were to be available if no other could be called upon. The 1894 contracts obligated tenants to harvest their cotton when it was in full bloom, and if they hesitated the penalty was heavy. A planter had the right to send pickers into the peasant's field. Afterward, he could take the wayward peasant's (i.e., one who failed to harvest the cotton when in full bloom) rent out of the proceeds from the tenant's field and charge the peasant's account at the daily labor rate for the labor the planter sent in. This was a harsh condition. The difference between family labor and wage labor was a great savings to fixed rent tenants. Add the rent payment, and the result undoubtedly would be irredeemable debt.

Other parts of the fixed rent contract gave added visibility to owner power. Owner rights included that of first refusal of surplus tenant cotton and first in receipt of debt repayments, "because the integral payment of rent is preferred and obligatory over and above all other obligations."[23] Owners held the power of consent over alternate use of the lands, especially in cases of subletting. Planters thus sought to block arrendatario attempts to overcome their debts by finessing the rent. At bottom, successful farming by arrendatarios and compañeros depended upon the ease of access to credit and labor. Arrendatarios alone were equipped by contract to make choices among these items. Compañeros could only rely on the plantation to supply them with labor and the tambo to meet their personal and farming needs.

LAND USE CHALLENGE

The turn in tenant policy had begun well, but within the first year owners and tenants clashed. Problems with rent collection, the volume of the harvest, and credit caused strong reactions by owners and managers against fixed rent. For the next two years the owners of Palto found themselves at odds with the arrendatarios in their fields. Rather than forcibly evict them, the owners negotiated, but the rift was not easy to bridge. In the end, it appears that the arrendatarios had their way with the owners, convincing them that the source of the problem was not the tenants but the manager. By 1901 Nestor Cerdeña, the trusted former tenant–turned–administrator of Hacienda Palto, had been fired.

Following the opening of new acreage, production rose sharply at Palto. Cotton began to crowd foodstuffs and grains out of the fields. Peasants did not provide full cooperation in the 1894 to 1895 Pisco valley drive to raise cotton production and join in the rush to meet new market demand. The steady exports at other venues were not consistent with the figures for the Pisco valley, and the difference may reflect the abrupt confrontation over land use.[24] At Palto, the Aspíllagas and their tenants engaged in a bitter dispute over rent increases. Much of the problem lay with the owners, whose mistrust and suspicion of the peasants nearly led them to close down the fields. An intense struggle at the onset of an era that held much promise for everyone illustrates clearly how important it was for cotton plantation growth that the peasants have opportunities for making choices, as represented by options for credit and field use.

The struggle began with arrendatario complaints about the poor condition of the land. Complaining that the lands they presently farmed were so muddy that they were willing to pay higher rent for better land, over a dozen tenants accosted the manager in early 1894, asking to be assigned fields in a newly opened section of the plantation. They promised fifty arrobas of cotton per fanegada, and they added that they would work in the irrigation channels. Unable to satisfy all of the complainants, the manager of Palto conceded a move to a few of them; then he compensated the remainder by reducing the rent. Still they balked until the manager agreed to a "dead year," during which they would pay no rent while cleaning the rocks and trash out of the drainage system. The manager complained that he could not control arrendatarios who refused to invest hard cash in irrigation, and he prayed aloud for the advent of a group of *Iqueños*, peasants said to be coming from Ica valley, who in his experience were more compliant.[25]

At the core of the problem were practices peasants had dreaded from the start: selective increases in rent and reductions in the size of fields. The increases of 1894 are recorded in table 3.3. In the cases of two arrendatarios, Dionisio Mendoza and Daniel Franco, rents were doubled. In the cases involving Juan Ramos and Macario Ascona, the manager reduced the amount of land allowed them by 33 percent without a commensurate reduction in rent, exacting the same rent from one-third less land. This action dramatically increased the amount of cotton expected from the arrendatarios. Two other men, Flavio Guerrero and Gustavo Buteler, argued that the manager halved their rentals without prior consultation. Altogether the simultaneous reductions of land resulted in huge rent hikes of over 27

Table 3.3 "Dos de Mayo" Rent Increases, Hacienda Palto, 1893–94

Tenant	Land (Has.)		Rent[a]		Rent/Has.		Annual Increase (%)
	1893	1894	1893	1894	1893	1894	
Macario Ascona	4.4	2.9	30	30	6.8	10.3	51.4%
María Avilés	2.9	2.9	30	30	—	10.3	0.0%
Gustavo Buteler	2.9	1.5	30	15	—	10.0	0.0%
Daniel Franco	5.8	5.8	30	60	5.2	10.3	98.0%
Flavio Guerrero	2.9	2.9	30	30	10.3	10.3	0.0%
Manuel Guerrero	2.9	1.5	30	15	—	10.0	0.0%
Nicanor Isla	—	2.9	—	—	30	10.3	—
Dionisio Mendoza	5.8	5.8	30	60	5.2	10.3	98.0%
Pedro Otoya	2.9	—	30	—	10.3	—	—
Juan Ramos	4.4	2.9	30	30	6.8	10.3	51.4%
Total land in use	32.0	23.2					−27.5
Average rent increase							+37.35

Source: AFA, Hacienda Palto, *Letterbooks*, April 2, April 12, May 2, 1893; May 22, 1894.
[a] Arrobas of cotton (one arroba = 25 pounds).

percent from 27.5 percent less land. Arbitrary rent hikes violated contracts, dangerously reduced arrendatario farming choices, and encountered strong resistance.[26]

At issue was the investment of cash to hire labor. Who would provide the cash to pay field wages, the owners or the tenants? The arrendatarios expected the owners to fund a harvest they would eventually control, but the owners withheld loans to force the peasants to invest in the harvest. Arrendatarios met this pressure by threatening not to cultivate the land. In March 1895, they once more requested cash, this time suggesting that the harvest might rot on the plants if they could not pay the field hands.

The Palto tenants pleaded with the manager to break the impasse. Following the dire prediction about the harvest, they focused on the loan. Without an advance, they would have to use cash rather than the customary cotton to pay the interest on harvest loans. For months the owners refused to budge, and the harvest ground to a halt. Alarmed, the manager pointed out that the fields already were turning to grass "that is hard to kill."[27]

Withholding of credit and labor became central tactics in the brief tenant-planter battle. In August 1895, some of the tenants had gone back to the fields with money in hand. Only seven of them stubbornly refused to plant, which was an indication that the others had found lenders elsewhere. Once asked, the seven holdouts replied that the field oxen were at pasture and could not be moved. When the owners charged the peasants with dissembling, the manager had to admit that "there are some fields that have been deprived of a planting of cotton for lack of oxen and rakes, and as [the tenants] have only gotten two ox teams from outside, they are working with these." Yet the pressure caused some of the tenants to relent. Thirty fixed rent tenants already had surrendered 2,605 arrobas (65,125 pounds) of cotton gleaned from nearly half their fields, and from which the rent of oxen had not yet been deducted. The thirty tenants rented over 47 fanegadas of land at 50 arrobas in various sections of Hacienda Palto.[28]

At this point manager and owners capitulated to the demands of arrendatarios. Business sense dictated the move. The problem was that the owners were determined to realize S/4,000 a year net, an overly ambitious goal at this early stage of expansion. The manager argued that this could not be done with arrendatarios, who left too much land fallow each year. At best, 109 fanegadas of land would give the owners 4,040 arrobas (101,000 pounds) of cotton per year.[29] To net S/4,000 the owners would have to shift from arrendatarios to compañeros because arrendatarios could not be forced to work the land: "As these men have no more guarantee than their person, between night and morning they disappear." He generalized the problem to the valley as a whole: "as there is no authority to make them comply, . . . each day [planters] become more demoralized . . . and tolerate disorder on their haciendas."

The solution, the manager argued, was to use more cash and return to the use of sharecroppers. The owners realized that, for all their inconvenience, the arrendatarios provided extremely cheap labor, a savings particularly when it came to cleaning the irrigation channels. At the end of 1895 the owners conceded defeat. Replying to an inquiry, the manager reported "as you ordered me, I am giving [the arrendatarios] advances in small quantities according to the numbers of peons they put [in the field] and . . . they are all working and content, and the greater part of them are planting new cotton."[30] Tenants held a slight advantage in this early phase of the plantation power struggle.

CREDIT

An especially critical aspect of tenantry after 1893 was *habilitación* (loan, literally enablement), the practice of making an advance to a tenant to enable cultivation of the next crop. Virtually replacing the enganche that had prevailed the decade before, habilitación took two forms. Its earliest form provided tenants with cash they repaid with interest once they met the rent and sold the remainder of the crop. At times it took the second form, a paper loan, a credit, and could be repaid in kind. This lien fell first on the crop and might successively fall upon the peasant's remaining possessions, including field animals. Either way he or she guaranteed to repay a loan, the tenant was a debtor before the seed entered the ground. Arrendamiento thus supported planter objectives and caused arrendatarios to fret that opportunities to escape debt might be closed. Cash advances were made with stipulations by lenders who commonly restricted use of the cash to the payment of harvest wages. Tenants who received such advances signed a promissory note to provide a certain amount of labor.

In effect, fixed rent tenants assumed the role that labor agents carried out a decade earlier. Equipped with an advance, an arrendatario sought out field hands. Family members — siblings, wives, children, in-laws, cousins, uncles — were first in line. These were the most trusted people for tilling the plots in a field under the tenant's supervision and the easiest with whom to strike a bargain. Various items in the social market basket might substitute for cash wages: living space, meals, labor, and numerous other reciprocal arrangements might be among them. For the planters, the cost and hazards of using enganchadores were eliminated. The tambo remained open; its net earnings now constituted pure profit.

The conventional view that credit — debt — entrapped peasants within the plantation and stalled plantation growth does not hold up when we examine how peasants worked with debt. All tenants did not have the same understanding about the handling of debt with the plantation owner, and differences surfaced among peasants when they calculated the usefulness of this instrument. In a buyer's market the availability of several sources of credit permitted tenants a bit of maneuvering room, and some of them used this space as a weapon to counter restrictions on their farming activities. Some peasants who held tenant contracts on Pisco valley plantations at the turn of the century found ways to turn debt into an asset.

The 1894 to 1895 problems at Palto compelled fixed rent tenants to seek financial backing elsewhere, and they turned briefly to cotton speculators in Pisco. The brokerage houses of Bringas, Venn Vargas, and Albizuri among others operating in the sur chico region, were important sources of funding for the peasants. These petty merchants took a profit from charging rent on cotton storage and transfer, and they sold to foreign houses for a further premium. A degree of independence put arrendatarios in a position to solicit loans from them.

Operating on a thin margin, the small Pisco merchants made short-term, high-risk loans to valley tenants at rates equal to those offered on the plantation or better. The loan usually came due at the end of the harvest. In the Pisco valley during the late nineteenth century the lenders charged interest rates of 15 to 20 percent. These small operators, often knowledgeable about national and international markets, were in a good position to speculate.[31]

Speculating in small lots was far riskier and more troublesome than buying in massive amounts from the plantation, and the difference was reflected in the attitudes of speculators toward tenant cotton. Some of them were downright unwilling to buy it. José Bringas of Pisco spoke for some of the speculators when in response to tenant inquiries he replied that if they could not get the money from the landlords they must not be trustworthy, and he refused to lend to them. Consequently, at Palto "the greater part of the arrendatarios" did not work their rented fields, leaving the harvest to be collected by the plantation manager, who hired day laborers at prevailing valley rates.[32]

This hardly settled the credit issue for the owners of Palto. They worried one moment that their policy might fail to attract sufficient tenants only to fear later that the tenants would squander the cash. To compensate, they ordered closer supervision of tenant activities. The Palto manager, who often made speculative loans to tenants himself, responded that he carefully reviewed each tenant's situation.[33] He made heavy demands on arrendatarios as well as compañeros, he said, "since I care most . . . that there should be no debts and that the accounts shall be clear."[34]

Valley landowners, disliking the competition from local speculators, meanwhile returned to the practice of offering credit to fixed renters. To cover the hazard, they increased field supervision and further discounted peasant cotton. A chorus of grumbling greeted the change in policy that followed the credit battles of 1895. One long-standing tenant of a large parcel, Luis Ferreira, voiced his anger directly to the owners. In one indignant letter he argued his trustworthiness:

All these years [the speculators in Pisco], who made me advances for my labors, have not taken a single cent in discount, and I have always found a way to cancel my accounts as quickly as possible, as I have done in this hacienda. I hope, Sirs, to hear that you will do me the honor of . . . [lowering] the interest on the renewal of my subscription.[35]

And in another letter, quoted from in this chapter's epigraph, he defended his honor to little avail. There is no evidence to show that the owners responded to his pleas, yet Ferreira did not leave Hacienda Palto to work on another plantation, as well he might have.

To provide a margin of safety against high-interest loans after 1895, tenant strategy moved in two directions. In the fields, arrendatarios practiced double-cropping. In the financial sphere, they manipulated credit. Contracts gave tenants control of what crops and how much to plant, stipulating only that rent must be paid on demand. Custom dictated that a certain amount of rent be paid within a given time period. In contrast to earlier years, when they had been told they must plant cotton, at the close of the century the tenants had more choices. The cotton market was feeble, leading the Aspíllagas to encourage the payment of rent in cash. Crop choice was up to the tenants: if they could meet the rent by selling sweet potatoes, corn, or pulses at the market, all the better.

Many fixed rent tenants paid off their debts in the time allowed with enough consistency to elicit optimism from the manager. He predicted that in 1898 nearly all outstanding tenant debts would be paid. He remarked that this resulted from the tenant practice of combining the yield from second-year cotton bushes, traditionally the highest yielding of this triennial variety, with income from other crops.

Yet when it came time to prepare the fields, the owners once again withheld funds. Some of the tenants threatened to leave for other plantations or to replace cotton with maize. When under orders the Hacienda Palto manager told the arrendatarios to sign contracts without advances, the tenants pleaded that they had no cash. The lending policy at Hacienda Palto was forcing tenants to devote all of the crop to rent, leaving nothing to cover the cost of labor and using up their reserves.[36]

In the absence of a strong market in cotton the owners' most important demand was the payment of rent in cash. Before 1907 their
primary strategy was to advance credit with great reluctance, leaving
it to others to bear the greatest burden of this form of risk. In view of
their wish not to encourage loan competition, the owners preferred
that the manager perform the credit-advancing function.

Managers moved cautiously in the early years of fixed rent tenantry. The Palto manager made few loans and for small amounts
to carefully selected tenants. Most of these advances were barely
enough to get tenants through an unexpected contingency. Along
with the negligible amounts involved, managerial loans carried a high
interest rate, often 20 percent. Arrendatarios maneuvered to find
alternative sources of lending to finance the coming harvest, but wid-
ening this channel toward freedom proved difficult. The manager of
the plantation became an increasingly important source of funds by
late 1902 and subsequently — with the assent of the owners — he became the most significant lender on the plantation. But his lending
activities favored compañeros over arrendatarios, which may explain
why managers disdained the use of fixed rent tenants.

Managers made small advances from the moment tenantry became
widespread. One might acquire four or five debtors when the plantation owners were reluctant. Managers viewed this activity as an opportunity and a right, and the advantages seem obvious. As the daily
supervisor of field labors, the manager was in a position to enforce
repayment. Manager involvement increased the complexity of the
lending circuit, but oddly enough his presence had some benefits for
the tenants. Tenants emerging from a first contract were willing to
accept a loan from the plantation manager. Rather than face the
higher risk of the marketplace, they preferred a creditor close at hand.
Striking a bargain with the owners or the manager gave a tenant a
stake in the crop and the land and made it more difficult to dislodge
him from his rented fields.

Tenants sometimes lost a field to the manager. The Palto manager
displayed considerable arrogance toward the ambitions of arrendatarios. Impatient with peasant efforts to improve their position,
and with his control of lending within the plantation threatened by
their independence, he remarked: "These people are difficult, they all
seem to want to make out well in four years."[37] The second round in
the credit struggle went to the plantation managers.

Differentiation

By 1898 arrendatarios were a sizable part of the farm labor force in the Pisco valley. At first glance they were indistinguishable from compañeros. Generally the fields they rented were no larger than those of a compañero, roughly two fanegadas, nor were they better located or more frequently tilled. Skills being equal, richer peasants seemed to have no advantages over poor peasants. But as distinct tenant sectors the number of fields they held differed sharply. The difference between them came down to mobility and access to more land. Such opportunities were linked to effective use of credit and labor.

A profile of Hacienda Palto tenants illustrates the situation. Of the thirty-eight tenants at Hacienda Palto, eighteen were arrendatarios and twenty were compañeros. The eighteen arrendatarios already rented far more land at Palto than did the sharecroppers. Of the 187 hectares of land plowed by Palto tenants in 1898, 163.3 were rented to arrendatarios. This contrasted sharply with Hacienda Palto tenants of the previous decade and reflected a shift in land use policy after 1893. Fewer sharecroppers also rented smaller numbers of plots.[38]

The rental contracts of Palto arrendatarios in 1898 ranged from 1.5 hectares to 4.8 hectares. Within two years the Palto manager saw the holdings of arrendatarios achieve a greater range.[39] An assessment of the holdings, debts, rent payments, and productivity of the same group in 1902 reveals that the largest Palto fixed rent holding was up to 22.7 hectares. The smallest was that of a man who contracted to deliver 250 pounds of cotton from 2.9 hectares.[40]

As a group, established arrendatarios viewed compañía as a labor opportunity. Unable to attract enough day laborers to the fields at low wages, they hired compañeros—a practice that met the terms of the contract. The hiring of other peasants by fixed renters as "partners" (in effect, subrenting), can be seen a number of ways. It opened an opportunity for compañeros who might not otherwise have been able to negotiate a rental contract, and it gave the subrenter a stake in the crop. To the fixed rent tenant as well as the owner it provided more labor without greater expenditures of cash. In this area of subrenting, managers and arrendatarios saw eye to eye.

Within a year after the tenants began to seek out compañeros, the number of subrenters at Palto matched the number of tenants, twenty-nine apiece. Compañeros underwent few risks save that of not meeting their agreed upon rent quotas. Adjudication in such instances was the responsibility of the manager, whose permission was needed for subrent to take place. Arrendatarios thus remained a social step below the manager of the plantation, diminishing the arrendatarios' "managerial" latitude and leaving the manager with a bit more leverage.

Arrendatarios sought to avoid cash outlays in their relations with compañeros. Typically, as was true of arrendatario Erasmo Arona, they took compañeros on as "partners," arranging for the compañeros to join them as sublessees. In Arona's case, this gave him sufficient labor (especially if the "partner" had a large family) to meet the rent. The partnership, a verbal contract that depended for success on the mutual guarantees the partners offered one another through family ties, provided generally for an exchange of labor for part of the crop.[41]

Subleasing arrangements were very helpful to arrendatarios, who found that compañeros added to their discretionary income. The success of subrenting also discouraged arrendatarios from hiring wage labor. Instead, they seized upon the new opportunities by renting other fields and growing supplementary crops. Arona compensated for his reduced cotton returns by raising maize on an additional field with still another partner. An obvious effort at diversification in a time of scarce labor and poor crops, the tactic worked in this case; the manager took "a little" of his corn, for example, to cancel Arona's debt.[42]

The manager of Palto viewed subrenting as a challenge to his control of the compañeros, and he sought ways to undermine arrendario use of it. He redoubled earlier efforts to convince the owners that subrent was of little use in the effort to expand the fields in cash crops and pleaded with the owners to withdraw their support for it. At the same time, he admitted the importance of the strategy for arrendatarios faced with labor scarcity, lamenting in the same letter that "in all the haciendas of this valley there has been much scarcity of harvest workers" and that crops were falling to the ground for want of fieldworkers to pick them. Indeed, some planters resumed the use of labor agents to bring in laborers from outside the valley.[43]

Several pressures worked against continued good relations between arrendatarios and compañeros. Antagonisms arose between them on issues of labor and pasture. Arrendatarios, viewed by owners as the most reliable labor force following the successful increase in cotton output after 1895, found credit easier to obtain than did compañeros.

Crop variation also highlighted the growing social distinctions among the two groups. Arrendatarios typically defended themselves from debt by changing crops or planting none. In the absence of a healthy market and plentiful labor, they preferred to plant vegetables and fodder over cotton. They sometimes allowed the fields to go to weeds for grazing in order to save the cost of fodder. Although these tactics endangered the arrendatarios' ability to meet the rent payment, they gambled that the plantation owners would give them an extension to get them through a time of scarce labor. The manager of Palto tried to combat this tactic with harassment and threats but to no avail. He made frequent comparison of the arrendatarios with compañía, and in a rage he once told the owners that arrendatarios would "try the patience of a saint but I will not leave them alone."[44]

The economic differences between fixed rent and sharecropping worked to the disadvantage of compañeros. They were required to make fiduciary agreements, for example, to insure that another person was available to uphold their contracts if they fled the plantation. Arrendatarios presented "no more guarantees than their person," and for several years they refused to take orders from the manager on when and what to plant. Compañeros, meanwhile, using equipment owned by the plantation and receiving plantation seed, were told what to do, when, and where to do it.[45]

Another important distinction between arrendatarios and compañeros was ownership of animals. Fixed renters sometimes owned relatively large herds. Ownership of animals gave a tenant a degree of independence from the clause of the contract that called for rental of animals to be paid in cotton. With these animals—rarely oxen but often mules, burros, donkeys, pigs, and other barnyard animals— they avoided insolvency in bad times. To avoid transport charges they used their own mules to carry cotton to the warehouse. When vegetable prices were down, the sale of a duck, pig, or chicken could make the difference between independent farming and controlled labor on the owner's fields.

Plantation demands on tenant labor increased at the turn of the century. Labor for flood control was always provided by the arrendatarios, and soon the plantation manager required fulfillment of this obligation. Tenants whose fields were closest to the river were especially affected when in 1903 the manager required them to contribute the labor of one peon per rented fanegada for flood control. Although this was compensated labor (the manager paid S/1.00 per day, a meal, and liquor), the arrendatarios grumbled at the imposition. The manager dismissed the rumble of discontent, reporting that "[the tenants] are very content."[46]

Fixed renters were better able to resist demands on the way they used the land. The manager of Palto demanded that they allow the fields to rest between crops. On the surface a reasonable plea, in fact it was an effort to make tenant lands available for foraging by plantation-owned cattle between cotton seasons. But the fixed rent tenants interplanted vegetables and cotton. The different growing periods overlapped, preventing the manager from turning the plantation animals into those fields after the cotton harvest. Compañeros had no such option, planting only vegetables or only cotton, as the manager ordered. In this state of affairs, the Palto manager once fumed:

[I]t will be different once the hacienda decides to work by its own account [with the use of compañeros], as is done everyplace; [the arrendatarios] must be dismissed, and [we shall] begin with those lands, and only be considerate to those who deserve it, and thus there will be order and respect."[47]

Despite the manager, the owners readily accepted the growing division of tenants into two ranks. The distinction had no social implications that seemed important, and they believed it might even prove beneficial to the plantation. They signified their satisfaction by ordering the compañeros to plant only vegetables and fodder. The manager claimed that he treated the two groups fairly, reviewing their labors with equal diligence and giving attention to the labor costs of both. He based the size of their advances on the going wage and the number of workers they put into the fields.[48]

Perhaps because of the crystallizing social divisions within the plantation, relations between the manager and all of the tenants grew progressively worse. In 1906 the arrendatarios were able to bring the hostilities to the surface. A few years earlier the owners had made an important concession: they announced that arrendatarios might pay rent in cash if they could not pay in kind. Arrendatarios recognized that this decision gave them some flexibility and a bit more independence. It also hardened the determination of the plantation manager to be rid of them.[49]

Steadily rising rent helped to bring on the confrontation. To increase land rents the manager used a technique today known as "ballooning." New tenants rented fresh fields for as low as ten arrobas of cotton per fanegada for the first year, after which the rent rose by 25 percent or more for the remaining two years of the contract period. Fields that initially had rented for forty arrobas of cotton the first year were assessed in 1905 at fifty and sixty arrobas per fanegada. When the manager heard complaints, he pointed quickly to the new concession made by the plantation, especially on the subject of drainage. Palto began covering the cost of drainage ditch cleaning. But the owners recovered that expense by raising the rent. Hence a cycle of costs was locked into place: the planter paid for cleaning the ditches on poorly drained lands, and later he raised the rent to cover the cost of cleaning drainage ditches.

Palto arrendatarios responded adroitly to this tactic. If the rent was raised, they cut back on cotton and planted more vegetables that brought cash more quickly in the local market. The cash then was offered in payment of the rent. In addition, once the crop was harvested, they offered the cotton stubble as pasturage to their neighbors or sold it to tenants on other plantations. Arrendatarios who owned cattle, and thus rented pastures from the plantation, used the pastures as a weapon. Though the connection between pastures and rent was rather obscure, the fields served the same purpose as did vegetables. That is, the peasants charged for the use of pastures to provide cash to pay the rent. Some arrendatarios had well-drained lands as well as access to a great deal of water, but like the other arrendatarios they used the stubble as a weapon to counter the plantation. When the manager accused them of misconduct, they claimed that everyone was doing it. Responded the manager, "[they are] throwing stones and hiding the guilty hand."[50]

Arrendatarios went on the offensive in 1906. They blamed the manager of Hacienda Palto for the spiraling rent increases and threatened to inform the owners about his bullying and threats. But the manager's practices continued because the owners ordered it, and fearful of retribution the tenants turned upon one another. Mutual hostility and suspicion split the Palto arrendatarios into two opposing camps, and in 1907 the two groups divided sharply along geographic lines. Led by Adrián García, who was raised from childhood at Hacienda Palto, the upriver section tenants competed intensely with those "from below," each hurling insults and accusations across the imaginary center of the plantation. Those on the upriver section claimed that the tenants in the lower section farmed richer fields; those on the lower section bemoaned the ruination of their fields by excess drainage from above. Each used the argument to seek lower rent. García, whose rent had risen sharply, spoke for his neighbors. To set an example of authority, the manager disciplined García by ordering him to switch lands with another arrendatario. This done, the manager hoped that the tenants would calm down.[51]

A serious flood in 1907 only postponed the hostilities. By that time Adrián García and his son, who together accumulated some savings, decided to seek funds elsewhere, and they were promised a S/2,000 advance from Pisco lender Leonidas del Solar. Del Solar was a relative of the political rival of the Aspíllagas, Vicente del Solar, owner of Hacienda San Jacinto. García made the same request of the Palto manager, who refused to make such a large loan. García thereupon demanded to talk to the owners. But by turning first to del Solar Adrián García had damaged his chances with the Aspíllagas. The Palto manager won this case in October 1908, when the owners ordered him to evict Adrián García and break up his holdings for rent to campañeros.[52] The order did more than simply undercut García. His was a test case for the owners as well as the manager, and his eviction from the plantation fields effectively crushed the second concerted resistance action led by fixed rent tenants at Hacienda Palto.

Conclusions

The forms plantation labor took in the 1880s — gang labor, compañía, and arrendamiento — provided ample tests of hegemony and domination in plantation society. Cotton planters and peasants challenged one another as both sectors struggled to survive the shrinkage of markets and a chaotic national currency. They needed one another, and once they found a mutually acceptable balance of inducements and penalties to plantation labor, each marked out his sphere of domination. The contract to rent land nodded mute recognition of those spheres.

Because the owners conceded many rights to fixed rent tenants, the landowner-peasant struggle took its clearest form in the two elements that represented the dominance of each sector within its sphere. Owner dominance was enforced by the plantation manager. When enganche lost favor, fixed rent tenants held sway over scarce labor. Understanding the opportunity created by low population growth, peasants acquiesced in many onerous tenant duties: they accepted harsh labor assignments, sold cotton below market price, and lived in makeshift housing. They balanced the minor drawbacks of tenantry against domination of the land. But their ultimate economic goal was control of a surplus product above rent. In short, for peasants power lay in the accumulation of savings.

Intervention by the plantation manager was a major obstacle to the tenants, and they confronted his power by challenging his actions, even questioning his authority. This tactic was a key weapon in a strategy to restrict managerial control without directly challenging the owners. Anytime the peasants found a rift between the planters and the plantation managers, they tested it.

Their quest did not make the peasants immune to avarice. They attempted to take over the lands of their less fortunate fellow tenants and tried to control the sharecroppers' crops, lands, and wages. These tactics became a regrettable part of the tenant struggle for domination of the land, sometimes severing plantation society along the lines of wealth and opportunity.

Meanwhile, for the first time since the abolition of slavery and the long, slow demise of Asian indenture, free peasants provided the cotton plantations with a stable, resident labor force. This was not inconsequential: above all, it meant that some of the social power inherent in the contract had been ceded to resident tenants. To reinforce this small sphere of power, the tenants gave close attention to the justice of the rental agreement. They insisted on control of planting rights, credit sources, and labor. By manipulating each item skillfully, tenants could avoid the familiar "debt peonage" conventionally viewed as the central mechanism of peasant history in Latin America. But after 1907 they could not avoid becoming the target in a realignment of plantation forces.[53]

CHAPTER 4

Plantation Growth and Peasant Choices

All the plantations have compañeros and [the hacendados] revert to them when the harvest is bad. . . . [E]ach compañero is [in reality] three people that are useful to the hacienda. . . . Fermín Tangüis says they are expensive bastards but they are ours.

— Tomás Acevedo, manager, Hacienda Palto, 1910

Gerardo Advíncula's advancing age made him vulnerable. A peasant who brought declining energy to his fields with noticeable regularity, he fell constantly behind on the rent. A fixed rent tenant of almost six hectares of prime land, according to the records Advíncula did not have many children nor was his a large extended family. He repeatedly faced charges of poor farming judgment, and soon his outside creditors abandoned him. In the end even the compañeros he had relied on — who were not family — left him. No one was available to come to his rescue when the manager of Hacienda Palto decided to eject him from his rented lands. As the 1910 season drew near, Advíncula begged not to be thrown off the land but to no avail. Deep in debt, he was humiliated by orders to become a compañero of the much younger Francisco Luján.[1]

Advíncula may have been a victim less of his age than of the manager's campaign against fixed rent tenants. When the Pisco River suddenly overflowed its banks in April 1907, major flood damage occurred at Hacienda Palto. The river cut a new channel where the borders of haciendas Manrique, San Juan, and Palto came together, and Palto suffered a serious loss of land and crops. The manager estimated that the river had overrun more than forty fanegadas of land, destroying cotton plants, vegetable fields, and pastures. It took fifty men working fifteen weeks to shore up the banks of the river's new course and to protect Palto fields now located in midriver. Thereafter those fields were accessible in the wet season only by bridge. In addition, poor drainage reduced by half the productivity of nearby land. The manager estimated a cost of S/7,000 for the labor of reconstruction.[2]

No doubt the most startling consequence of the Pisco River flood in 1907 was the attack it precipitated on arrendatario independence in the Pisco valley. A reaction to the widespread damange done by the flooding, the attack focused the blame on fixed-rent-paying peasants. The flood convinced the cotton planters whose lands fed from the Condor aqueduct that they must exercise greater supervision of land use, especially along the riverbank where they found the most careless attention to flood control and drainage. If drainage ditches had been dug deeply and cleared, they believed, river water would have flowed on through the plantations rather than spilling onto the fields. Thus owners blamed the flooding on the arrendatarios, who had failed to meet their obligation to properly clear the drainage ditches. They determined that hereafter, in contrast to their earlier views, the arrendatarios must share the cost of drainage.

Arrendatario Decline

The owners realized quickly that they could not resolve the drainage matter with fixed rent tenants, and they determined that sharecroppers would be in a weaker position to resist the demand that peasants clear their own ditches. Owners began to favor contracts with sharecroppers over those with arrendatarios. Continued arrendatario resistance came at a time of rising demand for raw cotton, and the owners were unbending. On the eve of World War I a renewed attack on the fixed renters completely destroyed the basis for arrendamiento. When it was over, fixed rent tenants found themselves reduced to the status and dependence of *yanaconas,* (singular, *yanacón*) the widespread term for sharecroppers in the Peruvian sur chico.[3] Some, like Advíncula, survived the attack by switching to *yanaconaje,* and those who stood their ground, like Juan Esquivel, did not. How the peasants fended off the landowner assault until 1917 is the subject of this chapter.

CHARGES AND COUNTERCHARGES

The insidious rise in the river, which had then seeped into the Condor channel floodplain, gave the manager of Hacienda Palto an argument for undermining arrendamiento. As good businessmen, the owners hesitated to make a radical change without good cause, but they slowly gave in to the manager's campaign in this instance. Like his predecessor, he argued heavily for a switch to sharecropping, buttressing his argument by blaming the arrendatarios for the 1907 flood. The owners of Palto, desperate for a quick recipe for overcoming massive flood damage, and unwilling to accept the blame themselves, listened with interest as Manager Acevedo harked back to the problem he all along had found insoluble in fixed rent tenantry: the tendency of tenants to underutilize the land.[4] Specifically, he attributed the damage of flooding to unwise use of the fields, poor crop choice, and general neglect. His reasoning was persuasive, and the owners of Palto decided to end fixed rent tenantry.

A group of the oldest, most important arrendatarios at Hacienda Palto were angered by the manager's accusations, and they took bold steps to stop him, hoping to trap their adversary into making a fatal mistake and falling of his own accord. A solid core of reliable arrendatarios, they commanded over sixty hectares of Palto's most productive acreage and they fast were becoming major employers of jornaleros. Their first move was a direct challenge. Each of them in turn, upon request by the manager denied him access to the fodder in their cotton fields. On June 4, 1908, the arrendatarios followed this rebellious act with a strong letter of protest to the owners to which almost all of them affixed their own signatures.

Accusing manager Tomás Acevedo of "threats and injustices," they declared that he treated them as if they were "not free men but only the most wretched of beings." Specific charges included introduction of hacienda cattle into the cultivated fields of arrendatarios, arbitrary raising of the rent without a warning, false accusations against a respectful and respected arrendatario, failure to clean drainage ditches, cheating, and mistreatment of the owners' cattle. Finally, they charged him with seeking to prevent them from seeking credit on the market and stated, "for the reasons we have explained as well as others, we agreed that it was opportune to direct ourselves to you, who are the owners, in demanding the justice that we hope to obtain."[5]

The tenant rebellion of June 4, 1908, and the letter that followed it raise an important psychological problem that goes to the heart of peasant tactics in the struggle to seize and hold the moral high ground on the plantations. The problem had arisen before in Latin American history whenever peasants and villagers found themselves under attack by those in authority, and it would surface again on the plantations. Acting on the assumption that the manager had made arbitrary decisions on his own accord without prior consultation with the landowners, the peasants phrased the accusations to convey a secondary message: that the owners were not aware of what the manager had done. Thus, the letter of inquiry contained not an accusation but rather an attempt to inform the owners that the rules of the game were being violated. Once the owners realized what their employee was doing, the unspoken message continued, they would right the wrongs and return the relations among owner, manager, and tenant to a proper balance.

Recent studies label the social dynamics of these conditions "triangulation." The term means that under certain conditions bipolar social dynamics are transformed into a more complex multipolar negotiation. One or more of the parties involved in a bipolar dialogue may find it necessary to call the extra party into the scenario. Such an action may reflect the need for realism or it may simply suggest a tactic used to equalize conditions perceived as heavily weighted against one of the participants in the dialogue.[6] Such a step ought not to be seen as a cynical effort at manipulation nor as an intention to dismiss participation in the negotiation by one of the parties. In this case, the peasants apparently were not questioning the right of the manager to exercise authority on behalf of the owners. But by conveying in the same breath the unspoken conviction that the peasants were fully confident of just treatment by the owners, the letter challenged the manager's judgment in a critical area of his responsibilities. This nuanced message was a sophisticated, modern rendition of the phrase so familiar to Latin American historians: "long live the king, down with bad government."[7]

As a call for justice, the peasant bill of particulars contained more of a plea for leniency than a hard bargaining position. They pleaded with the owners to stop the manager from ejecting them, because the peasants were about to put more peons on the land. In fact, the manager had forced the peasants' hand, and the owners knew it. Over the next two seasons the owners responded by undermining the social basis of fixed rent, reducing its economic power and its independence. Henceforth only sharecropping contracts would be issued at Hacienda Palto, giving the landowners greater control of field labor in an improving market. The intent of the owners was not to eliminate fixed rent overnight but to halt the growing independence of the tenants.

Though fixed rent remained the leading form of tenantry at Hacienda Palto and other Pisco valley cotton plantations as well for several more years, its practitioners would be much less independent. The manager of Palto especially wanted to gain control over loans, field care, and hiring of labor. A favorable outcome would enhance his monthly salary and if all went well help him to accumulate a modest amount of wealth. In the wake of understandable peasant reluctance to see the possibility of fixed rent eliminated after the 1908 rebellion, the owners of Palto turned once more to the manager, asking him to assess the consequences of a reduction of arrendamiento and greater use of compañía.

In two lengthy responses, the manager laid out a case for the complete and immediate abandonment of fixed rent tenantry, adding that "if there is one left that is enough to make a loss of everything." He blamed arrendamiento for all the plantation's problems, pointing out that they could not command fixed renters to work if they chose to avoid it:

[T]hey [arrendatarios] get money that they invest in whatever is convenient to them and they take little care of their *chacra* [plot of land sown in foodstuffs], and it is because from the start they owe for the advance, and what in the end they can get for the harvest they have already spent on everything except the chacra.

From the tenants' perspective, low cotton prices meant that the short-term loans they were offered would not be as attractive as they were when cotton had high value. The extra time they might spend on producing a surplus above rent would only benefit the plantation, not the peasant. The surplus would have to be surrendered in order to retire the loan and thus would not add to the peasant's wealth. Hence, the peasants decided to pay their rent as called for in the contract and to allow loans to remain on the books. They were, in effect, gambling that the payment of rent on time would deter the owners from ejecting them from the land.

Compañía promised the landowners better control of cotton. Mixing morals and economics, the manager cautioned that if the sharecroppers are "reliable ones who are not villainous, drunks, or vice-ridden as many are," this system of labor would be "most commodious to the proprietors." He recommended that each sharecropper receive one fanegada of land, seed, oxen, water, clean irrigation channels, and clean drainage ditches, as well as enough credit to support 190 work days (or rental of sixty pair of oxen) per fanegada and closer supervision. Control should begin with funds that, he warned, should be given to each debtor "on the table" before witnesses. He anticipated forming the laborers into *cuadrillas* (labor gangs) under the command of mayordomos de campo, working the chacras serially, always under his own watch and count, after which he would pay workers as well as tenants.

[Thus] one can ensure that there are always enough compañeros and none are lost, save by the will of God. . . . [T]his is the only manner in which a fundo can progress, working in sharecropping and giving credit, and if this is not the course pursued it would be better to make a gift of the money, so that all nuisances might be avoided.

Later he repeated this judgment, pointing out that nearby hacendados found themselves "most comfortable with . . . compañeros, who usually do not fail to work regularly, with care and cleanliness and do not lose their chacras because the *patrón* [owner] works . . . it with them." The manager also deemed it extremely important for the success of sharecropping that sufficient land be set aside for pastures.[8]

Despite the open conflict between the manager and peasants at Hacienda Palto, the owners hesitated to fully adopt sharecropping. Aware of the personal and business interests at play in the decision, and faced with the growing success of fixed rent tenantry, they temporized. Pisco valley cotton production had shown signs of improving before the 1907 flood, and the volume of cotton continued to rise at Palto unabated. The owners saw plainly that arrendatarios were not allowing land to remain idle. Other issues began to intervene. The cost of labor weighed more heavily on many sharecroppers, making it difficult, for example, to provide labor to meet plantation obligations. However, there were some sharecroppers who had no trouble hiring the labor they needed, and these individuals usually found new opportunities to rent more land. Those who could not pay larger numbers of jornaleros lost favor with lenders and soon were evicted.

Meanwhile, competition between plantations and arrendatarios to gain access to migrant labor periodically reached a high level of intensity. Even the most successful arrendatarios hardly could compete with the landowners for the time of jornaleros who circulated throughout the region, and in any case more labor did not by itself lead to successful increases in cotton output. Much depended on two related factors: the form of pay and the kind of labor undertaken. Labor performed for the plantation was straightforward and easily calculated. The plantations hired migrant labor to carry out the heaviest and most critical tasks, and they paid accordingly. The tasks that required the greatest amount of labor were the harvest and drainage maintenance. Harvest labor provided immediate, visible results whereas the benefits of drainage maintenance were difficult to see.

Landowners tended to ignore the drainage problem during the nonharvest phases of the agricultural cycle, and in fact only when flooding threatened the fields did drainage receive the attention of owners and administrators. But effective drainage labor might temper the worst effects of flooding, especially the transformation of loose soil into muddy fields and mud into hard-packed clay. In such fields accumulation of nitrates and salinization occurred more easily, depleting crop yields. Nonetheless drainage labor was seen as a drag on immediate returns and an expense that always could be postponed until a more convenient time.

Tenants viewed the hiring of labor for drainage and harvest labor as being in the same context but they treated the expense in another manner. From the time in the previous decade when multiyear contracts became available, tenants with large families had found rental attractive. Husband and wife would perform duties together when possible to reduce the time given to plantation fields and expand the hours available to the family garden and private crops. Family labor opportunities increased when it became possible to employ relatives.

Brothers, sisters, cousins, uncles, aunts, and more distant kin, including those gained by marriage, exchanged labor for a variety of reasons but mostly because the exchange avoided expenditures of cash and could lead to savings. Successful labor bartering among tenants on the cotton plantations required that the exchanges be roughly equal and that the timing and number of obligations not crowd the labors a family gave to the plantation's fields or to its own. A complex system, its most successful practitioners were those tenants who had access to the most labor. When children grew strong enough, large families found themselves in the best tactical position to succeed as tenants. With increased labor, *mutatis mutandis,* fixed-rent tenant savings became possible.[9]

Because animals represented savings to the cotton tenants, the problems of animal husbandry sometimes overshadowed land use issues. Intensive cotton farming required well-fed draft oxen to cultivate the fields and carry cotton to the barn. The care of field animals depended in turn on well-stocked pastures that could feed a dozen or more oxen. Pastures, commercial grains, and cotton thus competed for labor and space. As the land devoted to cotton increased, conflict over investment and labor issues on the plantation were sure to arise between arrendatarios and managers.

Tenants viewed rising tensions with managers as an assault on their dignity and their space. They looked upon the manager's tactics in handling these matters as crude and combative. Peasants held to the rule of common courtesy that dictated that a guest in one's house is due some respect merely by virtue of the guest's presence. Arrendatarios were offended by the insults and other crude tactics managers used in the headlong rush to find labor. They disliked the managers' dismissal of the rules of social colloquy.

Peasants also looked upon the customary rules of public discourse in the countryside as useful weapons in the struggle to preserve basic economic prerogatives. In danger were control of access to the fields, control over pasturage, and the right to use the animals as they saw fit. As arrendatarios, after the 1907 flood, peasants additionally sought guarantees of good drainage, particularly at riverain plantations such as Palto, and when those guarantees did not materialize they blamed the manager.

NODES OF RESISTANCE

Arrendatarios resisted the decline of their independence by exploring avenues of economic compensation. Their numbers down at Hacienda Palto from eighteen in 1898 to eleven in 1908, the survivors turned for income to food crops such as maize, sweet potatoes, and alfalfa. Others worked off their old debts by earning wages in the plantation-run fields. Fixed rent tenants with cash savings and those with independent creditors best absorbed the pressures of this struggle.[10] The manager of Palto persevered in his campaign against the arrendatarios.

Contests between managers and arrendatarios after 1908 did not always follow a clear and simple path. At Palto the administrator's campaign to replace arrendatarios with compañeros was complicated by the occasional emergence of a third position. Joaquín Gutiérrez, the least threatened arrendatario whose apparent status as a godson of Ramón Aspíllaga gave him a degree of immunity, watched for opportunities to provide himself with some insurance lands and even to bid for the managership himself. A fixed renter at Hacienda San José, Gutiérrez took advantage of the misfortunes of arrendatarios who had lost favor, volunteering to take up the duties — and the lands — of expelled peasants. When difficulties beset fellow tenant Daniel Franco in 1910, for example, Gutiérrez seized the moment to demand repayment of a loan, and Franco satisfied the debt by a signing over a fanegada of land. Later Gutiérrez coveted a parcel of old Advíncula's land, turning it into pastures of alfalfa and maize. He would have little difficulty paying the sixty arrobas a year rent, the manager surmised acidly, because he sought out "those meek ones that he always finds at his leisure, with whom he forms partnerships."[11]

Clearly desirous of the manager's job, Gutiérrez hired day laborers and sharecroppers with considerable success, and by 1912 he was much feared and respected among valley peasants. To the surprise of many of his neighbors, in 1909 Gutiérrez had acted as the spokesman of all the arrendatarios in another conflict with the plantation manager. He further alienated manager Acevedo by accusing him of mistreating all the arrendatarios and of "acting in league with David [del] Solar of San Juan" on the water distribution problem. Gutiérrez requested an audience with the owners on behalf of the arrendatarios of Hacienda San José "because they felt no support at all from Acevedo." Though serious, these accusations apparently elicited no response. Later when Acevedo quarreled with the San José tenants over the cleaning of irrigation channels, the Aspíllagas gave the manager their full support.[12]

Because Juan Esquivel lacked close ties with the owners, tenants watched his conflict with the manager more carefully. Receiving an arrendamiento contract at the turn of the century after the manager praised his thrift and "attitude," Esquivel rented a fanegada of land in a notoriously muddy section of Hacienda Palto.[13] With the help of his three sons, Demetrio, Ernesto, and Manuel, his wife (who regularly worked the harvests with her sons), and brother Apolonio, Esquivel paid off spiraling rent increases and large loans. To keep his income and obligations in balance, he used a number of tactics. At times he worked as an *arriero* (muleteer), sending a son or brother Apolonio when labor was needed on the plantation fields. He invested in cattle, and the amount of land he rented grew from the original fanegada in 1902 to over seven fanegadas by 1907, yielding an annual rent of 5,200 pounds of cotton. Esquivel rented four *yuntas* (pair) of oxen for several weeks a year, borrowing money to pay this fee from a lender in Pisco. His neighbors respected his skills, and though unlettered he was a leader of the June 4, 1908 rebellion.[14]

Relations between the Hacienda Palto manager and the ambitious Esquivel deteriorated after the tenant lost one-third of his fields in the 1907 flood. The manager's demand for rent did not take the flooding into account.[15] The two men argued loudly in the fields over rent and parallel claims the manager made on a personal loan. During these intense volleys, the administrator countered Esquivel's economics with epithets, denouncing the "black ingrate," and "speculator," whom he accused of lacking gratitude for the loan.

The proud tenant refused to be cowed, denying the manager access to fodder on his fallow fields but insisting in turn on his contractual right to cut firewood in the plantation woodlot. More serious accusations followed. The manager claimed that Esquivel had hacked the haunches of a plantation ox that had wandered into his field — a trumped-up charge, witnesses later said. But the manager nonetheless administered the degrading punishment of strapping Esquivel overnight into the plantation stocks.[16]

Undaunted, Esquivel finessed the manager at every turn. Despite the personal conflicts, he demonstrated a keen sense of timing, manipulating credit and crops with skill. He expanded his operations, taking over two new fields and adding a subtenant to help with a rent bill that had grown to 8,111 pounds of cotton.[17] His debts to several lenders mounted likewise, and to receive yet another loan he could not avoid guaranteeing part of the next crop with a pair of his precious oxen. Overcome by avarice, the manager took the offer of cattle as security to be a sign of failing resources, and he informed Esquivel that no more cash could be taken from local lenders until he had covered his existing notes.[18]

Plans to eliminate fixed rent tenantry in the Condor aqueduct floodplain received a setback when the river rose without warning once again on April 1, 1910. "On the same day and hour that it happened" in 1907, declared the astonished Palto manager, "an immensity of water arrived that . . . inundated the Acequia [irrigation channel] de Francia." He added: "they say these crests have never been reached before."[19] When it ended an entire section of the mainland portion of the plantation was underwater and nearly all of Juan Esquivel's recently planted cotton shoots were in danger of rotting.

In July 1910, Esquivel offered a crop of reserve vegetables to a Pisco lender, from whom he then sought an additional S/1,000 loan. Unsuccessful and now desperate he turned to the Palto manager, who saw this occasion as an opportunity to protect his earlier investment and to stake a prior claim to the arrendatario's oxen. Bemoaning his bad fortune and about to lose everything, Esquivel used the small postflood cotton crop to spread payments to all his creditors, angering the administrator, who had expected to exercise his rights as majority lender. The manager complained that Esquivel was impossible to deal with, as were other arrendatarios to whom the manager had loaned considerable sums and for which he was falling deeply into debt. Esquivel turned to the court of last resort. Traveling to Lima, he talked to the Aspíllagas and returned with another loan to start the new season. Upon hearing about this latest evasion, the manager cursed Esquivel as a "swindler" who "denies the amounts he received with great carelessness."[20]

Once recovered from the worst of the flood damage, Esquivel went on the offensive. In the next two years he consolidated his holdings, arranged for extensions on his debts, and made the payments on time. In 1913, Esquivel headed the list of Palto tenants with twelve fanegadas of land, and he increased his holdings to fourteen fanegadas before the next flood, all but a few hectares planted in cotton. Aside from the administrator, he was the largest, most influential tenant on the plantation. He solidified his position by regularly hiring more labor and producing far more cotton than any of the other arrendatarios.[21]

Confident now of his relationship with the Aspíllaga family, he retained a deep hatred for the manager and never missed a chance to communicate with the owners at the man's expense. On two occasions, in 1911 and again in 1913, he had complained to the owners that the real source of labor scarcity at Palto was the unwillingness of the manager to pay a decent wage. There was a simple solution the tenant said: "offer the peons enough soles and they will come to work."[22] Esquivel was deeply offended when the manager in 1918 announced another rise in rent. This announcement came in the wake of yet another damaging flood. Apparently certain it had not come from the owners but purely from the mind of a manager bent on vengeance, Esquivel overreacted. His letter challenged the administrator's rent hike, convinced that it was a repeat of the man's earlier designs on his cattle.

Respectfully but firmly Esquivel asked the owners if the administrator had received such an order as he claimed. His letter displayed a bit of the pride of one satisfied with his accomplishments, confident and certain that the owners would reciprocate. But he received no reply. Implied in the lack of a response to Esquivel's letter was a refusal by the owners to tolerate a tenant challenge to the authority of the plantation manager: Although he had mixed familiarity and deference in his letter in appropriate amounts, Esquivel could not believe that the Aspíllagas would turn their backs on him, raise his rent, and deny him the courtesy of an explanation.[23]

The boldness displayed by men such as Esquivel and Gutiérrez highlights the intractable dilemma cotton planters faced after 1910. The arrendatarios pressed the message that stable, reliable resident tenants meant greater care of the fields. But more accessible labor and a greater volume of production did not offset higher costs. Nevertheless, for a moment the owners of Palto abandoned the campaign to be rid of arrendatarios, and fixed rent tenants continued to grow in numbers throughout the valley.

In the years prior to World War I, arrendatarios dominated the landscape around the Condor aqueduct. Though the freedom to bargain for credit had been restricted, a buyer's market suppressed interest rates. Rent increases were a threat, but they too were limited by the market, and arrendatarios continued to thrive in the Pisco valley. Other aspects of fixed rent tenantry nonetheless continued to agitate the landowners. So long as arrendatarios could block access to fields by the plantation cattle, little could be done to achieve economies of scale through the expansion of operations.[24]

The arrendatarios of Palto drew very different conclusions from the sudden halt to the campaign to drive them out. They not only saw themselves as indispensable to good land management and productive husbandry of cotton cultivation, but they also concluded that the owners had learned a lesson from the perennial tenant alarms on the subject of drainage. The arrendatarios assumed drainage was an item too costly and important to be left to individual tenants, and that now planters would invest heavily in clearing the channels to prevent a repetition of such disasters as had occurred twice in a decade at Palto. Flood damage had received immediate attention and repair. The owners gave considerable time and investment to rebuilding the breakwaters that had been thrust into the river and the shoring along the riverbank where heavy currents carved away the soil after the 1907 and 1910 floods. But after 1910 owners and managers once more pushed flooding and drainage into the background. Preoccupied with control of labor, they subordinated drainage to the higher priority issues of credit and land use.

Yanaconaje

LOANS

A renewal of the debate over credit and its uses at Hacienda Palto in 1913 revealed the obstacles that lay before Pisco valley arrendatarios in the early years of World War I. The owners and manager discussed the importance of cash versus credit as tenant incentives. The manager argued that by halting the issue of cash advances the owners could end tenant independence. A cash loan was a "white elephant," he continued, primarily because the rented land units were too small to allow the tenants to quickly repay the loan. Defaulted debts, creating debt peonage, were a waste of capital. Default meant that tenants had squandered the advanced cash and then afterward hid part of the harvest, stealing the cotton "and [committing] a thousand barbarities." All the tenants, poor and wealthy, squandered it equally, "and the guarantor is the person who is ruined."[25]

Cash obtained in the marketplace suffered the same fate, charged the manager. Pisco lenders, who had loaned large and small sums to tenants throughout the valley, no longer made cotton loans save to those who could secure repayment with a mortgage, in effect drying up the valley loan market. Trust in the ability of well-off tenants to repay debts had eroded, contributing to the decline of fixed rent tenantry. Indeed, local lenders José Bringas and Venn Vargas, currently the only active *prestamistas* (money lenders) of the Pisco valley, by 1914 issued loans only to managers and owners.

In his subsequent remarks on the subject of loans, the manager revealed his growing self-interest in controlling credit. In prior years, the manager had commanded the borrowing practices of only those tenants to whom he was the compañero, but as the broader market closed down, the manager became a more important lender on the plantation. The Palto manager borrowed cash from Venn Vargas Cia. and loaned it to arrendatarios, developing a secondary market within the confines of Hacienda Palto. This was a highly speculative business, for if the tenants could not make payment in kind, the manager stood to lose the collateral he had offered to Venn Vargas.

But the attraction of a 20 percent return outweighed the risk. With better access to the market than the tenants had, if everything went smoothly the manager could supplement his salary handsomely.[26] He further reduced costs by charging penalties for late payment or hiring security to enforce compliance, as did private lenders. To keep track, he simply issued each debtor a book with the borrowed quantities inscribed in it, and when peasants surrendered the harvest, the rent and debts could be reconciled. The manager of Hacienda Palto expressed his satisfaction with the arrangement thus: "As this is so clear and is done in good faith I become angry with no one because nothing has happened to [let a debtor] deny me a quantity [of cotton] saying they have lost the book."[27]

It was not long before these conditions changed. Though the onset of war in Europe had created demand for many Peruvian raw materials in 1914, national exports surprisingly declined. The threat of war on the high seas generated a sudden fall in cotton prices, and owners had trouble selling off the large crops that had begun to issue forth. The fears of English and French merchants made them less willing to purchase Peruvian cotton, and Aspíllaga exports fell likewise.[28] Falling overseas demand for cotton occurred in tandem with the erosion of credit in the Pisco valley. By the end of October 1914, the manager complained that the drain on credit was hurting the arrendatarios and threatening a halt in cultivation for the new season. His own credit position made it extremely difficult for him to lend another sol:

[I]t . . . is the greatest and riskiest undertaking, this passing money that costs you your blood . . . into the hands of these faithless and shameless drunks . . . [which is what] I find so difficult about credit[; it is] like waving a cape at a lively bull or flying in an airplane [;] these days no one could earn a living doing either of those things."

Given the rapidly spreading world war's impact on the market, Pisco valley cotton planters thought once again about suspending cotton cultivation, a move they had not contemplated in twenty years. In those halcyon days they had weathered a poor cotton market by allowing sharecroppers to plant fodder or vegetables without loans. Now the landowners preferred fodder in order to build up the plantation cattle herd while the wartime doldrums passed. Meanwhile, many halted the issuance of credit to tenants altogether. As one of the owners of Palto put it, they would have to "take appropriate measures, and quickly, in retaliation for the problem of extended [debt] in our fundos."[29]

Under wartime conditions the owners' view of fixed rent tenants differed from that of the managers. To encourage the peasants to abandon cotton, they made it possible for tenants to pay the rent in cash as well as in kind. By reducing the possibility that managers could earn extra income from loans, the new lending policy predictably drove a wedge between tenants and managers. But the policy also widened the gap between a few wealthy arrendatarios who could afford to continue to market cotton and the majority of fixed rent tenants who were hard hit by the drop in cotton prices.

Cotton could be grown only on the largest holdings of the wealthiest arrendatarios. Many of them paid off loans by hiring the jornaleros that recently had grown in numbers throughout the valley, marking a rare departure from labor scarcity. Falling wages in the midst of the credit crunch saved numerous wealthy arrendatarios from terrible losses in the 1914 to 1915 season.[30] On other fields, tenants stopped growing cotton, turning to hay or vegetables to earn income. The possibilities that opened up under the new terms threw a different light on tenantry. Peasants explored alternative ways to earn cash, including the subrental of fields.

FIELD ENCLOSURES

As credit dried up, numerous arrendatarios relied on cattle to keep them afloat. Cattle ownership among peasants on plantations, conventionally seen as a burden on a backward peasantry and an obstacle to modernization, was to the tenants of Pisco valley plantations a storehouse of wealth. A sign of the competition to amass cattle was demand for pastures. When arrendatarios contracted to rent land before 1915, it was understood that a portion of the fields always would be set aside as pastures. Peasants grew fodder in those lots, usually alfalfa or hay. The clash between Palto tenants and the plantation manager in 1895 had shown that tenants enjoyed the right to refuse entry into the pastures by alien cattle, including those owned by the plantation manager and even those of the owners.

After the confrontation of 1908, peasants exercised the right of pasturage at Palto with greater resolve. Indeed, they fought off the owners by extending the right of pasturage beyond its earlier limits. Some arrendatarios rented pasture space to fellow tenants, and in a few instances they rented space to tenants from other plantations. Planters were slow to learn of this extracurricular activity, but as the pressure mounted on arrendatarios to renounce some of their long held rights the pastures became a focus of contention. The struggle to control plantation pastures joined the conflict over credit in the developing confrontation between owners and peasants.

A series of reports compiled between 1914 and 1917 by one of the visiting owners of Hacienda Palto puts the problem of land use into bold relief.[31] The issue was complicated, the report admits, by the existence on the hacienda of cattle with four different owners: the landowners, the manager, the family business accountant in Pisco, and the tenants, arrendatarios as well as compañeros. Calling the lack of fodder at Palto "deplorable," the reports contain orders that winter pastures be reseeded immediately in hay, and that the field oxen be farmed out to pasture at other haciendas, a practice "commonly done throughout the valley."[32]

Tenants as a whole owned large numbers of cattle. Altogether they totaled 191 head at Palto, including oxen, bulls, horses, cows, mules, donkeys, ponies, sheep, and calves, as compared to the herd of 62 fielded by the plantation. Furthermore, tenants of different statuses exercised separate customary rights in cattle. Compañeros kept cattle within their fields, grazing them at the edges of the irrigation ditches, and they did not have the right to refuse entry to plantation cattle. Arrendatario cattle fed in exclusive rented lots. As the owners saw it, the major problem was that each arrendatario owned but a few cattle, but the numbers of each always left an excess of forage in many fields. Moreover, the reports emphasized that the fixed rent tenants brazenly sold the forage rather than give it up to the plantation. This was unacceptable, and orders soon followed that would generate strong protest. Tenants were instructed to permit plantation cattle into the fields of forage wherever the fields existed on the plantation, and sharecroppers whose fields already were available to plantation cattle were commanded to open them whenever the manager wished.[33]

Crop choice also received attention in the business reports. Some of the arrendatarios in 1914 had forsaken cotton on the simple observation that it would not pay their rent and debts. Nonetheless, arrendatarios were ordered to plant cotton against their better judgment, and to protect themselves some took on supplementary jobs. Juan Esquivel, it is worth recalling, had started out as an arriero at Hacienda Palto, driving cotton to Pisco. In 1915 he returned part-time to this work when cotton was down. Pedro Otoya, a veteran of the 1908 rebellion, returned to work for the plantation as a shepherd.[34] But a command issued by the owners to open up the tenant pastures could not easily be enforced. Between visits by the owners, the Palto manager reported that the arrendatarios stubbornly resisted his orders on pasturage. The manager lamented: "I cannot count on more stubble than [that from fields] occupied by those [compañeros] to whom I give credit and with whom I have business."[35] The other tenants, he pointed out, refused to give up a single stalk of field fodder to the plantation.

Had the visiting owner of Hacienda Palto studied the past indicators of arrendatario response to owner attacks upon their rights, he might have been better prepared for the sight that met his eyes upon his return to Palto. A review of the records might have suggested the lengths to which arrendatarios were prepared to go to uphold customary rights. One long-standing arrendatario who lost most of his cattle in 1913 cautiously made a compañero contract with the Palto manager. He borrowed a sum of money from the manager and pastured his cattle in some of the fields. Telling no one, the manager then insisted that the compañero double-crop: cotton and sorghum on the high fields, cotton and hay on the low ones. To express their appreciation — and anticipating the pasturage opportunity — the owners insisted that the compañero be given an additional cash advance as a reward. The manager grumbled that all they had done was to give him the "rubber tit of spending for the fodder."[36] Later, the manager demanded payment in kind on the notes as though all the compañero's fields had been planted in cotton.

Accusations followed arguments, one louder than the next, and soon the puzzled and suspicious owners asked their business accountant in Pisco to intervene. The accountant called in the police commissioner, who walked the fields in question with the manager but could not make a clear judgment. The accountant supported the manager. Though the compañero lost the dispute, in principle he had won. He refused to allow the manager to dictate field use, and he lodged a key point with the owners that they had heard before: the compañero accused the manager of arguing on behalf not of the owners' animals but on behalf of his own. This compañero had been defeated primarily because he had no outside lenders or other plantation owners to stand behind his challenge. Forced soon thereafter to accept larger loans and to forage plantation animals, he could only declare angrily: "in the end God sees things; and he always sees them with justice."[37]

The effects of the latest confrontation stunned the Aspíllagas, one of whom returned to Palto before the next harvest ended. He found the replanted pastures to be "transformed into forests." Pastures in name only, they contained none of the high quality fodder he had expected the peasants to plant. The pastures needed new walls; drainage ditches and outlet sluices were clogged shut. All of them were in near ruin, and repair would be very costly. Not a fourth of the arrendatarios had been willing to give up their fodder to meet the needs of the owners. Cattle owned by tenants, meanwhile, had been used for every conceivable purpose. Their numbers had diminished by over 14 percent within the past year to a total of 162 head from overuse and seizure for debt.[38]

Palto's pasture struggle was the penultimate attempt by desperate arrendatarios to protect their rights. It had many distracting sidelights, but the main issue was provision of fodder for cattle, the most valuable aid to effective farm output in an otherwise human-labor-intensive industry. At stake in the argument over access to the pastures was not simply the validity of tenant contracts but ultimately control of the plantations. Because the owners retained the power to make the final decision about land use, the struggle was theirs to win or lose. But they had to do combat with a semblance of fairness or their advantage would disappear in a moment. Owners and peasants knew that and sought to avoid confrontation.

No doubt the field oxen at Palto were overworked: the manager repeated that he held them back from rental whenever possible for fear they would die in the harness. He preferred to work them a half-day at a time and feed them the rest of the day. The problem was where to find fields to feed them in. A large, fourteen-fanegada section of Palto was set aside for all the field oxen on the plantation, but the arrendatarios had accumulated such large herds that the manager realized they were making unbearable demands on the land.[39]

Scarcity of pastures continued unabated into 1915. Constant pressure from the manager finally yielded up some areas for the plantation animals on tenant lands, though not without cost. The manager reported that he was having to pay either in cotton or money for the pasturage and that no relief was in sight.[40]

CONTRACT RESTRICTIONS

In the midst of World War I, the cotton market reversed itself once again. When the sea lanes had reopened, European merchant houses once more placed larger orders for Peruvian raw cotton. The rise in demand for raw cotton made a favorable impact on the plantations of the Pisco valley but not necessarily on the peasants. Planters were cagey about opening the gates of the plantation to tenants with whom they had been carrying on a war of their own for some time. Besides, the labor picture, so recently brightened for the owners and arrendatarios by a rise in the jornalero population, just as suddenly faded. No doubt rising demand on the international market for Peruvian raw materials, including sugar, rice, and metals — especially copper, silver, and lead — reduced the labor population available for the cotton fields.[41] Competition for labor throughout the country and the reticence of cotton planters did not bode well for Pisco valley arrendatarios.

The owners of Hacienda Palto set out in 1915 to alter their relationship with the peasants who held contracts to rent land in the cotton fundo. But conditions were not ripe for an all-out assault upon fixed rent. Continued relative scarcity of labor caused the owners to fear a rise in wages if they were to open opportunities for direct plantation wage labor. Still, if the owners wanted a resident labor force and economies of scale, they needed to take steps to reduce the independence of the fixed rent population; in fact, no matter what they did by 1915 they could not avoid resistance from the arrendatarios. In a bid to cancel out one set of peasants with another, the owners attacked the issue of land use on two levels. First, they announced that preference in rental contracts and loans would be given henceforth to sharecroppers. Following that, they proclaimed that direct cash loans from the owners once again would be made available to the arrendatarios "but only under the most rigorous control." A signal of a change in attitude by the owners toward the resident labor population, the announcements contained barely a hint of the new direction the owners would take. Yet they suggested that the days of fixed rent tenantry in the Pisco valley were numbered.

In all new tenant contracts issued at Hacienda Palto in 1915 sharecroppers received improved conditions although the improvements were minimal. In exchange for land, seed, water, and oxen, the compañeros were obligated to pay only half the cost of the harvest (whereas earlier they had borne the full cost). Given that the cost of labor made up the bulk of the cost of the harvest, this was no small reduction, for sharecroppers were rarely able to shrug off the cost of labor. In return, they were required to plant the land only in cotton. Half the crop went to the plantation in rent under a two-year contract with a one-year renewal option. The plantation had the right of first refusal in the sale of any surplus.

Included among other important obligations in the new contracts were the duty to surrender to the planters one-fourth of any crop of fodder; to work on the irrigation ditches and riverbanks of the plantation; to maintain the roads, bridges, and other access ways on the rented lands; and to provide labor for such other tasks as needed. The planters agreed to hire resident sharecroppers first and to give preference in loans to the sharecroppers over arrendatarios. Debts could be paid in cotton at ten centavos per arroba below the market price.[42]

The critical item in the survival of cotton tenants through World War I was not productivity or the number of cattle a tenant held, but whether or not he or she had access to credit. The new compañero contracts, brought on largely by the determination of the cotton landowners to recapture full control of the expansion of cotton commerce without losing the capacity to maintain a resident plantation labor force, further reduced the independence of cotton tenants. It favored cotton over such crops as fodder and vegetables, and it encouraged rent in kind over cash. An Aspíllaga managed to express a combination of planter satisfaction at the new contracts with disdain for the tenants in the following manner: "in any other form, it would be advances of money the hacienda might make to inadvertently support the pastimes and vices of these people."[43]

Reverberations of the End of Fixed Rent

Economic and political judgments collided when Pisco valley cotton planters thought about adopting full-scale yanaconaje in 1917. A suddenly urgent market for raw Peruvian cotton, stimulated no doubt by scarcities as the world war drew to a close, encouraged some owners to quickly evict arrendatarios and rush headlong into the new contracts.[44] Others acted more coolly, waiting until political circumstances might allow for ejection with less fanfare. However the owners proceeded, there could be no doubt that fixed rent tenantry as it had been known for decades was near collapse. This time the owners of Palto and their neighbors were determined to command rising cotton volume and profits. With the labor reforms they had undertaken in the past two years, it seemed likely that they would succeed.

To consolidate their gains, the owners of Hacienda Palto took the final decisive steps in the process of deepening planter control: they notified all fixed rent tenants at the two fundos, San José and Palto, that henceforth they would be compañeros and if they did not like it they could leave the land. The manager made the announcement as the harvest of 1917 drew to a close. By November no further tenant contracts for fixed rent would be issued.[45] The new draconian land use policy took effect immediately. All tenants now fell under the same regulations. No one, not even arrendatarios of great age and lengthy service, escaped the change. Most notable about the new contracts were the changes in the rules of land use, credit, and loans. No tenant henceforth would be allowed to accumulate more than two fanegadas of land. Loans could no longer be arranged with lenders outside the plantation; henceforth only the owners would make loans to the tenants. The manager would handle the accounts, but all agreements would constitute a direct owner-to-tenant exchange. For the first time rent was tied to credit. The Palto owners announced that loan repayments would be deducted automatically from the cotton surrendered as rent at 20 percent below the market. The plantation retained the first right of refusal on the surplus tenant cotton and would charge a ten-centavo fee per *quintal* (100 pounds) for transporting the surplus to the ginning plant.

From late 1917 on, nearly all tenant contracts discouraged the peasants from holding personal cattle, and they soon found it necessary to rent almost all animals from the plantation.[46] Prospective tenants who were not interested in growing cotton thereafter were turned away at the gates.[47] Tenantry grew yet stricter when the owners added a few other key prohibitions and soon would be labeled yanaconaje. By the close of 1917 this form of tenant contract was in general use throughout the sur chico.[48]

The owners installed yanaconaje slowly and systematically. At the end of the 1917 harvest the new manager introduced yanaconas into two sections of Hacienda Palto. The affected fields recently had been converted from pastures after two years of fallowing, and the prospects for achieving a robust cotton crop, said the manager, were good. Another fifteen lots were set aside for future yanaconas, and the manager assured the owners that other fields could be converted with equal deliberation. The manager ended his latest assessment by opining that the high 1917 cotton prices would make yanaconaje advantageous for tenants and owners together.[49]

When one of the owners returned to Palto on the eve of the new season, he learned why yanaconaje could not be implemented at full speed. The old arrendatarios had finessed his plan to cut them off from outside loans by successfully arranging for cash advances from speculator José Bringas. Eager to oust the offending tenants, the owner was reminded by the manager that most of the arrendatarios were well along in the cultivation of their fields; removal now might prove complicated and damaging to the harvest. Some, like Esquivel and one or two others whose fields looked exceptionally promising, boldly requested more money from the plantation in order to continue cultivation. A few tenants newly arrived from the Chincha valley to the north also sought cash loans.

Despite their recent determined statement of opposition to alien loans for fixed renters, the owners approved the loan requests.[50] The following year numbers of new tenants applied for contracts on the fields of Hacienda Palto. The owners were pleased to learn that new tenants were coming from the Chincha area as well as from the upland interior reaches of the Pisco valley. The wider area of influence suggested that the Pisco region was gaining favor among a broader peasantry, and they announced repeatedly that the revised rules of yanaconaje governed local tenantry.[51]

Wisdom dictated that such a potentially disruptive change be made with sensitivity to its political consequences, especially given recent stirrings of political protest among the peasants. A strike, the first major protest action by the peasants since 1908, had occurred at Palto in April 1917. The manager provided little information on the event, but together with recent demonstrations in Pisco, it suggested a growing political consciousness among the peasants. Pisco valley yanaconas apparently had begun to suspect that economic problems on the plantations required a political response.[52]

Demonstrations in the central plaza of Pisco brought together dozens of yanaconas. In an apparent effort to unite tenants from several plantations in a common cause, the speakers passionately called for vindication of peasant rights in the land and an end to restrictive actions by the landowners.[53] Although poorly organized and easily repressed by mounted police, the demonstrations were notable for their purpose as well as for how the newly outspoken peasants voiced resistance. Shifting the focus of their discontent, the Pisco demonstrators blamed the landowners for placing limitations on yanacón independence.

Ever since the confrontations of 1895 that pitted new tenants against managers over questions of land use and contract rights, the peasants who worked in the Pisco valley plantations had suggested that their protests were a response to arbitrary behavior by the plantation managers. They insisted they had no quarrel with the owners who unknowingly had been led astray by their employees. Those pleas for justice were directed to the owners and against the managers. Off the plantation, however, the object of protest abruptly changed. The claim of managerial culpability was abandoned, and the peasants lay the blame for misery and injustice squarely on the shoulders of the landowners.

Two possibilities may account for the shift in peasant strategy from indirect to direct attacks on the owners. On the one hand, it can be read as the locution of an idea that could only be expressed through a political slogan; there seemed to be no other way to express the view that the managers should stand aside and let the landowners carry out a land reform. It was widely sensed that the owners were in command of the state and that all government authorities in the valley deferred to the landowners. But it was not generally agreed among the peasants that the landowners were the problem. Nevertheless, perhaps they believed that joining together to voice common complaints to the owners might better gain their attention.

After 1917 similar adjustments made throughout the cotton region further jeopardized fixed rent tenants. The few remaining arrendatarios found that they had to give more of their time to plantation labor in order to make up for reduced savings. If heads of household and other adults could not do the labor, children more likely went to the fields. Some resident tenants hired peons *de afuera* (from outside), as they were called, at pay rates that depleted arrendatario reserves.[54] The Francos, the Esquivels, and Gutiérrezes no longer felt secure about tenantry. At Palto, the only tenant with any sizable holding by the end of 1917 was Tiburcio Muñoz, a five-year resident who farmed a converted pasture near the plantation house.[55]

Assessment

In spite of a prolonged landowner attack upon peasant rights, Pisco valley arrendatarios made some notable gains in the early twentieth century. They withstood separate assaults on credit, cattle, and land, and they seemed to threaten planter hegemony in the countryside. The appearance was deceiving, as conditions at Hacienda Palto illustrate (see table 4.1). There were 32 arrendatarios at Hacienda Palto in a total resident labor force in 1898 of about 300 men, women, and children, and a dozen others at Hacienda San José, where altogether 90 peasants resided.[56] In 1909 the number of arrendatarios shrank to eleven individuals (including the administrator of the plantation), who held about 41 fanegadas (almost 120 hectares) of Hacienda Palto. In the next few years their numbers returned to 31 peasants, who together held rental contracts for nearly 97 fanegadas (about 280 hectares) of the cotton fundo.[57] The number of compañeros and arrendatarios at Palto rose in tandem until 1913, after which compañero numbers grew constantly until 1917.

Changes in the size of holdings dramatize the losses arrendatarios took for defending the rental contract. In 1898, eighteen arrendatarios averaged 5.44 hectares of land apiece, and a decade later ten arrendatarios held an average of 11.3 hectares. By 1913, thirty arrendatarios at Palto rented similar sized plots. That is, while the numbers of arrendatarios grew steadily in the early years of the expansion of cotton, the amount of land each rented changed very little. More telling is the fact that no arrendatario was permitted to rent a large section of Hacienda Palto until Juan Esquivel and Genaro Flórez took possession of significantly large fields in 1909. Yet in 1913 tenants held an average of 9.32 hectares each, a 21 percent decline in the size of arrendatario holdings over a four-year period. When tenants complained about repressive managerial seizures, the owners stripped them of the land. The uprising alone was not sufficient cause for the owners' action, but together with the floods of 1907 and 1910 the owners insisted on resuming control of the land.

Restrictions on landholding further divided the fixed rent tenants at Hacienda Palto. After 1913, they split into two groups, both labeled arrendatarios. But in fact those who rented within the last three years came under compañía-style restrictions. Even among those who held comparatively large tracts, land was distributed very unevenly. Of the seventeen large holdings, only Juan Esquivel (with 36 hectares) and Amancio Muños (with 52 hectares) held a substantial amount of land. Another five fixed renters held between 6 and 16 hectares each. The remaining twenty-three tenants held 82 hectares, nine of them holding over 5 hectares apiece and the others holding fewer than 5 hectares.

Looking closely at the rent requirements shown in table 4.2, it is easy to see why some tenants faced more difficulty than others in paying their debts. Without taking into account access to labor, soil conditions, and numbers of draft animals, some tenants started off with the balance tipped strongly against them. Here is further evidence suggesting that — when it came to survival on the plantation — the size of one's holdings mattered less than the size of one's obligations.

Despite the differences in size of landholding, tenants at Palto suffered equally in the seizure and redistribution of land after 1915. Although they remained on the plantation, the old arrendatarios, robbed of the hard-earned rights and privileges they held just a few years earlier, had reason to enthusiastically support the yanaconas who in 1917 took their dissent outside of the plantation and into the political arena.

It is difficult to assess relations between arrendatarios and compañeros. Little in the documents suggests direct antagonism. Anytime

Table 4.1 Changes in Landholdings, Fixed Rent Tenants, Hacienda Palto, 1893–1913

Tenants	Size of Holdings (Has., Known Years)			
	1893–94	1898	1909	1913
Tomás Acevedo*	—	—	20.0	49.3
Gerardo Advíncula	—	—	—	5.4
Mariano Albares	—	—	—	2.9
Agustina Alvarado	—	9.0	7.8	5.1
Isabel Alvarado	—	2.9	—	2.9
Erasmo Bernaola	—	5.8	—	—
Fermín Biscarra	—	—	—	5.8
Julia Bojorje	—	2.9	—	—
Seferino Borjas	—	5.8	5.8	5.8
Gustavo Buteler	2.9	—	—	—
Venino Cabral	—	5.5	—	—
Mariano Campos	—	—	—	5.8
Faustino Cavesudo	—	—	—	5.8
Eusebio Córdova	—	—	—	5.3
Pedro Cosme	—	1.6	—	—
Vicente Cosme	—	—	—	3.3
Apolonio Cruses	—	—	—	2.9
Clemente Cruces	—	—	—	—
Fernando de la Cruz	—	3.7	—	—
Vincente de la Cruz	—	3.7	—	2.9
Felipe Dias	—	—	—	2.9
Juan Esquivel	—	—	25.2	36.0
Genaro Flórez	—	—	17.5	—
Daniel Franco	5.8	—	—	—
Lisardo García	—	—	—	2.5
Flavio Guerrero	2.9	—	—	—
Manuel Guerrero	2.9	—	—	5.8
Anselmo Gutiérrez	—	—	5.8	7.7
Erasmo Horna	—	14.9	—	—
Juan Huamán	—	—	—	2.9
Nicanor Islas	24.7	11.6	—	8.1
Francisco Luján	—	—	7.3	6.7
Norberto Luján	—	—	—	2.9
Damaso Martínez	—	—	—	2.9
Valentín Mayuri	—	—	—	4.8

Table 4.1 *Continued*

Tenants	Size of Holdings (Has., Known Years)			
	1893–94	1898	1909	1913
Dionisio Mendoza	5.8	—	—	—
Abelardo Meza	—	—	5.8	—
Chino Moyanos	—	3.8	—	—
Amancio Muños	—	—	—	52.2
Jacinto Nieto	—	6.5	—	—
Pedro Otoya	2.9	2.9	—	2.5
Miguel Pachinga	—	5.8	—	—
Juan Ramos	—	—	—	5.8
Isabel Rosas	—	—	—	4.3
G. F. Victoria Santana	—	—	—	15.4
Enrique Siguas	—	5.8	—	—
Juan Tirao	—	2.8	—	—
Julio Torres	—	—	—	2.9
Luis Torres	—	—	8.9	10.1
Santos Valdivieso	—	—	9.0	—
Juan Vera	—	2.9	—	—
Total Tenant Land	47.9	97.9	113.1	279.6

* The plantation manager.
Sources: AFA, Hacienda Palto, *Letterbooks*, Palto to Lima, October 2, 1893; July 10, 1894; February 1, 1898; August 21, September 12, 1909; informe, September 8, 1913.

one person hires another relations between them must become some-what strained, but no clear pattern of claims by peasants against one another emerges in the records. In all likelihood the lack of evidence is due to the familial character of many subletting arrangements. On the other hand, several instances of arrendatarios' taking advantage of the bad fortune of less advantaged peasants did not go unnoticed. As we have noted, the manager of the plantation once voiced contempt for such behavior.

Antagonisms arose between tenants for reasons indirectly related to farming. Jealousies separated neighbors, husbands and wives acted adulterously, and the occasional alcoholic such as Daniel Franco made life a little more difficult for everyone around him. Complex

Table 4.2 Tenant Loans, Hacienda Palto, First Quarter (September), 1917–18[a]

Name	Land (Has.)[b]	Rent (Lbs. Cotton)	Rent/Has.	Loan (S/)
Benjamín Huarote	5.3	800	150.9	15
Isaías Ormeño	12.0	2,000	166.7	30
Benigno Piérola	8.9	2,500	280.9	35
Domingo Cabesudo	16.3[c]	4,875	299.1	15
Abraham Torres	[c]	1,750	301.7	—
José del C. Reyes	11.6	3,550	306.0	25
Daniel Franco	14.9	4,760	319.5	40
Cipriano Ramos	6.1	2,100	344.3	20
Nicanor Uribe	5.8	2,000	344.8	15
Eustaquio Reyes	6.0	2,500	416.7	15
Adolfo Gallardo	2.9	1,750	603.4	25
Vidal Aricochea	2.9	2,000	689.7	10

Source: AFA, Hacienda Palto, *Letterbooks,* September 15, 1917.
[a] Each holding consisted of two or more fields.
[b] These are arranged in order of highest to lowest ratio of land to rent.
[c] This tenant sharecropped 5.8 hectares with Abraham Torres.

kinship relations seem to have existed at Hacienda Palto, with a high degree of intermarriage among resident families. Indeed, the links between kinship and economic activities on the plantation beg for further study.

The judgment that conditions were ripe for improving landowner profits during World War I led cotton planters to reduce the independence of the arrendatarios, and the changes of 1917 to 1918 were a blow to their social standing. Most of the fixed rent tenants did not remain on the plantations once opportunities for farming independence were foreclosed.[58]

The Pisco valley landowners sought to cut losses by eliminating all distinctions between arrendatarios and yanaconas, and by 1920 they had succeeded. A typical tenant on a plantation in the Pisco valley in the decades after World War I was known as a yanacón. Such a peasant, the head of a sharecropper household, maintained his or her family in a condition of precarious but permanent residence as a plantation tenant.[59]

Plantation House, Pisco River Valley

Cutting old cotton, Hacienda Palto

Migrants gleaning cotton, Hacienda Palto

Yanacona families, Hacienda Palto

CHAPTER 5

Yanaconas, Mechanization, and Migrant Labor

[T]here is no better tractor than the oxen, the most practical [apparatus] at the moment.
— *AFA, Hacienda Palto,* Letterbooks, *Palto to Lima, January 3, 1920*

Pisco valley peasants dreaded the annual onset of deep winter. Humidity, light drizzle (*garúa*), and endlessly cloudy skies meant clammy discomfort, numbing cold, coughs, depression, and — mixed with poor health or infancy — the threat of death. The period of June through November along Peru's coast is the time of the infamous *helados,* or frosts. The helados are a product of several inescapable natural phenomena: for six months the cloud cover caused by the El Niño current hugs the coast, trapped by the Andes mountain range. Beneath the cloud cover nightly temperatures drop, creating a dense mist that irritates the lungs and weakens the resistance of cotton bolls.[1]

Tenants feared the helados on good grounds. Economically the frosts threatened to rot late harvested cotton, and sudden frosts regularly damaged cotton shoots planted early in the hope of raising yields. Frosts also took a toll on the mind. Months of cloudy, humid weather with occasional light rain left clothing and spirits permanently damp. When dampness combined with daytime temperatures averaging forty-five to fifty degrees Farenheit (ten to fifteen degrees Celsius), infants suffered life-shortening lung illnesses, children fell victim to common viruses, and no one escaped the numbing sensations the cold, damp weather inflicted on fingers and toes.

Peasants viewed nature and machines very differently. Nature was capricious in its treatment of man; owners and yanaconas felt its effects without regard for social position. Machines, however, could be seen as a product of the schemes of plantation owners to be rid of yanaconas. Relying on the same persistence with which they appeased the weather, yanaconas calculated the measures needed to minimize the impact of farm machinery on their lives.

Having witnessed the destruction of arrendatario independence in the years before World War I, yanaconas slowly lost hope that the plantations might accommodate their dreams of economic and social stability. In the exhortations of the owners, tenants sensed a growing belligerence. Fearful for their livelihood, they determined to protect themselves from the excesses they knew were common in the highlands, where gamonales and landlords ruled with armed gangs of hired thugs. Highland villagers and migrant laborers often lost their dignity and sometimes their lives to the combined forces of landlords and the state. Should those conditions prevail on the coast, peasants would lack the resources to resist them. Fear and indignation spread through the coastal countryside.

Planters could not have cared less. A robust market in late wartime provided a new opportunity to further rationalize cotton production. Owners removed the mechanisms of production and marketing from peasant control. They centralized ginning operations, introduced tractors and commercial fertilizers, and installed telephones to improve communication. The government standardized the fanegada at 50,000 square meters and soon decreed draft labor for road building and farmwork. In these measures the landowners foresaw increased profits and a long-awaited chance to establish their dominance in plantation society.

While cotton planters pursued economies of scale, the survival of yanaconas became problematic. At Hacienda Palto, where they were finessed out of growing cotton, yanaconas now planted only vegetables and tubers, which they surrendered to the owners in rent payment. The owners then used this product to feed migrant jornaleros, the meals an inducement to remain on the plantation through the harvest. Afterward, yanaconas cultivated the fields with rented oxen. The residents quickly learned that producing vegetables and cultivating the fields without access to cash made it difficult to meet their own subsistence needs. Plantation life with technological innovations and economies of scale began to resemble a maze without an exit.[2]

Yanaconas survived the changes that came with increasing technology and centralization by turning to wage labor. Giving the peasants a degree of flexibility, access to wages ironically provided a hedge against marginalization and proletarianization. Rather than signal that yanaconaje would pass from the scene, wages allowed peasants to survive the introduction of economies of scale. Before the end of the decade, cotton landowners returned to yanaconaje contracts.

How yanaconas survived economies of scale and became a key element once more in cotton production after World War I is the subject of this chapter.

Technical Changes

Pisco valley cotton plantations reached new levels of production during World War I. In 1920 the Aspíllagas alone sacked a high of 528,806 pounds, a figure unmatched since before the war with Chile.[3] But the postwar market was erratic. Production fell off abruptly after 1920, then recovered steadily for years. The sudden postwar decline was a function of the reopening of world sources of raw cotton, particularly in Egypt and India. Despite a reduced volume of cotton in the Pisco valley, the owners found increased profits in technical improvements, and they continued to invest in such changes. New housing and schools were opened on many plantations, telephones and shortwave radios were installed, better disease control became possible, and rational land use and administrative techniques became common.

Such changes supported increased profits, but they also had a deleterious effect on plantation labor. Successful reduction of fixed rent tenantry gave the cotton owners an opportunity to increase control of the peasants, essentially by stripping them of any capability of resisting landowner designs. Opportunities arose to restrict the peasant economy to the confines of the plantations, and landowners seized the moment. In the meantime, when landowners sought greater amounts of migrant labor the migrants balked. The objectives of rationalization and cheaper labor often clashed with one another, reawakening old animosities. In the space between more wage workers and fewer tenants, it became possible for yanaconas to dodge the restrictive regulations.

In the Pisco valley, yanaconaje took two forms after World War I. One group of yanaconas went virtually unsupervised, while the other was more closely watched. At Hacienda Palto the unsupervised yanaconas farmed the "Isla," the forty-fanegada section of land left in the middle of the river after the repeated early twentieth-century floods. They produced cotton along with vegetables, double-cropping in every row, partly for subsistence and partly to help feed the migrant laborers on the mainland. The supervised yanaconas (formerly "compañeros") worked as "partners" of the plantation manager. They grew vegetables and fodder according to the plans of their host with few opportunities to do anything else. None of the yanaconas could seek out loans on their own account; both groups were dependent on the plantation for advances of cash, and neither could find many ways to set aside gains. Although the unsupervised yanaconas had their own oxen, pasture areas had shrunk to the edges of their culti-vated fields, severely limiting herd size.

Meanwhile, migrant laborers became more visible on the cot-ton plantations. Gradually migrating coastward since the War of the Pacific, increasing numbers of highland villagers descended into the Pisco valley from neighboring Castrovirreyna province. Driven partly by the need for cash, they did field work on the cotton planta-tions. On weekends they celebrated in Pisco, and some of the youths among them occasionally landed in jail. Although local police rec-ords are scant, those available support the observation that a trickle of migrants in the 1880s had by the 1920s become a steady stream.[4]

Plantations hired massive numbers of highland migrants during the cotton harvest. As the cotton plants bloomed, the traditional harvest-er's sack became visible once again. The large migrant labor popula-tion, locally called *nómadas* (nomads), supplemented the residents for the harvest period, then left after the cotton was in storage and ac-counts were settled. Plantations quickly reduced the resident force to a skeleton crew that carried out interim cultivation duties and main-tenance labor. This labor rhythm displayed the balance that land-owners had sought for so long. Anticipating a constant flow of mi-grants, Pisco valley cotton planters undertook to further restrict the options available to yanaconas. The project was delayed in the early 1920s as the cotton bubble burst and markets returned to prewar conditions. Yanaconaje remained a fixture on Pisco cotton planta-tions as wages rose once again. Despite delays, the plantation owners were determined to introduce mechanization into cotton agriculture.

TRACTORS AND CATTLE

At the turn of the twentieth century, newspapers and agricultural journals, some of them sponsored by the influential Sociedad Nacio-nal Agraria (SNA; National Agrarian Society), were filled with arti-cles that discussed mechanization and technological progress in agri-culture throughout the world. The machinery promised to extend acreage and achieve economies of scale.[5] American and European merchants hawked mechanical rakes, harrows, gins and similar implements that performed arduous farming tasks in far less time and with less expense than could be done by hand. Letters to the editor in *La Vida Agrícola* debated the pros and cons of competing brands of farm machinery. The claims of the manufacturers elicited the envy of planters, who complained bitterly of having to rely on peasant labor and to compete in a market that often discouraged risk and yielded relatively low returns.[6] Once the war ended, the continuation of labor scarcity under conditions of increasing demand for raw cotton encouraged the planters to continuously explore mechanization.

Sectors of the peasantry reacted differently to the mechanization of cotton. Introduction of machinery reduced the numbers of tenants who sharecropped the land, and yanaconas rightly opined that the machines threatened their livelihood. In contrast, migrant field hands more readily looked upon tractors as a positive addition to cotton agriculture. Tractors meant the clearing of more fields, increasing the demand for field hands and potentially raising wages.

At Hacienda Palto a debate took shape over the place of cattle in tractor-dominated farming. On this issue the exasperated manager stood with his "compañeros." He pointed out that tractors were too much trouble. A mechanic had to be hired, tractors always broke down, and parts and gasoline were costly. Any tractor could become bogged down in the muddy fields, requiring the labor of a large group of men for many hours to extricate it.

The Palto manager held ambivalent views on mechanization. He once gleefully informed the owners that the tractor at neighboring Hacienda Urrutia lay "paralyzed" in the field and that other managers nearby complained that the machines caused irritable delays. But he relented when the owners admonished him to use them whenever possible. Abruptly at one point he agreed that tractors made yanaconas superfluous, but then he remembered that tractors and tenants could not coexist. Tenants meant cattle, and in early 1920 he preached that the hacienda should exploit the land "in compañía," rather than directly. Revealing his fear and suspicion of machinery, he remarked: "there is no better tractor than the oxen, the most practical [apparatus] at the moment."[7]

Only an increase in the number of field oxen might raise production to meet post–World War I demand, argued the manager. Reports cautioned that if the Palto owners wanted to reorganize tenantry to keep yanaconaje central to the operation, they must buy ten field oxen to supplement the plantation herd. Yet for a number of reasons an adequate herd never developed at Palto. One impediment was the threat of disease. A bull ox had died recently, probably of anthrax, and owners feared the spread of the disease through the valley. In subsequent years, as tractor use grew more common, the manager of Palto saw his procattle arguments further eroded by epidemic diseases. In 1924 aftosa, the dreaded foot-and-mouth disease, made mechanization yet more attractive.[8]

Space limitations along with the vulnerability of animals figured in the adoption of tractors. As planters extended fields to maximize the land planted in commercial crops, pastures began to look wasteful. In contrast to the pre-war years, Hacienda Palto reserved the right to pasture its cattle on the fields of tenants after the harvest, forcing tenant cattle to compete for fodder. Peasants sometimes have favored the mix of planter and tenant cattle in the hope that interbreeding might improve the health of peasant herds.[9] But on the plantation, cattle mixture was a restriction, not an opportunity. Stock owned by the planters seems generally not to have been much different in quality than that owned by the tenants. The more important problem for the tenants was how to avoid further loss of space. The new practice effectively closed tenant garden plots, and when double-cropping ended yanaconas began purchasing food with cash.[10]

GINNING AND PLANTER CREDIT

Centralization occurred somewhat differently in cotton production than it did in sugar production. In sugar, highly capitalized producers forced out those with less access to credit. Further rationalization included a total shift to massive, migrant wage labor. *Centrales,* or large mills, commanded the sugar harvested in growing plantations.[11] In cotton agriculture, centralization occurred at the level of ginning. Planters troubled by mechanical breakdowns and costly repairs looked outside the plantations for further mechanization after World War I.[12] The moment was opportune. Processing costs were driven down by competition among ginning plants, exemplified by a prolonged bidding war in the town of Pisco and the surrounding area in 1918 to 1923 that pitted local ginning establishments against one another.

A few firms emerged triumphant. Thereafter ginning costs stabilized somewhat and were disturbed only by successive years of poor harvests. One firm that survived the bidding, the locally owned Fábrica "La Industria," won the right to receive, store, gin, and transship the cotton of Hacienda Palto. By 1925 the company transported ginned cotton to the port by means of rail lines that ran up to the warehouse doors. Owners "shared" the cost of ginning with the tenants, adding another burden to those already borne by the cotton tenants.[13]

Centralization of ginning reduced the number of jobs on the plantation. When the ginning shed closed down, four to six jobs that provided cash to supplement field earnings disappeared. Ginning shed dangers had meant higher pay than that earned by field hands, and this money could not easily be made up by other work. Only the equally dangerous river jobs — building bridges, dikes, and embankments against flooding — paid as well, but they could not regularly be counted on.

Planters found state support for centralization in the form of government credit. After a few false starts, the government made public credit accessible through the Banco Agrícola.[14] Loans also became available to planters from foreign shipping consignees. Until this point foreign merchant houses largely stayed out of the local economy save for occasional personal loans, but they now sought to control cotton before market prices were quoted in Europe. Companies like Duncan Fox Ltd., a British merchant and shipping house that had taken cotton consignments and made loans to landowners since World War I, began entering the cotton business through the ginning factory.

Impressed by the Duncan Fox facility, Aspíllaga Hermanos contracted to place the raw cotton of haciendas Palto and San José with the British firm's ginning operation in the town of Pisco in 1933. The local effect was highly visible; the rates offered by the local "La Industria" ginning firm could not match those of the newly opened Banco Agrícola of Peru or of the British giant.[15]

OTHER ADJUSTMENTS

Security   Administrative reforms introduced a higher degree of oversight into the Aspíllaga cotton fields. In 1920 the owners separated the administration of their two Pisco valley plantations, Palto and San José. For the past two decades arrendatarios of the two properties had answered to the Palto administrator. Further, the two cotton harvests had been ginned, baled, and transported together to Pisco.[16] But now, although cotton from both plantations continued to be transported and ginned together, administrations were separated and the number of security employees at both was increased. More oversight required another layer of field supervision. In response to frequent managerial complaints about the disappearance of cotton and tools, and damage to equipment, the owners hired more mayordomos de campo. It was easy to conclude that sabotage was at play here, and within the next two years the manager supplemented the longtime mayordomo de campo, Agapito Díaz, by hiring two more mayordomos de campo, bringing the total at Hacienda Palto to three.[17]

In contrast to yanaconas, migrant workers were not viewed as "family." The manager explained to Máximo Gómez, one of the new mayordomos, that "he must not mix with the people of the *ranchería* [housing for field hands] except in his position as commander of labor."[18] The distinction drawn here is symptomatic of an expression of feelings that rarely would find its way into the public sphere. The costs of security had perplexed the Pisco valley planters since the War of the Pacific. They were not satisfied with the rural police nor their surrogates, none of which seemed to intimidate the restless peasant population. Flight from contract was a constant nuisance, and a traffic in contraband cotton seemed to live a healthy existence whenever prices moved upward. But after World War I this problem seemed to the manager to have gotten worse. Owners and managers were convinced the problem was a function of migration. Far greater numbers of people were leaving the villages, especially after 1925, and entering the lower valleys to work temporarily on the plantations. They usually planned to stay a short time and then to return to the village, perhaps only long enough to complete a single harvest, some staying for as long as two or three. The duration of a family's stay on the plantation depended largely on how great a need it had for cash and, as Peter Blanchard reminds us, whether the family was clever enough to avoid burdensome debts. As several scholars (Klaren and Smith among them) have demonstrated for Peru, and others for similar countries, the process of migration, possible resettlement, and return, was a long and difficult one. From the perspective of the manager, migration meant that a lot of people were passing through the plantations who were not familiar to him and the strangers often stayed only a short time. He would never know their habits and customs, and he would always remain suspicious of them. Increased security was but one of the measures he could take to try to control their activities while they were on his payroll.

Owners customarily compensated for their absence from the plantations by taking numerous security measures. A certain amount of loss could be expected, and planters sometimes paid tenants "under the table" to inform on their neighbors in the hope of reducing offenses. When that did not work the owners assumed losses, as occasionally occurred at Palto. Further losses were attributable to the failure of owners ever to reach a satisfactory agreement on how to share the cost of valley security. Each planter had to judge for himself how many employees were needed to get the fieldwork done, bring in the cotton, and truck it to the Pisco warehouse.[19]

With large numbers of migrant laborers living at the plantation only during the harvest season—and the yanacona population pared to a minimum—managers argued for increases in the number of field security employees. Cotton might be but one potential object of theft; tools, cattle, and similar capital goods might also be stolen. Evidently, peasants who felt mistreated took retribution on the goods at hand. With the enactment after 1920 of national labor registration and vagrancy laws by the Augusto Leguía regime (1919–30), numerous labor control devices became available to the planters. Working in cooperation with recently expanded rural police forces, they exercised greater watchfulness over migrant laborers.[20]

Fertilizer A rising volume of cotton production soon took its toll on soil quality. This was particularly true at Hacienda Palto, where managers consistently delayed soil conservation measures. Yet soil nutrition was a perennial problem. For years the Palto administrators handled the issue by closing down a field whose soil was thought to be *delgado* (thin) and exhausted. Fields were returned to systematic planting after a year or more of "rest." But in the expansion of land use to its limits during the postwar boom, the owners of Palto—and planters throughout the valley—considered the possibility of more systematic use of fertilizer on the plantation fields.[21] Addressing the matter for the first time in years, in 1923 the Palto manager applied forty-eight tons of guano to the fields of the plantation, up twenty-three tons from the previous year. Another seventy-six tons were left in reserve for the coming year. He had spread the guano over the more than 160 fanegadas of the plantation and passed the entire cost on to the tenants.[22]

Virtually all the harvests at Hacienda Palto prior to World War I were completed without application of much extraneous nutrient other than water and animal manure. Even animal manure was applied to the fields only on occasion as a by-product of fallowing. Like most landowners in the sur chico, the owners and managers of Palto were convinced that the cotton fields did not suffer from a lack of nutrients. Indeed, from the early part of the century, agronomists were astonished that the *guano de las islas* (from the islands) the famed fertilizer that in the mid nineteenth century had been in such great demand around the world, cheap as it had become, was not more rigorously used by coastal cotton planters. Fernando López Aliaga, a noted specialist on cotton, admonished the landowners that the lack of land fertilization reduced the size of the crops and the quality of the cotton. His warnings were ignored. Periodic evaluation of field conditions by managers and owners (whose visits became more frequent) gave every indication that a sufficient equation existed between fallowing, animal manure, and plant nutrition.[23]

The decision to apply fertilizer to the fields of Palto was an important social and technical step. A subject rarely discussed in the past, fertilizer gained attention as pastures disappeared, the draft animal population declined, and land use became more intense. Thereafter the planters urged that guano "from the islands" be applied. Manager Max Alcántara urged in 1923 that in the future the plantation issue guano to the tenants and admonish them to use it. The order to do so represented yet another invasion of the rights of yanaconas.

Increased fertilizer use did much to determine which tenants would survive the process of expansion after World War I, but in spite of the stress laid on the practice in the cultivation of cotton, the tenants applied it to the fields reluctantly. Fertilizer application meant yet another block of time had to be spent on cultivation, and by this point tenants lacked confidence that it could reward their labor. The manager, himself suspicious, provided them with little evidence of its value. Planters demanded enforcement of the procedure and yanaconas were burdened with its cost.[24]

Tambos and Peasant Credit   Yet another change narrowed tenant opportunities: planters repeated a prohibition of earlier years against the use of commercial land for subsistence crops. The prohibition had been allowed to lapse, but the new announcement, coupled with the imposition on a tenant's time represented by fertilization, forced yanaconas to rely more frequently on the plantation tambo. Tambos, the proverbial company stores of plantation infamy, had been in existence at Hacienda Palto since the inception of enganche. Examining the logistics of debt peonage, students of plantations view the company store as the central coercive device that prevented peasants from leaving the plantation. If tenants were indebted to the company store, so the thinking goes, they were legally at risk if they fled their debts, and the landowner had the right to hunt them down and punish them for the transgression.[25] Contemporary intellectuals such as Joaquín Capelo, Aurelio Denegri, José Carlos Martiátegui, and Víctor Raúl Haya de la Torre, all pointed to enganche as the linchpin in a dreary life of peasant debt peonage. Their writings and speeches depict the tambo as the institution that trapped wage migrants, especially sugar field workers. They emphasized entrapment over the reciprocal potential of debt, misreading a critical social distinction between migrant labor and yanaconaje.[26]

But in contrast with the oft-expressed view that tambos were a key device in the process of tenant indebtedness, before the 1920s Pisco valley tambos seem not have served a central purpose. Under the early tenant regime the Palto tambo, located near the ranchería, sold an array of goods for domestic as well as recreational and field use. Supplied by the tambero in arrangement with the administrator (not the owners, who left this matter largely to the employees), tambo goods were a convenience provided by the plantation. Not surprisingly, goods sold at considerably higher prices than those in the pueblo of Pisco, perhaps a 20 to 50 percent markup, but convenience made them attractive. The tambos undoubtedly were a lucrative operation, but planter profits do not seem to have relied on debts owed to the tambo by tenants. Although no individual accounts survived for us to examine, peripheral evidence suggests that the company store did not effectively entrap peasant labor.

Through the early twentieth century, two tambos operated at the Aspíllaga holdings in the Pisco valley, one at San José and the other at Palto. Lisardo García controlled the tambo at Hacienda Palto for many years, and he passed it on to Carlos Sánchez. Both men were long-term tenants of Asian descent, who the manager claimed never made more than a "modest" living from this monopoly. The "modesty" of their circumstances may be understated, however. Though tamberos may not have expected to accumulate great fortunes, one of the owners could report in February, 1919, that the tamberos of Palto not only paid a "modest" rent to the plantation manager punctually, they also provided "coin to the administrator, for the pay" of the day laborers. Yet tambo collections did not satisfy the entire payroll of the day labor force, and the plantation manager complained that the collections often gave him more trouble than they were worth.[27]

Pisco owners and managers viewed tambos as a minor source of plantation income. The tambo produced "small change" that allowed owners to avoid some measure of direct cash outlays for wages. It also was a convenience, a magnet, that attracted labor to the plantation. A tambo whose goods were sought by field hands reduced the cost of enganche to owners. The high prices charged at the plantation tambos were not always controlled by the owners. Pisco landowners apparently preferred to charge tamberos rent for the privilege of setting up business on the plantation grounds, leaving prices to be set by the tambero and the market. At Hacienda Palto, the owners charged the tamberos 20 percent of the proceeds, a cost the tamberos undoubtedly passed on to their customers. Prices also could be influenced by competition between tamberos within a single plantation. Although not the linchpin of enganche, the tambo contributed to the woes suffered by the yanacón, whose choices in the 1920s were increasingly limited.

Precisely how the tamberos used credit to gain possession of yanacón valuables is subject to conjecture. Did tamberos accept cotton and cattle for debts in lieu of cash? By sharing a contract with the tambero, did a yanacón become his compañero? Did tamberos take over contracts in payment of debt? Once again, scanty evidence suggests that the landowners permitted transfer of contracts from parent to child and from compañero to arrendatario. At Palto some evidence hints that tamberos, in the manner of a petty entrepreneur, sometimes negotiated to assume a contract upon the inability of a tenant to cancel plantation debts. These questions beg further study of the variables at work in defining precisely the part tambos played in the creation of debt.[28]

Between gardening and double-cropping, peasants sought to provision themselves. They further fought the tambo by renting out parcels of the land for use by subtenants. Two tenants would share the crop of the rented field, allowing the yanacón to make use of his neighbor's labor time. This was not a new phenomenon in the postwar decade. Indeed, subrenting was practiced to some degree almost from the beginning of modern fixed rent tenantry. In the 1890s these agreements required the consent of the planter to be legitimate, and it appears that for the most part the stipulation was adhered to. But planter involvement became unnecessary. The planters at first denied few of such requests because only wealthy fixed rent tenants could take on subtenants.[29]

With demand for labor running far ahead of supply during World War I, the practice of subrenting became more widespread. In the 1920s it was the poorer yanaconas, those less independent, who seemed most in need of subtenants. With the only capital left to them (their field oxen) in jeopardy of being taken for rent payments, yanaconas found subtenantry useful for further spreading risk. Subtenants usually were fellow yanaconas who gave up their lands when debts reached impossible size or former compañeros. As we have seen, under conditions in which success depended on a high degree of mutual trust between the participants, yanaconas preferred relatives to strangers.[30]

At the end of the decade, Palto yanaconas divided their time between cotton and marketable foodstuffs. Depending on how much concern the owners expressed for pasturage and fodder, the yanaconas marketed several vegetables locally, paying the plantation a fee for the privilege. The most favored crops were vegetables and maize. Although the owners sometimes demanded that the yanaconas plant alfalfa, ordinarily they left the choice of crop to the peasants. Not all the yanaconas seized this opportunity, but the more risk worthy among them continued to make such choices after 1925, even within the limited parameters of mechanized cotton agriculture.

Yanaconas: Isolation and Revival

REDUCED ALTERNATIVES

In addition to providing for two types of rental tenants in 1917, the Pisco valley planters distinguished among them in other ways. At Hacienda Palto, for example, they designated certain sections of the plantation as the *sección yanaconizada,* and another they reserved for the tenants called compañeros. A third area, the vast central section of the plantation with its fields planted in cotton, were worked through the 1920s by "direct cultivation." Only migrant wage laborers worked this section.

Important details separated the otherwise indistinguishable contracts of yanaconas and compañeros: compañeros were "partners" only of the plantation manager, and they received loans from and were responsible for repayment directly to him. The other group, the yanaconas, were responsible directly to the plantation owners; similarly, they received loans granted by the planters. These yanaconas held lands that isolated them from the compañeros and migrants at Hacienda Palto — they settled and worked "La Isla," the section of land surrounded by the Pisco River. Their virtual independence of the manager reaffirmed yanacona privilege as it had existed in the past and emphasized the status of the group apart from the compañeros and jornaleros.

Compañía seems to have been the means used by the owners of Palto to meet two needs. For one, it assuaged the manager, whose power and income were endangered by yanacona independence. Compañía contracts and loans, furthermore, provided the manager (who charged 6 percent interest) an opportunity to supplement his monthly salary. For another, compañía was an instrument for reducing landowner costs. Compañeros planted only foodstuffs that they were forced to sell to the plantation. By this means the owners provisioned the migrant wage hands. The symbolic geographic distinction made between different types of tenants through their designation to exclusive sections of the hacienda, perhaps was unique to Hacienda Palto. But the distinction made between them based on privilege was widely practiced on Pisco valley cotton fundos.

In contrast to the nearly permanent resident laborers called yanaconas and compañeros stood the migrant laborers. They were hired to perform "direct" cultivation and harvesting. Direct cultivation meant simply that no individual or group mediated between wage hands and the manager or owners. Field hands were paid in cash directly out of the plantation coffers, and they answered only to the plantation employees. Hence two groups of labor — one composed of the resident yanaconas and compañeros, the other consisting of the migrant field hands — with different interests and economic goals, and somewhat divided from within, cultivated the fields of the Pisco valley as a result of the consolidation measures adopted on the plantations.

The migrant workers lived on the plantation only for the length of the harvest. Managers and owners used revealing descriptive terms in talking about the jornaleros. *Gente de afuera* (outsiders) was a common derogatory phrase; "nómadas" was another term, signifying the temporary nature of their hiring and setting the migrants off from the resident population. Such designations inadvertently implied that the yanaconas were settled and "at home" on the land. This distinction, disparaging the nonresident character of migratory labor, throws light on a perception that cotton planters nurtured from the early days of tenantry under conditions of labor scarcity. They hoped from the start to develop a population of reliable and trustworthy peasants who saw themselves as residents, a group that might view themselves as an intrinsic part of a vigorous, rationalizing enterprise.

Migrant jornaleros entered the plantations for brief periods, living in sparse huts built especially to house them, leaving after the harvest for another plantation. Indeed, more people — especially young men — began migrating between valleys as roads improved and national labor laws intervened more fully in their lives. Gathering for hire at locales conveniently positioned near clusters of plantations, the migrants eked out a living and returned to the highlands when the first opportunity arose. Competition for these workers among the plantations was intense in times of scarcity but not so when there were plenty of migrants around.

Yanaconas found independence to be more precarious than ever within this fragile labor mix. They found their numbers reduced when owners awarded contracts in 1925 that were designed to provide insurance against flood damage. In the negotiations, the owners insisted that independent tenants make labor available for "defense against the river," for the labor of drainage, and for fieldwork, especially the harvest. The planters further demanded one-half the cotton and one-third of the season's vegetables as rent. Any remaining cotton also became an option of the owners, who could claim it at the local spot price.[31]

Yanaconas meanwhile gave high priority in these negotiations to a restoration of mixed croppage. They realized that they were being made to choose double-cropping over cash labor. The possibility of working on the plantation fields for cash seemed to have been ruled out. Meanwhile, if peasants demanded space for raising foodstuffs, landowners conceded it. After World War I they chose rental contracts in accord with a calculation of how well the household could survive without cash. Such choices, like those made by planters, reflected a knowledge of labor, food, and crop prices. To attract reliable tenants, owners allowed compañeros and yanaconas to choose an appropriate crop mix for themselves. One Aspíllaga brother compensated Palto tenants for the loss of cash income in 1925 by permitting them to mix vegetable plantings within the cotton fields in the Isla section of the plantation.[32]

Off-Plantation Labor   Independent yanaconas sometimes earned cash by leaving the home plantation to work at other fundos. On its face a strange solution, this signified a search for cash to maintain independence in the face of restrictions and fluctuating prices. To lure yanaconas back home, managers offered them tasks for wages. Such tasks as digging postholes, organizing feed lots for the plantation oxen, and weed removal in cotton fields were part of the morning routine. At Palto, dependent yanaconas already heeded this schedule. If the manager could lure independent yanaconas back into the fields under this regimen, he might be able to cut back on hiring migrants.[33]

The Palto manager was preoccupied with the independent yanaconas. He conceded that they had suffered the most from the floods, but he chafed at how they continued to draw on the plantation's resources. Nearly all the new housing went to independent yanaconas. He noted that increased expenditures on them reflected higher labor costs, not loans. He pointed out that weekly advances to the yanaconas amounted to only 10 percent of the total annual expenditures of the plantation for the year, whereas wages accounted for most of the remainder. Those wages were paid to independent yanaconas.[34]

The weekly advances mentioned by the manager, requiring more attentive bookkeeping, signaled the flexibility of independent yanaconaje. In prior years loans had been made for the length of the season, rarely fewer than three months, but after 1925 they became a weekly payment. Peasants saw that a major advantage of short-term cash advances was greater flexibility to move about in search of supplementary work. Provided one did not fall behind in payments, a tenant could move from plantation to plantation seasonally throughout the valley without losing residence.

Flooding cut deeply into the cotton livelihood of peasants in mid-decade. A few long-term yanaconas left Hacienda Palto when La Isla flooded in 1923, but most tried to ride out the loss, determined not to lose their precarious foothold on the land. They worked on the owner's fields daily, harvesting cotton, while on their own fields they switched from cotton to vegetables in an effort to cut losses. This strategy for survival cut into the ability of many Isla yanaconas to repay their debts on time.[35]

Theft Yanaconas who accumulated high debts sometimes fled the contract. Such flight created a large security problem that managers simply could not handle. By itself flight did not disturb the plantation rhythm. The manager could call upon the rural guard for help, and in the years of the Augusto Leguía dictatorship (1919–30) state security expanded to meet a wider need. By far a greater problem when cotton harvests became larger was labor mobility. Plantation managers noted that the number of field hands they knew personally was dropping, and the problem multiplied when yanaconas fled or terminated rental contracts. Mobility itself, of course, need not have given rise to theft, but if a market existed for stolen goods then theft was sure to occur. As Pisco and surrounding towns grew in size and anonymity in the 1920s, a rise in crime could be expected.[36]

Increased cattle and cotton thievery hit the valley in the same decade. Periodically, the manager of Palto bemoaned a loss of cattle by the plantation or by a yanacón. Animals disappeared during the night, and the circumstances suggest that the culprits were fellow tenants, not organized cattle thieves. Seen in this light, cattle rustling had political overtones. Cotton theft can equally be linked with tenant protest. Although plantation managers and owners voiced fear and frustration at cotton theft, peasants did not complain to the manager that cotton had been stolen from them. In all likelihood, cotton theft was a sign of peasant retribution against being cheated of their rights by the cotton plantations. In the absence of a reliable court of justice, tenants perceived that theft was an effective way to exact vengeance against an increasingly oppressive plantation regime. The manager of Palto did not say so directly, but his statements leave little doubt that he saw tenants behind every missing boll of cotton. His pleas for hiring more security men increase the likelihood of that sentiment being present in his comments on theft.[37]

Theft was not the only response by yanaconas to feelings of entrapment in the early 1920s. As the possibilities for subsistence narrowed, flight from the contract became equally common. When the harvest of 1923 reached its final weeks, the manager found the experienced independent yanaconas leaving Hacienda Palto. Floods had destroyed their plants and many well-known families had already left. These tenants had converted pastures into producing cotton fields but hereafter they sought wage labor. By November, La Isla was virtually abandoned. The yanaconas now cultivated only 8 or 9 fanegadas where before they had cultivated 17 or more.[38] Indeed, of the 165 fanegadas of Hacienda Palto, only 80 were under cultivation and another 7 were in use as pasture. Another flood in 1925 (perhaps the last of a series of major river invasions of the farmland) further reduced the size of the island and triggered a rash of abandonments.

Such instances of flight, coupled with the mid-1920s hiatus in the use of sharecropping as valley plantations turned to wage labor, left few peasants residing on the valley cotton plantations. The speed of the plunge into a nearly total wage labor force was unsettling: plantation labor needs called for the appearance of large amounts of cash in the valley, leading to renewed fear of a return to banditry. The logistics of housing, food supply, and other basic elements of plantation life were strained by the sudden ballooning of the labor force. The crop year of 1925 to 1926, in the words of the Hacienda Palto manager, was "a disaster."[39]

REVIVAL

In the late 1920s the compañeros of the plantation manager (dependent yanaconas) became the instrument of plantation policy. Their farming activities held down the cost of both rent and wages. For a few years, though the planters found it necessary to provide compañeros with costly equipment and services that yanaconas provided for themselves, the compañeros' continued presence also held down the numbers and size of loans. Independent yanaconas could not demand larger cash advances, because the "dependent" compañeros asked for less. The latter had less reason to hire wage laborers, and so they sought fewer loans.

After the 1925 to 1926 crop "disaster," the owners of Palto joined the other valley cotton plantations in balancing their labor force. Slowly but surely, in the next two years independent yanaconaje contracts were issued with more enthusiasm, and after 1926 yanaconaje once more became the pivotal form of labor on Pisco cotton plantations. It was the form of labor around which wages circulated. The owners of Hacienda Palto continued to believe that a movement from tenantry to full use of wage labor was desirable and possible, but like the other cotton planters throughout the valley they were unable to move in that direction.

When the Aspíllagas created the conditions that would make the plantation attractive to an elite corps of tenants and large numbers of wage workers, they severely reduced the amount of land planted in cotton. They used sixty-two fanegadas to cultivate first- and second-year cotton plants, and another fifteen fanegadas were planted in cotton intermixed with vegetables and fodder. The largest portion of this acreage, for the first time in Palto's modern history, was devoted to "direct cultivation," meaning that the landowners paid field hands directly with cash. Wage laborers, the plantation's "floating population" as the manager once phrased it, emerged briefly as the predominant labor force.[40] Yanaconas and compañeros did not disappear; nor did they devote the bulk of their time to the lands planted by the owner. The 113 residents and their families continued to form the core of the plantation labor force in two senses: they were the workers most familiar with the plantation, and as tenants they were the group most interested in bringing in the largest possible harvest. The opportunity to do so would come from hiring the migrants provided by the plantation owners.

Concessions had to be made in order to placate the yanaconas, whose previous importance to the owners was their social stability and usefulness in hiring labor from among the migrants. For the remainder of the decade, valley landowners found themselves rebuilding favor with the yanaconas while they refurbished the plantations after the floods of 1925. Palto's La Isla, now reduced in size to thirty fanegadas, once again was the sección yanaconizada. Yanaconas responsible to the manager of Palto — "dependent" yanaconas — were relegated to the seventeen-fanegada pasture located just north of the plantation house. Here they farmed what the manager of Palto described as *trozos de tierra* (bits of land), hardly large enough to be identified as individual plots. Meanwhile, the mineral-laden Isla fields in midriver were planted in cotton and vegetables by the independent yanaconas. Each set of tenants then made themselves available for part of the daily labor that farmed the remaining mainland sections, thus providing the owners a needed service while they earned cash.

A Palto report of April 4, 1927, indicated a change in the plantation strategy for recovery. In this plan the compañeros of the plantation manager planted only vegetables on small patches of land within the seventeen-fanegada section, and the yanaconas of La Isla regained the right to double-crop. With new cash advances that gave them a wider measure of independence, they mixed vegetables and cotton. But double-cropping alone could not guarantee the survival of the new yanaconas. The more successful among them realized that this form of tenantry was severely constricted when it was seen against the more ample market of the 1920s. It could only be attractive to an ambitious peasant if tenantry's demands were sufficiently flexible to allow for other kinds of cash-earning work.

By late in the decade the compañeros performed beyond expectations, and the manager felt vindicated for pressing this form of yanaconaje upon the owners.[41] Greater control of the resident labor force rewarded the cotton planters with an unexpectedly large crop. Competition among peasants for compañero contracts became intense; migrants took them whenever they were offered. At least they allowed for a pause in the otherwise relentless migration cycle, providing a respite for children and the aged.[42] In turn the competition lowered the cost of day labor to the independent yanaconas and encouraged them to hire more migrants during the harvest in order to speed completion of the contract. It appeared to the owners of Palto that they were closing in on a high level of cotton output without significant increases in labor costs.

This conclusion became more apparent as calculation of the cost of raising cotton became more precise. According to figures submitted to Aspíllaga Hermanos in 1927, the cost of labor to produce a fanegada of cotton was S/869.50. The elements of this calculation can be seen in table 5.1. Calculated per fanegada, the expenses divided production into four operations: preparation of the soil, seeding, harvesting, and transportation. Predictably, most of the costs came from the preparation and cultivation of the soil rather than the harvesting and transporting of cotton. Labor costs were more clearly related to the condition of the soil than to the quality of the seed or the speed of the harvest. When the cost of seed, at S/13.50 per fanegada (for the necessary three quintals), is removed, the total preparation cost is

Table 5.1 Cost of Producing 2.9 Hectares (1 Fanegada)
of Cotton, Hacienda Palto, 1927

Task	Wages
Tillage	S/406.50
Cultivation	180.50
Seed	13.50
Fertilizer	150.00
Harvest	80.00
Transportation	39.00
Total	S/869.50

Source: AFA, Hacienda Palto, *Letterbooks,* Palto to Lima, informe,
April 4, 1927, appendix.

lowered to S/856 or about S/7.58 per resident yanacona (at 113
residents) per fanegada. Included in the labor cost was the cost of
irrigation, figured at the cost of hiring gate operators and the like in
the preparation and cultivation phases. Also to be noted are changes
in the calculation of costs from previous years. Newly included was
the cost of commercial fertilizer. Commercial fertilizer cost S/6.00
per sack, and twenty-five sacks were used per fanegada. When the
cost of fertilizer is deducted from the bill for the labor of cultivation, it reduces the total labor bill seen in table 5.2 by S/150.00,
making the cultivation bill (where fertilizer was listed prior to 1927)
S/180.50 and further reducing the cost of labor per yanacón per
fanegada to S/6.25.

The biggest labor bill involved raking the fields with a tractor,
represented in the tillage task cost in tables 5.1 and 5.2. At S/220.00
it was the largest factor in the calculation of the per fanegada labor
cost. Starkly dramatizing the progression of technical change in cotton commercialization, the cost of producing a fanegada of cotton in
1927 on the fields worked directly by the plantation had been reduced significantly from the First World War. According to the data
of Hacienda Palto, valley planters could expect seventy-five arrobas,
or 1875 pounds, of raw cotton from a fanegada of land for S/6.25 in
labor, plus the cost of goods and marketing.[43]

Meanwhile, for peasants yanaconaje became a regular means by

Table 5.2 Per Tenant Cost of Producing 2.9 Hectares
(1 Fanegada) of Cotton, Hacienda Palto, 1927

Labor	Cost
Tillage	S/3.60
Cultivation	1.59
Harvest	.70
Transportation	.34
Total	S/6.23

Source: AFA, Hacienda Palto, *Letterbooks*, informe,
April 4, 1927, appendix.

which a family could supplement its income within the plantation
without resorting to temporary labor elsewhere in the valley. In effect, for those peasants fortunate enough to repeatedly win sharecropping contracts, life became as stable as possible in an otherwise
volatile commercial cotton setting. There were a number of measures
that could be taken to get oneself into this position and others to keep
oneself there as a tenant. A few individuals succeeded admirably at it.
They became the elite "wealthy" sector of the plantation's resident
field labor population. Those who migrated seasonally from fundo to
fundo and valley to valley often worked solely for a daily wage. Any
social security to which they might have access outside of the harvest
season likely was related to their ability to sustain ties with the highland communities from which they migrated. Seasonal migration of
this sort brought about many quandaries for families who relied
upon it for income. It is not hard to imagine that migrant children
particularly suffered in comparison to those who maintained residence in one or two plantations over several generations.[44]

Conclusion

The end of labor scarcity coincided with the adoption of new machinery on Pisco valley cotton plantations. The coincidence sustained the
overall costs of production and drove down the price of labor. Deep
social effects followed. Plantation owners no longer felt the need to

give way to tenant demands for space and privilege. They gave less attention to tenant privilege based on tenure or familiarity, and the general position of labor deteriorated. Debt peonage grew more common as the labor pool expanded, its composition changed, and its mobility increased. Landowners sought to retain control of a portion of the more mobile population under conditions that, ironically, demanded that migrant farm laborers move about frequently in order to ensure an adequate income. Despite such crosscurrents, in the mid-1920s the "dependent" yanaconas formed an accessible pool of plantation labor.

Attractive profits could best be made from Peruvian cotton and sugar when planter costs matched those of overseas competitors, and growers invested further only when they could anticipate reduced costs. Until World War I, high returns in cotton were achieved largely with rudimentary technology, hand labor, and limited production. Only when demand rose to a level sufficient to force planters to introduce technical changes to compete successfully, as happened during the war, did planters introduce tractors, risking the radical effects of mechanization on plantation society. Meanwhile, a more extensive and powerful state in postwar Peru limited the risks for cotton planters of increased mechanization.

The adoption of new machinery proved detrimental to the yanaconas, reducing their autonomy and their latitude to select crops and thus to provide for their own subsistence. The basic modernization elements — tractors, centralized ginning, improved communications, and a stabilized credit structure — displaced yanaconas from playing a central role in cotton production. But yanaconas maneuvered to counter the social effects of displacement.[45] Although their resources shrank, plantation conditions opened up two further routes of resistance against total planter domination of their labor: they might work the land of several plantations or, failing that, they might flee their contract responsibilities. In the second case former yanaconas joined the wage labor forces working under harvest contracts and living temporarily on Pisco valley plantations.

The changes of the late 1920s constituted a notable return to a form of land use recently abandoned. For more than a generation yanaconas stood at the pinnacle of society within the plantations. They were the most trusted sector of the laboring population and were perceived by the owners — and by their fellow tenants — as the most reliable and most knowledgeable farming group in rural society. Then in the postwar rush to expand and centralize, the cotton planters swept all that aside. Yanaconas lost social standing as well as economic and residential stability. At Palto the distance between direct and indirect cultivation widened: the quantity of wage-labor-produced cotton moved higher in relation to that produced by tenants.

But when the owners realized how flexible yanaconaje allowed the plantation regimen to be, they eased the restrictions against double-cropping and gardening. Late in the decade at Hacienda Palto and several neighboring plantations, rental contracts once more were made attractive to deter "independent" yanaconas from further abandoning the plantation. As the decade closed wage labor once again lost its attractiveness, a turn that reflected the coordination of yanaconaje with the mechanization of cotton.

CHAPTER 6

Yanaconas, Migrants, and Political Consciousness

[A]ll the yanaconas are now working as peons, and their families too, on their lots and on the fundo in general.
— *AFA, Hacienda, Palto,* Letterbooks, *Palto to Lima, November 11, 1934*

Daniel Franco the younger was worried. As he looked at his shrunken fields, his thoughts drifted back to those halcyon boyhood days when his father, a tenant since the 1890s, commanded many head of cattle on a large plot of land at Hacienda Palto. Despite the father's habitual, belligerent public drinking, the manager competed with planter Vicente del Solar of rival Hacienda San Jacinto to put cash in Franco the elder's hands. Neighbors had watched incredulously as Franco the elder cursed the Palto manager roundly when he questioned the peasant's methods; after their dispute, Franco turned to the manager and paid him a huge rent. Once, the son recalled, his father got into a violent, drunken argument with a neighbor, slashing his stomach nearly open. Somehow — probably because the manager intervened — his father narrowly avoided arrest for attempted murder.[1] The elder Franco died a tenant, and he would not have recognized his son's situation. In contrast, Franco the younger was a yanacón, who shared a shrunken set of fields with his mother. The family herd long since had gone to pay loans and wages, and the children — although nightly in school — were in the fields every day. At this moment the family's cotton receipts were threatened, and there seemed to be nowhere to turn.

Pisco valley cotton tenants greeted the spread of the worldwide depression into the countryside with a mixture of relief, bewilderment, and anxiety. A feeling of relief came over the peasantry during the 1930s as plantations made more land available for rent. Relief turned to bewilderment when they found that rental conditions made it virtually impossible for a family to subsist without sending all but the infants to work in the fields, and anxiety mounted as the shortcomings of this tenantry arrangement became clear. In the end, rental contracts no longer provided yanaconas with the social stability and income they promised in the past. Even the fragile comfort of knowing that they could survive while their more nomadic compatriots would suffer was wrested away from the yanaconas. Cotton landowners resorted to harsher repressive and manipulative tactics to control labor under the market pressures of the decade between the world wars. Those tactics, and the unsuccessful peasant struggles to counter them, will be examined in this chapter.[2]

Expansion of Cotton

Most studies of rural Peru give primary attention to the sugar regions of the coast and little if any to the areas where cotton prevailed. The result has been to limit our view of agrarian change in the depression decade to what happened in the north coastal valleys. But as national commerce gained strength in the 1930s, cotton played at least as great a part in growth as did sugar. During the 1930s the impact of sugar on the economy as a whole declined whereas that of cotton grew. The area of cane production shrank to occupy only the north coastal departments of Lambayeque and La Libertad, and while large amounts of sugar continued to issue forth from the north coast mills, cotton from the central coast and the sur chico overtook it. Before long, cotton outpaced sugar as Peru's fastest-growing agricultural export.[3]

Behind the shift in position was a fall in the international price of sugar as world currencies weakened and overseas markets collapsed. The drop in sugar prices reportedly prompted many of the remaining south coast sugar growers to convert fields from sugar to cotton plants. Results came shortly thereafter. A contemporary observer, not a person given to exaggeration, judged that half of the coastal population earned a living from cotton. He surmised that the cotton harvest influenced nearly all of Peru's economic life, from the value of land to the exchange rate of the sol, to the buying power of large sectors of the urban population, and perhaps even to that of some elements in the highlands.[4] Rosemary Thorp and Geoff Bertram gave attention to another angle of the shift, saying that cotton derived its key place in the Peruvian economy at that point from its high re-

Table 6.1 Total Land Planted in Cotton, Peru, 1930–40

Year	Hectares	% Change from Prior Year
1930	133,688	0.0
1931	126,890	−5.1
1932	123,065	−3.1
1933	130,481	+6.0
1934	148,517	+13.8
1935	162,088	+9.1
1936	165,530	+2.1
1937	157,021	−5.7
1938	190,792	+21.5
1939	177,483	−7.0
1940	180,135	+1.4
Average annual increase		+3.0

Source: Horacio Pinto, *Estadísticas históricas del Perú. Sector agrícola-algodón* (Lima, 1977), 15.

turned value in Peru in comparison to other products and the relative equality of incomes earned from it.

Peruvian merchants were the leading South American cotton exporters in 1930. They benefited when rapidly recovering world demand and U.S. restrictions on American exports doubled the country's share of the world market from 1.5 percent to 3 percent. Brokers formed a local futures market, and planters took advantage of the opportunity, thus securing a portion of necessary working capital well in advance of the season. These developments became noticeable in the pattern of land use throughout the coastal valleys of Peru where "a massive transfer of land into cotton" took place.[5]

The surge in prices stimulated the expansion of cotton lands. The price of cotton fell slightly from 1929 to 1934, then rose strongly. After another brief dip, prices rose steadily until 1939. It has been estimated that by then nearly half the total available land on the coast was planted in cotton (table 6.1). Furthermore, increased investment and greater use of fertilizer meant improvement in yields per hectare by 1935 of between 30 and 40 percent above the levels of the mid-1920s. The establishment of the government-sponsored Banco Agrícola as a credit source was another important factor in the expansion of cotton acreage and its domination of the coastal economy.[6]

Yanaconaje Revised

The rising value of Peruvian cotton stimulated planters to redouble their assault on the independence of yanaconas. They pounced with a vengeance upon the labor costs that they viewed as an impediment to ever higher returns. To control costs, the planters more readily manipulated labor and, in a turnabout in methods, they took to alternating forms of labor more quickly in tandem with the market. In rapid succession, they abandoned direct wage labor, reverting once more to yanaconaje, again placing the cost of fieldwork squarely on the shoulders of the tenants. Granted not all the cotton planters joined without hesitation in the adoption of these tactics. Indeed, many of those who had grown accustomed to migrant wage labor returned to tenantry with great reluctance. Such inconsistency among the landowners, at first glance puzzling, reveals the continuing lack of unity within the dominant agrarian elite. Those who sought to further rationalize plantation cotton were countered by those who sought immediate advantages in the foreign market.

One of the owners of Hacienda Palto illustrated the fissures that could occur even within a single family of owners. Working hard to make a case for yanaconaje to his co-owners, Antero Aspíllaga Anderson, son of the late patriarch, argued that the sharp rise in cotton volume between 1929 and 1931 justified a return to the use of this form of labor. In a report from the plantation, Aspíllaga Anderson dwelled on the incessant dilemmas of land use. Aspíllaga was not in favor of drastic change. Rather than commit themselves to any single form of labor, he advised his relatives that Hacienda Palto's labor force should continue to consist mainly of short-term wageworkers but that 10 percent of the nearly 100 fanegadas of land should be rented to yanaconas.[7]

From the standpoint of the yanaconas, rumors of a major rise in demand and renewed vigor in the plantation valleys meant new opportunities to return to farming after a long drought. Wage labor and restricted yanaconaje had pushed many families out of tenantry in the previous decade. An opportunity to return to the fields as residents reawakened old longings to live on the land. But a sense of caution toward tenantry was well founded, for old problems remained unsolved and unfamiliar voices were proposing new solutions.

In the late 1920s peasants listened more carefully to voices from outside the plantation. The outlook of many peasants soon changed. Political movements that sought the attention of peasants, with the Alianza Popular Revolucionaria Americana (APRA) leading the way, worked hard to bring national power struggles into the daily purview of the people of the Pisco valley. Political consciousness had risen somewhat among the plantation peasants briefly during World War I, but once the war ended, interest faded. Media attention and political activity concentrated on the crowds in the cities, especially the growing numbers of Lima industrial workers, and left peasants to their own devices. The peasants were not ignored, of course, and throughout the 1920s new magazines, pamphlets, and newspapers brought political news to the Pisco countryside.[8]

The political campaigns of the 1930s and growing awareness of political events created a new consciousness on the cotton plantations. Migrant workers and plantation tenants received attention from factory workers and urban cadres representing APRA and the Community Party. APRA appealed to the plantation labor force with promises of free popular education, land reform, anti-imperialism, and attractive social programs. Many peasant leaders became convinced that foreign involvement in the agrarian economy was the major culprit behind the social distance that separated owners and workers.[9] Henceforth yanaconas and migrant workers alike looked for political allies to support their quest for just conditions of life and work on the plantations.

Conditions on the plantations diverged somewhat from the developments shaking the cities and towns after 1934. In part the difference can be attributed to the astute tactics pursued by the owners, who began to pay more attention to the noneconomic needs of tenants. Also, peasant incomes were increasing as cotton output rose, a tendency that could dampen political enthusiasm. Divisions within the peasantry also muted the force of politics. Meanwhile, tenants sought to avert the eviction that would occur if they did not increase production, and the result was a dizzying mix of intensified labor use and peasant maneuvering that was not well understood in the political realm.[10]

EVERY BIT OF LAND

Land use at Hacienda Palto, shown in table 6.1, followed the general pattern of the region during the 1930s. By 1935 the amount of Palto land in cotton had grown substantially, with more than ninety-five fanegadas under cultivation. Of the total acreage cultivated at the Aspíllaga fundo, fully seventy fanegadas were in the hands of yanaconas. Only twenty of those fanegadas were cultivated directly with wage labor, while another five and a quarter fanegadas were set aside for grazing the plantation-owned cattle. This pattern contrasts sharply with the way the land was used just a few years earlier, as shown in map 4. Note the L-shaped plantation house on the left, the diagram of field use, and the damage from the 1925 flood on the right.[11]

Cotton yields, although high, provide no clue to the efficacy of a single form of labor over any other. At Hacienda Palto and throughout the Ica region, yields were erratic during the early 1930s. After jumping to a total 620,023-pound cotton harvest in 1929, the yield at Palto dropped the next year by nearly 24 percent. In contrast, the 1931 harvest of 503,295 pounds would be exceeded only once during the remainder of the decade. In the Ica region as a whole, table 6.2 shows there were peaks and valleys early in the decade but then a leveling off of production became widespread.

Near the end of the decade, another report based on a tour of the Pisco valley by one of the owners indicated that the Aspíllaga's practices were typical of their neighbors. Almost all of Palto's land was rented to yanaconas, who replaced subsistence crops with cotton. Most of the fields of former sugar plantations (including huge Hacienda Caucato at the mouth of the Pisco valley) and vineyards throughout the valley likewise were converted to cotton. Production at Palto and many other fundos steadied, supporting the general rise in prices and prompting the Sociedad Nacional Agraria (SNA) unabashedly to declare the 1930s the "golden age of cotton" in Peru.[12] The SNA failed to point out that a higher degree of labor control by the planters was a key element in the success of that "golden age."

CONTRACTS AND CONDITIONS

The tactics pursued by Pisco valley landowners in the early 1930s failed to halt the upward spiral of wages. At fault in part was an intense search for labor in several competing industries, most notably textiles, where Lima factories experienced a surge of activity that doubtlessly contributed to the high return value noted by Thorp and Bertram. Also, the floodtide of migrants from the sierra in the 1920s slowed, no doubt contributing to the rise in wages. Migration from village to city and back had not ended but merely experienced a slowdown due to a change in direction. Highland mineowners paid wages attractive enough to slow the pace of migration to Lima and the coastal valleys. Plantation pay rates and tenant conditions no longer competed equally with the cities and the mines. Exasperated, the manager of Palto groaned that "*serranos* [highlands dwellers] are not coming anymore."[13]

The owners viewed higher wages as a drain on the favorable cotton market, and after a few years of steady erosion of profits they wasted little time in shifting from wages to rent. Yet a return to yanaconaje would be problematic. A tenant contract no longer held some of its earlier unspoken benefits. The owners' insistence on maximizing the land devoted to cotton meant almost total elimination of pastures and subsistence fields. Without pastures, the peasant dream of reviving cattle herds went unfulfilled. Indeed, peasants found it necessary to rent oxen to plow the fields and to rely more heavily on the plantation tambo for tools and foodstuffs. With prolonged tambo use came further debt. More debt in turn delayed and discouraged repayment. The cycle made so familiar in the literature of debt peonage, including higher levels of intimidation and repression, more uniformly than ever before governed exchanges between peasants and plantations.

To the astonishment of many, the peasants were undeterred by the deterioration of the rental contract. There is no doubt about the greater difficulty involved in meeting contract terms. In addition to the items already noted, the contracts were more financially precarious. Carryover of debt after the harvest season became more difficult, for example. One or two fanegadas of rented land did not allow a yanacón to raise enough cotton, and other means of making interest payments could not easily be found. The loss of personal field herds also was high on the list of peasant anxieties. Fewer yanaconas found it possible to retain animals: those who retained them to 1935 lost them shortly thereafter. Tenant pleas for a greater share of available water also added tension to the deteriorating relations between planters and peasants.

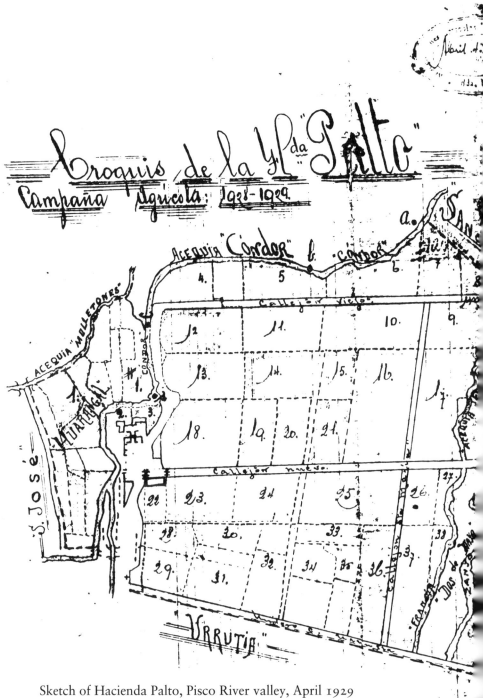

Sketch of Hacienda Palto, Pisco River valley, April 1929
(*Note the L-shaped plantation house drawn on the left, the diagram of
field use, and the damage from the 1925 flood depicted on the right.*)

Signos convencionales

Plantadas
Socas
Chacaras
pastos
en blanco
Compañias de
Algodón
Sangraderas
acequias   comunales
Tomas   a. b. c. d.
callejones
Rio nuevo
La Cuchilla
Isla litoral
toma y defensa
Francia: I. a.
Monte
defensa litoral
Palto: I. b.

Rio Pisco
S.Juan Cultivado
Rionuevo o S.Juan
Acequia Francia
San Juan
Isla
O Quiebra
Rionuevo o Quiebra
Acequia Francia
Isla
Monte de la Isla
Urrutia
Palto, abril 1929

Rio Pisco
Quiebra
Rio Pisco
Montte
zona de 1905 – Quiebra de 1905 la de
Dos de Mayo
Zanjones
Hoyada

Table 6.2 Volume of Cotton Production, Ica Department,
1929–40

Year	Tons
1929	21,583
1930	17,097
1931	13,722
1932	—
1933	16,686
1934	20,541
1935	—
1936	—
1937	20,024
1938	24,437
1939	23,253
1940	24,261
Average	20,178

Source: Horacio Pinto, *Estadísticas históricas del Perú. Sector agrícola: algodón* (Lima, 1977), 13.

Yet when new fields opened, many peasants who were relative strangers applied to the managers for rental contracts. The new arrivals were seen as a greater lending risk, and hence they paid higher interest rates. Also, the owners abbreviated the length of the loan period. Short loans and short contracts would, they suspected, more quickly winnow out "careless" and "unworthy" tenants, meaning those who were most likely to abandon the fields once they realized the hopelessness of the long-term prospects for success.

But those peasants who bore up under the unfavorable conditions of the early 1930s found solace in a few gains. Concern had been voiced often in the past for the education of the young and medical care for all. Education was ignored by the landowners until the national political stirrings of the twenties gave rise to a complaint that the children of plantation families were working full days throughout the seasons, perpetuating peasant illiteracy in the countryside. APRA won many adherents to its ranks by offering evening classes in popular universities, essentially an adult literacy program. The Aspíllagas, who built the plantation's first school in this era, like their neighbors put off giving the matter any more attention. But under pressure from the APRA's popular universities, Hacienda Palto hired a teacher to give reading and mathematics classes to the peasants in the evening. By 1934 students began passing through a rudimentary curriculum.[14]

After 1934 tenant complaints became more audible and found a more receptive audience. Sensing that owners hoped to undercut political activism, the tenants pressed for advantage, especially aiming at the contract. At Palto those peasants deeming the hard-packed sections of the fundo unsuitable for cotton could not be convinced otherwise. The owners addressed the problem with surprising haste, directing that those fields be rented as vegetable gardens with contracts that gave the tenants access to the local market after they had paid rent in kind. This left the bulk of the produce in the hands of the owners, but in all other respects, the vegetable tenants received contracts matching those of cotton tenants, even as the volume of cotton production reached unprecedented heights.[15]

After 1935 wages reportedly fell to levels more suitable to owner pocketbooks, and rental contracts gained greater attention. For the yanaconas, the land use issue took on a political dimension. A rising volume of peasant claims against the land in the very period when the cotton plantations returned to yanaconaje puzzled and irritated landowners, who hoped to stop vegetable production altogether. Many yanaconas opposed such a move on what seemed like straightforward grounds. Although vegetables yielded less cash than cotton, they sustained the family and provided its members with a foothold on the plantation. From there family members could move more securely around the valley earning cash in neighboring cotton fields to supplement income at the home plantation. Meanwhile, as table 6.3 suggests, cotton wages continued to be relatively steady throughout the decade.

In mid-decade long-sought efforts at collusion among the valley cotton planters finally achieved results. The most visible evidence of new tactics on the part of owners was the appearance of greater amounts of security on the plantations. But when in 1933 the landowners of the lower Pisco valley agreed not to pay more than a set price for tenant cotton, the tenants were slow to learn of it. Once the valley owners felt they had this agreement in hand, they found it easier to abandon vegetables in favor of cotton. The owners of Palto joined their neighbors in ordering all the yanaconas to plant only cotton.[16]

Table 6.3 Cotton Prices and Wages, 1930–41

	Prices	Average Wages (S/)
1930	—	—
1931	9.5	1.11
1932	—	1.35
1933	—	1.54
1934	—	1.55
1935	—	1.73
1936	11.8	1.73
1937	—	1.24
1938	—	1.30
1939	—	—
1940	—	—
1941	14.8	—

Source: Baltasar Caravedo Molinari, *Burguesía e industria en el Perú (1933–1945) (Lima, 1976)*, 60–61.

Next they turned to the field maintenance problem. Yanacón lots notoriously were the costliest to maintain and least productive. Located at the plantation's geographic core, these sections badly needed the drainage ditches cleaned as well as other essential refurbishment. By insisting that the yanaconas bear the costs for drainage maintenance, the landowners stirred up an issue that had long lain dormant. In the past the peasants considered this task a matter for the plantation. Drainage, as everyone knew, was an expensive, labor-intensive operation, and the peasants could not be convinced that a network of ditches that linked the river inlet at one end of the plantation to the swamp that drained it down below as their responsibility.

Landowners possessed two instruments that might convince the yanaconas to invest time and expense in drainage. They could raise prices at the tambos, or they could require peasants to finance drainage repairs out of their own pockets. Raising tambo prices would place the tenants in a quandary, but it might not solve the problem. They might feel a need to clear the drains only if poor drainage rotted their plants, a condition that would not befall all the tenants at the same time. The second option was not likely to guarantee greater success to the landowners. If peasants paid for repairs from their own pockets, they would find it all the more difficult to repay loans. Owners forbade the use of loans for anything but cotton harvest labor, we may recall, and perhaps owners felt the limited use of loans gave them leverage. At any rate, after a brief delay, the valley landowners once again passed the coast of drainage to the tenants.

Responsibility for a number of other items previously provided by the owners soon fell to the yanaconas: seed, guano, transportation of cotton to the ginning plant in town, and the rental of oxen at high interest outstanding among them. For the independent yanaconas the resumption of tenantry without cattle was hard to swallow. More than other tenants, they were aware of the cost to peasant independence. Several families of independent yanaconas sought to ease their predicament by joining together to rent a team of field oxen in common from the owners, sharing the cost and dividing their use among them.[17]

Sub-yanaconaje

WAGE HANDS

Despite the small victories experienced by the yanaconas on a few items important to their lives on the plantations, the profile of tenant income grew flatter. When yanaconaje reigned in the early 1920s, rent and loans circulated on a seasonal basis. Planters carried over debts that often were not paid when nature intervened, although much depended on personal relations between the manager and the tenant. Even when the owners revised yanaconaje in 1927 to prevent tenants from obtaining loans in the open market, money remained available for relatively long periods and the terms allowed tenants to make ends meet. That sort of flexibility ended in the middle of the following decade.

But along with the growth in landowner power over the peasants came a greater intensity of competition for labor among the mines and textile factories, and the continuation of demand for Peruvian cotton further complicated the search for workers. In fear of a return to labor scarcity and the independence it had afforded the peasants, Pisco valley planters once again devised one of their idealistic common hiring plans. Or so it seems. In practice the new plan for landowner collusion was an alteration in the terms of yanaconaje. Blaming the labor problem on an ineffective enganche system, the owners acknowledged that yanaconas who contracted labor elsewhere were poorly rewarded. Enganche was nearly at a standstill in the valley. For that reason, they provided the yanaconas with a new version of a familiar incentive. They dangled wages before them. But in contrast to past practice, they offered to pay wages to yanaconas for labor performed on the fields they rented for themselves as tenants.[18]

At first glance this device appears implausible. What purpose would it serve if a tenant collected wages? What advantage could an owner derive from such an arrangement? Where in the past the tenant left his own fields and spent several days a week working the "direct" fields of the plantation for wages (or assigned family members to work them in his stead), he now no longer left his own fields nor sent representatives. Now he would work for wages on the parcels he had rented. Indeed, the entire family labored on their own rented fields as wage hands employed by the plantations. What earlier had been an activity that supplemented tenant income had become a necessity of yanacón survival.

Contractual arrangements made in earlier years, when peasants frequently found it possible to rent parcels of cotton plantations in sizes exceeding three fanegadas, often reflected the amount of labor the prospective tenant might bring to the land, including his grown children and other relatives. Adrián García or Juan Esquivel, for example, could argue that their labor resources provided them with access to more than five fanegadas. Such families met their rent and credit obligations with little difficulty and sometimes, as we have seen, found it possible to accumulate small amounts of savings in the form of cash or cattle.

Critical in the previous equation was the unpaid labor of children and spouses.[19] Yet on a leasehold reduced in size to one or two fanegadas, the unpaid labor of family members no longer contributed to tenant independence. In order to pay the rent, tenants had no choice but to send their families to work in the fields for cash. The new rental conditions also meant that the yanacón's share of the cotton harvest fell further than ever, and that wage rates likewise were lower. More than the ratio of rent to income was at stake. Planters had turned the slowdown in migration and the availability of family labor time to their own advantage. Managers extended supervision throughout the plantation, virtually erasing the difference between dependent and independent yanaconas.

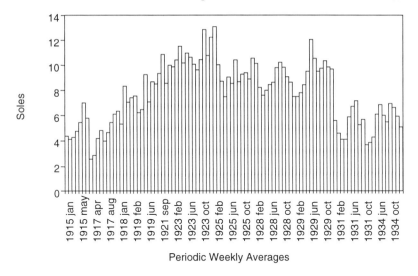

Figure 6.1 Cultivation Wages, Hacienda Palto, 1915–34.

Indeed, a plantation supervisor visited each yanacón's plot on a regular basis. Landowners could now draw upon the families and relatives of yanaconas the year round, supplementing their labor in the harvest season with as many migrants as necessary.[20] The family labor of each tenant was paid for by the plantation, not by the yanacón from his own funds. Cotton plantation managers meted out pay on a sliding scale that varied downward with age and sex. Palto manager Max Alcántara, a former fixed rent tenant, drily summed up the situation: "all yanaconas are now working as peons, and their families too, on their lots and on the fundo in general."[21]

The wage curve undoubtedly reinforced the valley owners' decision to reduce the terms of yanaconaje. At Hacienda Palto, the owners pegged wages to the going valley rate. Figure 6.1 illustrates the general pattern of field wages that allowed the landowners to manipulate yanaconaje. More specifically, wages began the decade at the low level of S/1.00 to S/1.70 a day and climbed sharply to S/3.00 a day by 1933, then dropped off once again. By 1935 the daily wage fell to under S/2.00 a day and remained there through the end of the decade, fluctuating within a range that reflected temporary scarcities and specific types of fieldwork.

By linking larger numbers of peasants to the cash economy, wages created a broader, more competitive labor pool in agriculture. But whether cash signified an improvement in the position of the peasants is problematical. Thorp and Bertram ascribed the renewed emphasis on cash to the "growing political strength" of tenants and the institution of a new system of rural credit, implying that wages were preferable to rent and perhaps that migrants had more political strength than tenants. It is also possible that the turn to wages altered the peasants' perception of the political problem and encouraged them to listen more closely to the arguments of political parties. An Ica valley peasant rose to leadership within the ranks of the Communist Party of Peru in the 1930s, for example, as the appeal of popular reform programs widened under the repressive Benavides military regime.[22]

But the link between wages and the political consciousness of the peasantry seems only to have shifted the contest between the powerful and the powerless to new ground. Like the political movements and parties, private lenders as well as the government Banco Agrícola also encouraged cotton growers to use wage labor despite its high cost. The thinking in this case was that wages made labor susceptible to more precise accounting. The bank viewed with anxiety the independence of sharecropping a practice bankers saw as removing the crop from direct planter control whereas wages did not.[23]

Yanaconas of the late 1930s played a more critical part in cotton production than was true of their forebears. The clearest indicators of one's position were the uses a tenant could make of wages and loans. After 1935 these sources of income served several purposes, for — like the owners — tenants operated in different economic spheres throughout the agricultural year. At some points they acted as farmhands, at others as employers, and yet at other times as brokers. When they were farmhands they tilled the rented fields under the direction of the plantation administrator, seeding the plowed and neatly terraced rows and spreading a thin layer of guano on his orders. For three months the manager paid them in cash, and they performed other jobs for wages as well. On the fields for which they were held responsible through a contract, they worked on irrigation, cultivated new plants, and pruned second- or third-year cotton bushes.

Before the crop came in, tenants abandoned the lampa for a moment and donned entrepreneurial hats. Hard talking, based on knowledge of field conditions, weather, seed, and costs — in essence futures bets — ended with the awarding of a loan. Usually this was the first in a series of small loans advanced to pay harvest workers. Once again tenants switched hats, this time wearing that of a broker. With the loan funds in hand the tenant-brokers then assembled a team of field hands from among family, relatives, friends, and migrants, setting labor terms and wage rates in conformity with the market, ready to pay wages for field labor. Cotton gathered on the family fields went for the most part into the stockpile that the tenant carried to the plantation warehouse for weighing and settlement of accounts with the plantation manager. Having redonned a tenant's hat to carry out the latter tasks, the peasant returned to his or her familial role only after the manager accepted cotton against interest, loans, rent, and debts.[24]

Once they closed the plantation doors to outside lenders, cotton fundo owners pressed their new advantage. They raised interest rates on the harvest and shortened the loan period to three weeks or a month. Peasants were forced to accept interest rates of up to 3 percent per period. Annual rates effectively climbed from 15 and 20 percent in the era of World War I to a new rate of 36 percent, an all-time high for the twentieth-century tenant.

At those rates, rent became difficult if not impossible to pay and for most yanaconas entrapment in perpetual debt seemed unavoidable. Between reduced cotton prices and high-interest loans, fortunate tenants could hope only to meet their rental obligations and pay off personal debts. Little attention could be given to equipment and family responsibilities beyond the provision of food and a few other necessities. The numbers of loans and their amounts grew precipitously over the decade. Loans in 1931, the first year of the revised practice, with tenants at minimum numbers, amounted to slightly over 4,600 soles, a paltry sum. By 1933 when larger numbers of tenants were returning to the plantation fields, the amount rose to over 18,000 soles, and two years later the total of loans outstanding at Hacienda Palto had doubled.[25]

Determined to survive within the more repressive order on the cotton plantations, peasants in large numbers made use of a final instrument left open to them by the new yanaconaje regulations. In a sense, the instrument was a variation on a time-tested method of tenant survival. Driven into the smallest possible landholdings and forced to deal in cash in ways that left them uncomfortable, peasants shifted back and forth between one way of making a living in agriculture and another. Mixing cash and cotton, yanaconas developed a kind of flexibility toward farming on the plantations that earlier was missing from the cotton valleys. Out of necessity and calculating with small parcels of land and a lot of farming sense, yanaconas subrented in the 1930s. Those yanaconas who survived remained on the plantations, reinforcing their claims to the land. The vast majority migrated, worked for wages, and found themselves more subject to a wider set of forces: the plantations, the state, and the growing industrial economy of Peru.

YANACONAS-PATRONES

Some yanaconas feared debt so badly, they paid off their cash obligations and relied upon subrent. The practice was not new; nor was it peculiar to the Pisco valley. Called *allegadía* in some parts of the Andean highlands and *sub-yanaconaje* in the wider sur chico region, it had been practiced in the Pisco valley since at least the turn of the century.[26] In this arrangement a tenant rented a small parcel of his contracted lands to another peasant. Subtenants tended to be young or not well established enough to apply for tenantry in their own right. For a brief time before World War I, arrendatarios had split tenantries with compañeros in the same manner. The difference between the two eras lay in the uses to which the arrangement was put. Earlier usage signified an effort by arrendatarios to reduce the size of loans they contracted, limiting their liability and enhancing capital position. In the 1930s simple lack of solvency usually was behind subrenting. Tenants who found it impossible to meet the family's basic needs by farming one fanegada of land resorted to sub-yanaconaje.

Documentation has not yet surfaced to provide detail on sub-yanaconaje in the sur chico, but studies of more recent agreements of this nature in other regions of Peru outline how it worked.[27] Based on mutual trust between the participants, sub-tenantry most frequently occurred between relatives or compadres.[28] Observers perceived a shift in social relations as tenants resorted to this practice. Sub-yanacón returns fell as the dependents failed to meet the requirements of land use, rental of tools, machines, field oxen, and transport costs. Sometimes the contracting parties disagreed strongly over details of the arrangement, but given the informality of the terms, yanaconas had something of an advantage. Subtenants surrendered cash or a cash crop for use of the land, providing that they might grow foodstuffs among the commercial plants. Most of the foodstuffs were sold for cash if possible, the return going to the lessor. Even if the parties shared the essential tools of farming, the advantage lay with the yanacón.

In 1938, the landowners joined progressive legislators in the National Assembly to pass a law providing government protection for sub-yanaconas. The preamble of the bill claimed that *yanaconas-patrones* (yanaconas who rented land to subtenants) were giving insufficient attention to the welfare of subtenants. The law required yanaconas to provide social security coverage to the subtenants, a moot issue given the general poverty in which peasants were immersed at the end of the depression decade. Although the law passed, it contained no enforcement provisions and had little effect. Yet for a brief time it enabled landowner representatives to deflect criticism away from their own dominance of the land and onto the "dominant" sector of the peasantry.[29]

Despite the absence of clear evidence that significant numbers of subtenants worked the cotton fields at Hacienda Palto, their presence can be surmised. Although space was at a premium, there was sufficient capacity for them in the farming areas. Sub-yanaconas could not hope to subsist from the product of the land alone; they also expected to earn cash by working the fields of the plantation. By 1940 the owners of Palto had stretched the cotton fields to cover over 97 of the fundo's more than 165 fanegadas, and the sub-yanaconas were most likely found on many of those fields.[30]

Rather than hire labor contractors all year around, cotton landowners encouraged sub-Yanaconaje. The practice allowed them to delay hiring extra migrants until the last moment. Although it did not resolve the general scramble for scarce labor at the onset of the harvest, sub-yanaconaje shifted the preoccupation with temporary cotton labor from the owners to the yanaconas. As migration slowed, Pisco valley landowners derived some satisfaction from reports like that submitted in 1940 by the Palto manager, who noted that "almost all" of the fundo was rented to yanaconas.[31]

Yanaconas took steps to adapt to the deteriorating conditions of tenantry. The most frequent decisions they faced at this juncture concerned not so much the crops to plant and when to harvest them, or even the amount of ready cash they needed to undertake cultivation. The most important question was how best to generate income so as to keep from falling into unrelieved debt. Evidently sub-yanaconaje

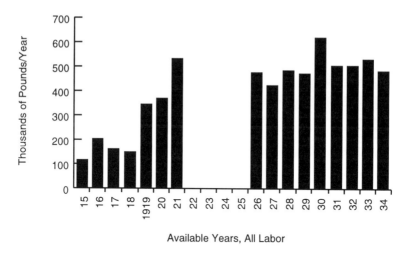

Figure 6.2 Total Raw Cotton Harvested, Hacienda Palto, 1915–34.

did not provide the help that was hoped. Conditions of tenantry decidedly had shifted for the worse, and by the end of the decade debt peonage became a widespread reality.

The achievement of a long-term resident labor population burdened by debt was a hollow victory for the cotton planters. With more intensive land use, other factors took a toll on cotton. Soil deterioration, plant disease, and fertilization costs, all combined to reduce output and profits. Having failed to reduce costs despite passing many of the burdens of cotton planting to the peasants, some landowners found themselves worrying over the fate of cotton. Later, in 1947, a new law written by socialist reform legislators regulated yanaconaje to the detriment of landowners, and shortly thereafter some owners began backing away from direct involvement in cotton. At that point, the Aspíllagas decided to lease all of Hacienda Palto to an experienced and ambitious tenant.[32]

Conclusion

By the late 1920s sharp distinctions separated yanaconas from Pisco valley migrants. Key plantation practices accounted for the distinctions, none more conspicuous than credit. Lending practices on the

Pisco plantations changed after the last contract revisions in 1925, when lending was restricted to the plantation. At that point peasants received loans for cultivation from only two sources, the owners and the manager, who did not compete with one another. Dependent yanaconas, the last campañeros at Palto, borrowed only from the manager and did not have the right to borrow from the owners. Independent yanaconas similarly borrowed only from the owners. Both forms of credit carried appallingly high interest rates and very short terms.

After 1931, with the return of yanaconaje, cotton planters pressed their monopoly of lending to full advantage, combining it with reductions in the size of rental plots in a final effort to entrap the peasants. Although the strategy worked, driven in part by the greater availability of migrant labor, its effect on output disappointed the cotton landowners. Despite the fall in output, which owners blamed on increasing land use for subsistence and the use of sub-yanaconaje, the owners raked in high returns as labor availability kept wages low.

For the yanaconas and migrant workers, resistance had reached its nadir by the end of the decade. Slowly the noose of debt encircled the valley population until by mid-decade yanaconas were isolated in the spectrum of rural society. The political voice they looked for in the APRA movement and the Communist Party was dimmed after both movements were diverted to industrial issues. The land reform problem did not die, but its place on the list of priorities fell as parties sought political power and listened more intently to miners and factory workers. Agrarian reform bills taken up in the National Parliament after 1935 strongly reflected the voice of the Sociedad Nacional Agraria, the landowner lobby, and the laws frankly reflected landowner concerns.

The key to understanding why peasants returned to yanaconaje despite the deterioration of tenant independence after 1935 lies in the general economy. Population growth apparently outpaced the availability of jobs in the depression decade, while an inexperienced and harassed labor movement sought wages and other improvements for industrial workers. In short, no clear voice expressed the political significance of the ties between the rural economy and the living conditions of labor. Competition for jobs and land in the cotton valleys intensified divisions that had existed for decades within the rural population and undermined the independence of yanaconas. Debt peonage followed.

CONCLUSION

Plantation Society and Peruvian Culture

The story told in these pages about peasant activities in the lower Pisco valley calls attention to several propositions about peasants and plantations, especially cotton plantations. There is little disagreement anymore that plantations were key to the growth of a national economy in republican Peru, but what has not been clear is the part peasants played in the growth process. Until now convention had it that growth depended on a repressed or co-opted peasantry. The evidence seems to show otherwise: that the peasantry was not uniformly repressed and, further, that not all peasants submitted to or collaborated with planter control of growth. More to the point, it appears that the peasantry was critically involved in the formation of Peruvian society from the mid nineteenth century at least until World War II.

If peasants noticeably were not co-opted nor submitted to planter domination, then how can we accurately describe their part in the process? If neither co-optation nor submission occurred, then what happened? A satisfactory response to this question calls for bringing into play two concepts referred to often throughout this study: hegemony and resistance. The two concepts travel well in tandem, and they are critical for understanding relations between the powerful and the powerless sectors of agrarian society.

Planter dominance of rural society declined soon after indenture. The wartime flight of contractees tore a veil from before the eyes of the cotton planters, and the owners found it necessary to abandon the coercive labor practices to which they had become accustomed. The planters found their choices narrowed to two: they could improve mechanization, or they could employ the free peasant population. Given the high cost of mechanical improvements and the perception that the market could not absorb such expenses, planters turned to the free peasants as the most convenient source of labor at hand. A new labor strategy focused on various techniques of persuasion and deception.

To stoke the furnace of growth by hand would require among other things that the planters demonstrate a degree of confidence in the fieldworkers. Yet as is widely known, planters traditionally have held peasants in utter disdain.[1] Pisco valley landowners were no different in this respect from their counterparts elsewhere in time and space. Cultural prejudices played a critical part in determining the cotton planters' practices. True to the paternalistic character of creole culture, the owners treated the peasants like children who, given their "races," were thought to be incapable of understanding the economics and management of farming.[2] Although relations between the two primary sectors of rural society were filtered through the discourse of race, it was a discourse no less shaped by law.

Not that the peasants were free of racial prejudice. The people of the sur chico in the 1860s, largely the descendants of Afro-Peruvian slaves and former indentured Asians, were joined by a steady twentieth-century stream of highland villagers, descendants of pre-Hispanic natives, who migrated down into the Pisco valley in search of plantation work. Although some of the highlanders returned home regularly, increasing numbers remained on the coast. The combination made this region one of the more ethnically and racially diverse in the country. After 1895 the social order on the cotton plantations underwent the sort of changes noticed by Rebecca J. Scott on sugar plantations in Louisiana, Cuba, and Brazil, where society was reconfigured as agricultural capitalism matured.[3] Within the next two generations — and in the face of internal conflicts of many sorts — the three groups intermingled and intermarried on the plantations.

Meanwhile, creoles stood at the apex of rural society, visible only as holders of privilege and wielders of power. Included among them were plantation managers, accountants, judges, local officials, and representatives of the national state.[4] Not surprisingly, they walked the high social tightrope with some ambivalence and uncertainty, claiming the right to rule yet finding it demeaning to assert the claim before the population over which they ruled. They preferred intermediaries.

The landowners conveyed their ambivalence to the peasantry through many intermediary instruments. On the cotton plantations these began with the presence of the managers and continued through a constellation of signals. The manager's arrogance, the practices of cultivation and harvesting, the patronizing exhortations to work harder from managers and owners alike, the use of various forms of security on and off the fields, preference for children as labor, and preservation — and occasional use — of the stocks from the days of indenture (and perhaps earlier) into the early twentieth century, made it clear that the planters had little appreciation for the persistence, tenacity, and wisdom based on experience demonstrated by farmers in the sphere of land use.

On the other hand, the planters encouraged the most productive peasants and rewarded their market-oriented achievements with more land, more privileges, personal greetings by the owner, attentive greetings by the manager, and other marks of high status. These rewards unquestionably were made in the context of a paternalistic, creole society keenly conscious of racial and cultural differences between its members and the peasantry and prepared to maintain those distinctions. The landowners were far from proposing social democracy on the plantation. But they recognized that the appropriate social and economic incentives would stimulate the more skilled peasants to improve their farming operations and thereby raise production.

By their actions, peasants were perhaps less ambivalent in their feelings toward the dominant sectors but no less willing to accommodate. They spoke politely and rarely unless spoken to; they waited patiently for the manager to discuss contracts and revisions. Admittedly, some peasants exhibited more audacity and arrogance than others, but the Joaquín Gutiérrezes and the Daniel Francos were few and far between. Perhaps only the most independent of them, the Juan Esquivels at the top of the social pyramid, dared confront the manager with the latter's shortcomings or complain directly to the landowners. The rebellious organization effort of the 1908 cohort of rebels at Hacienda Palto best illustrates their own recognition of the powerlessness of their social condition.

When confronted with opportunities to maximize their power over the land or to improve their position in the market, however, the peasants, particularly the well-placed fixed rent tenants, worked quickly. Peasant actions in the credit market provide interesting insights into the tactic renters and sharecroppers used to minimize threats to their independence. The more successful of them avoided the domineering plantation manager and sought independent creditors by negotiating the sale of their cotton, or they dealt directly with the owners. In the tactics used to maximize the effectiveness of pastures and credit, we can see the designs peasants had on the land, their respect for it as their major provider, and the limits placed upon farming skills in an increasingly commercial plantation economy.

The motive for peasant behavior ultimately can only be guessed at.[5] It may be possible to argue that to the extent that peasants accepted the rules of the plantation game, they were collaborating with the landowners in the business of deriving profits from the maximization of returns. However, there is much evidence that collaboration was not the most important of the peasants' goals and that their designs on the land were of a different order from those of the landowners. The most important evidence come from the owners themselves, who right up to the end complained that there were insufficient instruments — be they incentives or deterrents — to make the peasants work hard enough and with enough consistency. Our sources are skewed on this point. The owners complained only about those portions of the plantation where crops were raised for the direct benefit of the owners. They rarely complained about the garden plots under peasant control, and only when peasants failed to pay the rent did they turn to look at the lands the peasants farmed under contract.

Cultural distance figured heavily in the hegemonic design of the landowners. They were determined to create a reliable, stable labor force out of a population whose cultural credentials they disparaged and demeaned. In their view the African, Chinese, and pre–Hispanic American biological inheritance of the rural laboring population — and its farm-laboring proclivities — ill prepared it for the civilized art of learning. Yet coercive tactics had proved to be inconvenient. The task for the landowners was to devise a combination of incentives and obstacles that would create a sufficient level of trust to convince peasants that life on the plantation could be no worse than life outside its walls. In short, they expected to limit the terrors of the plantation such that peasants would curb their own freedom to move on. This was no easy task, and it took much experimentation and adaptation on the part of the owners, much of it represented in the alterations made in the wage and rental contracts, the loans, the crop requirements, and the herd provisions that were part of the bargaining process carried on almost daily throughout the period under study. Whatever understandings and values both sides brought to the process, the negotiation became the discourse of plantation society. It is a small wonder that planters and peasants alike associated skin color with culture and culture with power.

In that fashion, the hegemonic project of the landowners created the space within which peasants carried out a prolonged resistance. Once again the question arises: If the peasants accepted the terms of the bargain, be it the wage or the rental contract, how can their commitments be termed anything but collaboration, or adaptation, to the larger demands of the plantation? Perhaps, when rural day laborers bargained in the 1880s for wages, and struck when they felt deceived by the length of the work day or the nature of the task, one could talk about resistance in the confrontational manner James C. Scott intended. This was plainly resistance to coercive practices. Peasants may have bargained over the elements of the contract, but once a contract was accepted they in effect had played into the farming rules of the plantation. Peasants, in truth, always were at a disadvantage in the contract and they undoubtedly knew it. Why should a tenant's farming choices be seen as resistance to the plantation?

Alan Knight's analysis of dominance offers a compelling response to this question. Knight invokes the conditions wherein dominance often gives way to hegemonic social relations. As Knight put it, hegemonic relations between planters and peasants occur most often where peasants see opportunities to maximize individual interests in a society ruled by a supposedly heavy-handed ruling sector. Indeed, plantation society seems especially to call forth elite behaviors calculated to persuade and convince the peasants to join the planters in a process that, ultimately, may be seen as opposed to the interests of the peasants. It is important to point out that Knight rejects the explanation of "false consciousness"; that is, peasants in the Pisco valley were not misled to think that they might seize direct control of the plantations. The planters were leery of this possibility from the opening years of tenantry. However, it is also necessary to recall that peasants — indeed, both sides — knew the old adage: that possession is nine-tenths of the law.

Almost from the start of tenant contracting, peasants demonstrated that they knew their rights under a contract and they sought to invoke those agreements whenever a question of possession or use became an issue. In their most assertive moments, they left the plantations at the end of the harvest, shrugging off the demands made by plantation managers that they accept another contract. They protested aloud the devaluation of the coin in which they were paid, and they complained vehemently when managers tried to cheat them in the weighing of cotton and the use of pastures. If a landowner failed to redress specific grievances, the peasants simply left that plantation for another. Those with contracts fled them, abandoning crops to rot in the field and planters to bellow helplessly about the inconstancy of labor.

A pattern of peasant resistance emerged within the varied and scattered forms of protest that peasants carried out under fixed rent and sharecropper contracts. The peasants did not view acceptance of contracts as an agreement to submit to daily supervised labor. Everyone on the plantations was conscious of rank, a structure imposed not by the planters alone but by the conviction on the part of some sectors of the peasantry that they could best be satisfied by renting land rather than working the fields for a wage. A contract for long-term rent undoubtedly signified a high degree of farming skill, while sharecropping — especially as a debtor to the plantation manager — and subrenting — conveyed lesser stature within the plantation hierarchy. High rank under a capitalistic regime was not associated with birth but with merit, and it followed that social position imposed certain responsibilities of group leadership. Meanwhile, the techniques — from foot dragging to displacement of protest into carnivalesque and theatrical displays — raises the possibility that other worlds exists alongside and within the dominant one. It becomes the task of the student of subordinate culture to re-create the outlines and fill the spaces of that inserted resistive reality. Sharecroppers living on the plantations voiced little protest in the early twentieth century, and by the 1920s and 1930s they found it expedient to take their protest in the direction of off-plantation labor. Migrant fieldworkers were much less ready to voice complaints within the plantation hierarchy; they preferred to protest on a more political level. Of course, the lower ranks of the peasantry also felt far less commitment to the land and a surplus.

Resistance among high-ranking peasants arose when plantation authorities violated the tenant contracts. The goals of tenant resistance appear generally to have been simple and predictable. Foremost in a peasant's eyes was the satisfaction of familial needs in the domestic sphere and the exercise of farming choice in the fields. Tenants felt satisfied when they could pay the rent and make a surplus, and they became agitated when debt became unmanageable. Long-term residence on a plantation carried with it a certain ambivalence.

It might leave a tenant vulnerable to entrapment, especially if the tenant balked at the responsibilities of larger loans and higher rent. On the other side, long-term residence also made the peasant a familiar figure, suggested reliability, and improved access to credit. Peasants who stayed in one place long enough found the plantation rental contract to be a negotiable and flexible instrument. These conditions, so critical to the effective functioning of peasant rentals, largely went unspoken. The failure of contemporaries to accept the possibility that peasants found a flexible contract not to be a violation of an agreement has misled serious students of enganche to give undue emphasis to its use as a weapon of landowner control and to deny its potential as an effective weapon of resistance in the hands of insightful peasants.

Perhaps least well understood is the relationship that developed among tenant contracts, enganche, and credit. Conventionally the latter two institutions are viewed as one. Enganche, the advance on wages or credit against a future payment of rent, too easily is seen as a snare from which peasants could not extricate themselves, a never-ending debt. Credit, so goes the standard view, could only be arranged within the confines of the plantation. In the Pisco valley, however, peasants experienced the two institutions differently. They served quite distinct — if related — purposes. Enganche was indeed an advance that indebted the peasants, but it also threatened for a time to clog the cotton plantations with an overly large resident labor force. Peasants accumulated debt in order to remain in residence on the plantations when wage rates fell. The planters undermined enganche of their own accord when they canceled debts to relieve themselves of labor costs in years when cotton production stagnated.

Credit sometimes became an instrument of protest and resistance to plantation rules in the hands of the peasants. In the early twentieth century, Pisco valley tenants played the local credit market well enough that the momentum of power on the plantations momentarily shifted away from the planters and toward the peasants. True, the moment passed by quickly and the peasants soon lost what leverage they held. But credit remained the linchpin of tenantry in the cotton regions. When access to credit ended, yanaconaje finally took the form that its later students would erroneously assume to be its form throughout the entire history of the institution.[6]

This is not to argue that cash wages played little part in cotton farm labor. In the era between the War of the Pacific and the close of the nineteenth century, mobility and freedom from entrapment were very important to the Pisco valley peasants looking for jobs. Wages freed them from the barter economy and gave them access to goods in the towns such as Pisco, where they purchased necessities that no longer could be made in the home or found in rural markets. But Lima fiscal policy and market conditions soon undermined the choices that wages made available. Later, when the planters choked off peasant access to credit, wages again became an instrument of survival and a means for peasants at the apex of the plantation hierarchy to ride out changes that drove most labor into the sector of rural society that had no resources but its own labor.

What, then, was the meaning of wages under a system that has been called "coerced labor"? By now we ought to be able to provide a tentative answer to this question. Even under indenture, wages performed at least one important business function. They helped the owners of the cotton plantations keep track of their returns. Wages also measured the degree to which labor performance matched its cost. Put another way, wages could be compared to production to determine whether the indentured Asians were slacking. The greater the ratio of returns to wages, presumably the more productive the manager could surmise his laborers were. Without this element in the effort to measure profits, the owners could not determine if their investment in cotton was worthwhile. Whether or not the wages entered the market and were spent was immaterial; what was important was that a wage signified the output value of labor.

There were also important social reasons for paying workers, even indentured workers, on the plantation. Wages served as an inducement and discouraged flight. We have seen that flight was a serious problem in the Pisco valley after the end of indenture, and the managers of the cotton plantations hoped to stem the exodus of Asians from the work regimen by dangling the prospect of higher wages before them.

After the War of the Pacific, wages declined in importance. At first, owners paid wages to stabilize the labor force and to slough off related living expenses. They found that labor contracting absorbed wages, however, and with labor continually scarce planters passed the wage problem on to the tenants. The wage inducements formerly associated with indenture ironically would have secondary importance in a market dominated by rent.

Realizing that wages continued to be a useful instrument for attracting extremely scarce and highly mobile labor, the cotton planters never fully abandoned wage payments. And they found that if they sacrificed their hold on the land temporarily they could pass the burden of wages on to the renters. The trade-off of wages for tenantry remained central to the growth of export cotton until the rural labor population became plentiful and wage rates fell. At that point, having weakened peasant claims by persistent attack, the owners resumed control over land and wages.

Wages also were one of the two major instruments that shaped peasant society on the plantation in the years of cotton export growth until World War II. As independent tenantry declined, wages became an instrument of labor negotiation and mobility. Between the world wars, when labor became plentiful, the choice between cash and rent narrowed to the point of being indistinguishable. A clear pattern of labor use, reflecting the abandonment of rent in favor of wage labor on the plantations, failed to emerge in the sur chico before the Second World War. Even when in late 1934 dependent yanaconaje once more came into full-blown use, it had evolved into a set of social relations that masked the importance of wages.

A fine line existed between tenant stability and entrapment. Tenantry became usable when landowners and peasants found the institution to be a means to a greater end. To the landowners this meant that the state had recovered sufficiently from the war with Chile to underwrite a three-year renewable contract. To the peasants it meant that an extended contract would reliably support subsistence. As the tenant uprising at Palto in 1895 showed, the peasants perceived that the danger of entrapment had passed only when the landowners made credit available. At that moment tenantry took hold on south coast plantations — before Peru experienced significant population growth and before the avalanche of mass migration from highland communities to the cotton valleys.

Proper financial conditions were but one aspect of farm management. For peasants to act on the opportunities made available by credit with some expectation of success, they would need social support. Ordinarily peasants would be able to rely at such moments on the protective cushion of the community. The independent communities of the coastal valleys long since had given way to the expanding plantations, however, and they no longer could be a source of social strength. Tenants had only their individual guarantors, their families and their neighbors. Perhaps, as events at Hacienda Palto suggest, when the villages disappeared peasants sought to re-create them within the boundaries of the plantations.

The rewards of family cotton tenantry potentially were high. Protection of tenant rights was temporary and unpredictable, and tenants had little to fall back on in times of failure save their farming skills. Despite the risks, capital accumulation in the form of cattle occurred. Under the circumstances this was no small feat. Cattle permitted tenants to bargain in the marketplace off the plantation, giving them access to credit, goods, and lower prices that a lack of capital would otherwise deny them. Those tenants, Juan Esquivel and his cohorts, for example, who marshaled their resources well and displayed an ability to bargain for credit while they brought in large harvests, became known for their skills. They amassed wealth and won prestige from owners and fellow tenants alike.

Another item of importance to the peasants is discernible within the volatile agrarian growth process. The peasants wanted tenantry to provide them with stability of place, and the best way to meet that need was through permanent residence. For peasants, continued residence at a single plantation through two contract periods could provide opportunities to marshall resources and avoid the losses that inevitably occurred when large families moved from one location to another. It meant opportunities to become familiar with the peculiarities of the soil and the details of cultivation in a designated area, increasing the chances of farming success. It meant greater familiarity with one's fellow tenants as well, although familiarity did not necessarily lead to friendship and support in the face of authoritarian threats.

The planters found it necessary to modify and adapt the tenant contract, especially when they feared that cotton grown on the plantation might not be subject to their control. The timing of the decision suggests that they hesitated to encourage resident tenantry as the central labor force in cotton until they could be reasonably certain that a nonintrusive state was stabilized and the cotton market improved. Once so assured, a judgment severely tested by the Piérola uprising at the end of the nineteenth century, the planters then were in a position to encourage the formation of a resident tenant population without fear that peasant claims to the land might provoke social upheaval and civil war.

Under a fragile planter hegemony, an era of opportunity arose for peasants in the two decades after the turn of the twentieth century. The opportunities for peasants to make extraordinary advances on the plantations continued for a surprisingly long period of time. The Pisco valley provides a showcase of that phase. Between 1895 and 1915 the most interested sector of the peasantry, the fixed rent tenants, seized opportunities available on the cotton plantations and made the most of the chance within the limitations of rented land and the tenant contract.[7]

Numbers of peasants at Hacienda Palto and other Pisco valley cotton plantations repeatedly took initiatives that placed their families at risk. They challenged the manager and the owners when it seemed that contractual rights were endangered by plantation policy. In response, the planters reaffirmed their control of cotton, and in the aftermath of this struggle tenant independence was severely reduced. Fixed rent tenants gradually disappeared from the scene and their place was taken by yanaconas, who commanded far fewer resources.

By the mid-1920s the typical cotton plantation tenant was a yanacón. This individual's rights were negligible; most especially, he or she had seen a dwindling of opportunities to accumulate savings in the form of cattle. Almost as if to emphasize that point, the owners brought tractors to the cotton plantations. At the same time labor scarcity became a memory as the population trend reversed. Yields improved gradually, and in 1934 the owners of Hacienda Palto and their neighbors learned with satisfaction that tractors, the reduction of yanacona space, and other technological refinements increased cotton returns dramatically throughout 1929.[8]

The resistance tactics pursued by individual peasants crumbled finally when the rural labor supply became plentiful. Scarce labor had led peasants and planters to compete with one another for migrant labor in the early 1920s, driving production up to the limits of technology and splitting the peasants into wealthy and poor sectors. After 1925 heavy migration favored the owners. Peasants were deeply divided, finding it impossible to complete individual contracts and to pursue their goals through collective means. Tenants feared ejection, and migrant laborers responded more favorably to the arguments made by APRA, the Communists, and the Socialists, but the moment for a blending of peasant needs under the leadership of popular politicians and parties apparently had passed.

Knowing that peasants initiated events helps to undermine the argument that the masses of people were acted upon rather than active in the creation of Peruvian history, but the initiatives described here raise further problems. Pisco cotton tenants did not rise up in spontaneous rebellion against the injustices they faced, nor did they link the problems of plantation tenantry so clearly to a political agenda, at least not for many years. On the contrary, they struggled quietly, often as individuals though sometimes in orchestrated cooperation with one another as the dramatic Hacienda Palto demonstration of 1908 illustrates.

Peasants clearly undertook this struggle for power at an enormous disadvantage. They had no connections to powerful politicians or to banks as a source of agricultural credit. Few owned the necessary cattle and tools to cultivate the fields. Nor did they own their houses, determine when to plant and sow, or take their products to market. Their burdens were spelled out with ever greater clarity in each new writing of a contract. Individualization of contracts discouraged cooperation among tenants and maintained a competitive atmosphere in the fields. Meanwhile, greater clarity and specificity in tenant contracts over the years homogenized tenant conditions and gradually reduced the negotiating flexibility of the yanaconas.

Despite the imbalances in the struggle, it was one thing for cotton planters to state the rules; it was quite another to gain the willing submission of the tenants to those dictates.[9] Hegemony theory proposes that civil society — where a majority consents to values and perceptions proposed by a minority — is accomplished when the consenting majority is free, yet without access to economic and political power. T. J. Jackson Lears links consent more clearly to culture by noting that "legitimation, not manipulation, is the key to cultural hegemony."[10] Lears thus helps to clarify a key element of this study: that although a landowning elite held power over the peasantry in ways that did not require enforcement, it does not follow that the landowners were at all times dominant.[11]

To argue that power in Peru was consistently in the hands of the few families at the top of the social order, as typically has been done, does not squarely hit the mark. In the sphere of cotton commerce, landowners wielded power through the diffused, overlapping circles of the oligarchy. Within those circles divisions arose in part as a product of personal jealousies and conflicting political ambitions between families. The divisions surfaced in the sur chico valleys in the form of quarrels between planters over water rights violations, irrigation and fencing disputes, wage agreement violations, and labor provocations. The rivalry between Antero Aspíllaga and Augusto Leguía is well known. Though less well known, the Pisco valley discord between the Aspíllagas and the Del Solars that shattered the public calm from time to time did as much as the Aspíllaga-Leguía split to undermine the dominant position of the Peruvian oligarchy and delay its hegemonic project.[12]

Throughout this study evidence shows that the peasants who settled in the Pisco valley were enormously adaptive. The plantations made their lives more difficult, but they struggled to keep their heads up. They often maintained a decent sense of life's importance and its traditions in the face of repressive and humiliating assaults intended to channel and control their labor. The plantation population rarely struggled in a unified manner toward a commonly accepted goal, an observation that comes as no surprise if we remember that the rewards of plantation residence were individualized in the rental contracts.

Yanaconaje reflected the social dynamics of agricultural capitalism. In the form that became familiar in Peru in the 1920s, after the writings of José Mariátegui focused on it as an inhumane, repressive institution but before Hildebrando Castro Pozo began to draw attention to it in the National Congress, yanaconaje was a new version of an old relationship. It had provided peasants with an alternative to the mid-nineteenth-century independent communities in the coastal valleys that in many cases were destroyed as the plantations expanded. But after the mid-1920s yanaconaje became more restrictive. Yet even in its most repressive form, it was not a rigid institution. Between 1927 and 1940 yanaconas responded nimbly to a number of changing circumstances on the plantations, from the depressed conditions of the late 1920s, signaling the exhaustion of the postwar boomlet in commercial agriculture, through the surge in population and burgeoning demand that enlarged Peruvian textile manufacture in the mid-1930s.

Resistance is a complex phenomenon, as the evidence presented hre suggests. When searching for its elements at levels more obscure than open mass rebellion, we ought not to define it too strictly. James C. Scott used the phrase "arts of resistance" to convey the wide range of tactics that may come under study, and his use of the term seems accurate. Above all, resistance involved the fine art of remaining alive and relatively free while engaging in forms of rebellion against authority that are not easily recognizable as resistance — at least that is what the actors hoped.

In some cases, rebellion was expressed through the instrumentality of the very institutions designed to hold resistance in check: contracts, loans, and credit served that ambiguous purpose. Sometimes the so-called resistors collaborated with those in authority. Resistance also could be seen occurring as a process some call "triangulation," in which scapegoating became the preferred instrument of communication. A great deal about the place of resistance in the formation of Latin American societies has yet to be understood.

In the end it is important to focus on the contract, perhaps the greatest symbol of the space between dominance and hegemony. A failure on the part of planter or peasant to properly negotiate this instrument could do serious damage to the cycles of cultivation and cotton harvest. The result might easily be a loss of advantage — a loss of power in the relentless struggle for command of production. Indeed, the centrality of the contract in cotton plantation society dovetails so conveniently with the definition of hegemony that one may be startled. Raymond Williams placed legitimation at the heart of hegemony. Similarly, the tenant contract was the key to legitimacy and power on the plantations.[13]

NOTES

Preface

1 On the geography of the valley, and particularly of the Pisco River, see Instituto Geográfico Militar, "Mapa de la cuenca del río Pisco" (Peru, 1955); and see especially the colored pencil sketches of the river drawn by the manager of Hacienda Palto in the early twentieth century, separate unpaginated items in Archivo del Fuero Agrario, *Hacienda Palto: correspondencia y cuentas, 1867–1949* (Lima). Hereafter AFA, Hacienda Palto, *Letterbooks*. [*Letterbooks* is a shortened translation of *Correspondencia y cuentas*. Account statements accompanied letters sent by plantation managers to the owners of the plantation at least once a month.] Unless otherwise noted, dated letters and statements of account flowed from the plantation manager to the Lima office of the Aspíllaga family operations.

2 Criticism of the 1969 agrarian reform from the perspective of its effect on economic structures is in Rosemary Thorp and Geoff Bertram, *Growth and Policy in an Open Economy: Peru, 1890–1977* (New York, 1977), chaps. 14–16. Early social policy critiques were led by Colin Harding, "Land Reform and Social Conflict in Peru," in *The Peruvian Experiment: Continuity and Change under Military Rule,* ed. Abraham F. Lowenthal (Princeton, N.J., 1975), 220–53; DESCO, *Estado y política agraria: 4 ensayos* (Lima, 1977); David Guillet, *Agrarian Reform and Peasant Economy in Southern Peru* (New York, 1979); and Cynthia McClintock and Abraham F. Lowenthal, eds., *The Peruvian Experiment Reconsidered* (Princeton, N.J., 1983).

3 Roger Ransom and Richard Sutch appropriately titled their study of sharecropping in the United States as *One Kind of Freedom: The Economic Consequences of Emancipation* (Cambridge, 1977).

4 José María Caballero, "Sharecropping as an Efficient System: Further Answers to an Old Puzzle," in *Sharecropping and Sharecroppers,* ed. T. J. Byres (London, 1983), 107–9; Joseph Reid Jr., "Sharecropping in History and Theory," *Agricultural History* 49.2 (1975): 426–40. Some might argue, as did Eric Wolf, in *Peasants* (Englewood Cliffs, N.J., 1955), that when people entered the plantations they ceased to be peasants. Wolf later modified his position: see Magnus Mörner, "Latin American 'Landlords' and 'Peasants' and the Outer World during the National Period," in *Land and Labour in Latin America,* ed. K. Duncan and I. Rutledge, with Colin Harding (Cambridge, 1977). Sidney Mintz succinctly outlined the main features of the problem of definition in "A Note on the Definition of Peasantries," *Journal of Peasant Studies* 1.1 (1973): 91–106. See also James Scott, "Hegemony and the Peasantry," *Politics and Society* 7.3 (1977): 262–96; William Roseberry, "Images of the Peasant in the Consciousness of the Venezuelan Proletariat," in *Proletarians and Protest: The Roots of Class Formation in an Industrializing World,* ed. Michael Hanagan and Charles Stephenson (New York, 1986), 149–69; and William Roseberry, "Peasants, Proletarians, and Politics," in *Power and Protest in the Countryside: Rural Unrest in Asia, Europe, and Latin America,* ed. Robert P. Weller and Scott E. Guggenheim (Durhan, N.C., 1989), 106–31. A thoughtful addition to the literature is Ben Orlove, "Against a Definition of Peasantries: Agricultural Production in Andean Peru," in *Peasant Livelihood: Studies in Economic Anthropology and Cultural Ecology,* ed. Rhoda Halperin and James Dow (New York, 1977), 22–35.

5 See Ralph Bolton and Enrique Mayer, *Andean Kinship and Marriage* (Washington, D.C., 1977), and Raymond Smith, *Kinship Ideology and Practice in Latin America* (Chapel Hill, N.C., 1984). James C. Scott, *Domination and the Arts of Resistance: Hidden Transcripts* (New Haven, Conn., 1990), refers to rituals performed in subordinate circumstances as "hidden transcripts." Some Peruvian terms found in the sources used for this study may be unfamiliar. See the Glossary at the end of the text. The terms are italicized on first appearance only.

6 Detailed studies of Gramscian hegemony that my conception relies on are Perry Anderson, "The Antinomies of Antonio Gramsci," *New Left Review* 100 (November 1976–January 1977): 5–80; T. J. Jackson Lears, "The Concept of Cultural Hegemony: Problems and Possibilities," *American Historical Review* 90.3 (1985): 567–93; and Chantal Mouffe, "Hegemony and Ideology in Gramsci," in *Gramsci and Marxist Theory,* ed. Chantal Mouffe (London, 1979), 168–204. Particularly illustrative recent discussions of hegemony and resistance that take gender into account are Ana María Alonso, "Gender, Power, and Historical Memory: Discourses of *Serrano* Resistance," in *Feminists Theorize the Political,* ed. Judith Butler and Joan W. Scott (New York, 1992), 404–25; and Florencia M. Mallon, "The Promise and Dilemma of Subaltern Studies: Perspectives from Latin American History," *American Historical Review* 99.5 (1994): 1,491–1,515.

7 Contrasting conceptions of patriarchy are reviewed in Veronica Beechey, "On Patriarchy," *Feminist Review* 3 (1979): 66–82. Richard Sennett, *Authority* (New York, 1980), 19–24, elaborates on some variants. For Peru, see Florencia M. Mallon, "Gender and Class in the Transition to Capitalism:

Household and Mode of Production in Central Peru," *Latin American Perspectives,* 13.1 (1986): 147–74.

8 Arguably the most influential work of the past generation on segmentation and power in peasant society is Eric R. Wolf, *Peasant Wars of the Twentieth Century* (New York, 1969). Recent literature on the economic theory of tenantry took a significant turn with Stephen N. S. Cheung, *A Theory of Share Tenancy* (Chicago, 1969); Reid, "Sharecropping in History and Theory"; and José María Caballero, "Sharecropping: A Survey of the Issues," Wolfson College, Centre of Latin American Studies, Cambridge University, (1982) manuscript. It culminated in Juan Martínez-Alier, *Haciendas, Plantations and Collective Farms* (London, 1977). Magnus Mörner introduced a dozen models of tenantry in "A Comparative Study of Tenant Labor in Parts of Europe, Africa and Latin America, 1700–1900," *Latin American Research Review* 5.2, (1970): 3–15. Arnold J. Bauer, in "Rural Workers in Spanish America: Problems of Peonage and Oppression," *Hispanic American Historical Review* 59.1, (1979): 34–63, thoughtfully rested distinctions he noted among different strata of tenants on criteria that could be analyzed in plantation records; Caballero, in "Sharecropping as an Efficient System," 107–9, questioned the conventionally accepted distinctions between farmers and peasants, a position that I view sympathetically.

9 Scott called attention to the importance of peasant resistance in *Weapons of the Weak* (New Haven, Conn., and London, 1985); drew compelling comparisons in "Everyday Forms of Resistance," in *Everyday Forms of Peasant Resistance and the Arts of Resistance: Hidden Transcripts,* ed. Forrest D. Colburn (Armonk, N.Y., 1989), 3–33; and explored his ideas in more detail in *Domination and the Arts of Resistance: Hidden Transcripts* (New Haven, Conn., 1990). Knight wrote with particular insight on what might be called "passive resistance" in "Weapons and Arches in the Mexican Revolutionary Landscape," in *Everyday Forms of State Formation: Revolution and the Negotiation of Rule in Modern Mexico,* ed. Joseph Gilbert and Daniel Nugent (Durham, N.C., 1995), especially 44–54. Also beneficial has been William Roseberry, "Beyond the Agrarian Question in Latin America," in *Paradigms, Peasants, Labor, and the Capitalist World System in Africa and Latin America,* ed. Steve J. Stern et al. (Madison, 1993), 318–70.

10 The phrase was used by Ranajit Guha in "Dominance without Hegemony and Its Historiography," *Subaltern Studies: Writings on South Asian History and Society* 6 (1989): 210–309. See also Partha Chatterjee, "More on Modes of Power and the Peasantry," *Subaltern Studies: Writings on South Asian History and Society* 3 (1983): 311–49.

11 Much of this analysis relies on the ideas developed in Ranajit Guha, "The Prose of Counter-Insurgency," in *Culture/Power/History: A Reader in Contemporary Social Theory,* ed. Nicholas B. Dirks, Geoff Eley, and Sherry B.

Ortner (Princeton, N.J., 1994), 336–71. For a more concrete treatment, see William Roseberry, *Coffee and Capitalism in the Venezuelan Andes* (Austin, Tex., 1983).

Introduction: Peasants, Plantations, and Resistance

1 This is not to exaggerate the turnover. Many creole owners remained on the land and retained full title to it. The Elías family of Ica, whose principal figure was prominent and powerful through mid-century, exemplified this group. See Alfonso Quiroz, "Estructura económica y desarrollos regionales de la clase dominante, 1821–1850," in *Independencia y revolución, 1780–1840,* ed. Alberto Flores Galindo, 2 vols. (Lima, 1987), 2:201–67, and on highland land problems at the turn of the nineteenth century, see Karen Spalding, "Class Structure in the Southern Peruvian Highlands," in *Land and Power in Latin America,* ed. Orlove and Custred (New York, 1980), 79–98.

2 See Peter Blanchard, *Slavery and Abolition in Early Republican Peru* (Wilmington, Del., 1992). From the perspectives of the slaves, see the recent seminal work of Christine Hünefeldt, *Paying the Price of Freedom: Family and Labor among Lima's Slaves, 1800–1854* (Berkeley, Calif., 1994), and Carlos Aguirre, *Agentes de su propia libertad: los esclavos de Lima y la desintegración de la esclavitud, 1821–1854* (Lima, 1993). A recent general study of the movement of plantations through cultures is Phillip D. Curtin, *The Rise and Fall of the Plantation Complex: Essays in Atlantic History* (Cambridge, 1990). Latin American plantation studies are viewed in a comparative framework in Enrique Florescano, ed., *Haciendas, latifundios y plantaciones en América Latina* (Mexico City, 1975), and are analyzed as the context of several forms of rural society in Martínez-Alier, *Haciendas.* In the present discussion, examples are drawn from Kenneth Duncan and Ian Rutledge with Colin Harding, *Land and Labour in Latin America* (Cambridge, 1976).

3 Manuel Burga, in *De la encomienda a la hacienda capitalista* (Lima, 1976), and Eduardo Arroyo, in *La hacienda costeña en el Perú: Mala-Cañete, 1532–1968* (Lima, 1981), provided illustrations of the expansion process that overwhelmed villages throughout the coastal region in the colonial and republican periods. Peter Klaren, in *Modernization, Dislocation and Aprismo: Origins of the Peruvian Aprista Party, 1870–1932* (Austin, 1973), found this process to be fundamental in explaining the rise of a political constituency for the Alianza Popular Revolucionaria Americana (APRA; American Popular Revolutionary Alliance) movement among the sugar plantation workers of the north coast. See also José Matos Mar, comp., *Hacienda, comunidad y campesinado en el Perú,* 2d ed. (Lima, 1976).

4 Jean Piel, "The Place of the Peasantry in the National Life of Peru in the

Nineteenth Century," *Past and Present* 46 (1970): 108–33; Pablo Macera, "Las plantaciónes azucareras andinas (1821–1875)," in *Trabajos de historia* 4 (1977): 9–308. Early republican cases of plantation survival in the midst of social change are in Burga, *De la encomienda.*

5 Useful global comparative studies of world peasantries are Joel S. Migdal, *Peasants, Politics and Revolutions: Pressures Toward Political and Social Change in the Third World* (Princeton, N.J., 1974), and Jeffrey M. Paige, *Agrarian Revolution: Social Movements and Export Agriculture in the Underdeveloped World* (New York, 1980). A highly influential, landmark comparative study of peasants is Barrington Moore, Jr., *Social Origins of Dictatorship and Democracy; Lord and Peasant in the Making of the Modern World.* Boston, 1966. Peasant conditions on the eve of major plantation expansion in late nineteenth and early twentieth-century Mexico are examined in John M. Hart, *Revolutionary Mexico* (Berkeley, Calif., 1989), chap. 7. Detailed plantation comparisons are made in Kenneth Duncan and Ian Rutledge, with Colin Harding, eds., *Land and Labour in Latin America* (Cambridge, 1977) and Brij V. Lal, Doug Munro, and Edward D. Beechert, eds., *Plantation Workers: Resistance and Accommodation* (Honolulu, 1993).

6 See Eric Van Young, *Hacienda and Market in Eighteenth-Century Mexico: The Rural Economy of the Guadalajara Region, 1675–1820* (Berkeley, Calif., 1981), on population decline and demand for rural labor. Another angle on the problem is given in Jeremy Baskes, "Coerced or Voluntary? The *Repartimiento* and Market Participation of Peasants in Late Colonial Oaxaca," *Journal of Latin American Studies* 28.1 (1996): 1–28. See also studies of peasants and low population growth in Argentina and Mexico, especially Nicolás Iñigo Carera, "Génesis de un semiproletariado rural: la incorporación de los indígenas a la producción algodonera chaqueña," *Cuadernos de CISCO,* Universidad de Buenos Aires, Serie Estudios 4 (Buenos Aires, 1975), and Harry Cross, "Living Standards in Rural Nineteenth-Century Mexico: Zacatecas, 1820–1880," *Journal of Latin American Studies* 10 (1978): 1–19.

7 Witold Kula, *An Economic Theory of the Feudal System: Towards a Model of the Polish Economy,* trans. Lawrence Gardner (London, 1976).

8 The classic, highly influential texts in this vein are Andre Gunder Frank, *Capitalism and Underdevelopment in Latin America: Historical Studies of Chile and Brazil* (New York, 1967), and, with greater attention to social repression, Stanley J. and Barbara H. Stein, *The Colonial Heritage of Latin America: Essays on Economic Dependence in Perspective* (New York, 1970).

9 One widely reprinted source of this analysis as it is applied to Peru is Julio Cotler, "The Mechanics of Internal Domination and Social Change in Peru," in *Peruvian Nationalism: A Corporatist Revolution,* ed. David Chaplin (New Brunswick, N.J., 1976), 35–71.

10 A widely accepted, inclusive definition of "peasants" by a historian is in

John H. Coatsworth, "Patterns of Rural Rebellion in Latin America: Mexico in Comparative Perspective," in *Riot, Rebellion, and Revolution,* ed. Friedreich Katz (Princeton, N.J., 1988), 21–64; see also Andrew Pearse, *The Latin American Peasant* (London, 1975), and John Tutino, *From Insurrection to Revolution in Mexico: Social Bases of Agrarian Violence, 1750–1940* (Princeton, N.J., 1986).

11 As one can imagine, a vast literature seeks to place boundaries around the idea of a peasantry, and with regard to Latin America some was mentioned in the preface (see note 4). Other important influences on my thinking have been Teodor Shanin, "Defining Peasants: Conceptualizations and De-conceptualizations Old and New in a Marxist Debate," *Peasant Studies* 8.4 (Fall, 1979): 38–60; his views are joined in debate with Hamza Alavi, "Peasant Classes and Primordial Loyalties," *Journal of Peasant Studies* 1.1 (1973): 23–62, and with the more gender-oriented Claude Meillassoux, "The Social Organization of the Peasantry: The Economic Basis of Kinship," *Journal of Peasant Studies* 1.1 (1973): 81–90. See also the more comparative work edited by Teodor Shanin, *Peasants and Peasant Societies: Selected Readings* (Harmondsworth, England, 1971), and by Jay O'Brien and William Roseberry, *Golden Ages, Dark Ages: Imagining the Past in Anthropology and History* (Berkeley, Calif., 1991). More specifically for Latin America, see Eric Wolf, "Types of Latin American Peasantry: A Preliminary Discussion," *American Anthropologist* 57.3 (1955): 452–71, and Pearse, *The Latin American Peasant.* For comparison with the Caribbean, see Sidney W. Mintz, *From Plantations to Peasantries in the Caribbean,* (Washington, D.C., 1984).

12 The most widely known works that introduce ideas about the social dynamics of peasant society are E. P. Thompson's *The Making of the English Working Class* (New York, 1966); "The Moral Economy of the English Crowd in the Eighteenth Century," *Past and Present* 50 (1971): 76–136; "Patrician Society, Plebeian Culture," *Journal of Social History* 8.1 (1974): 382–405; and "Class Struggle without Class?," *Social History* 3.2 (1978): 133–65. See also the critique of Thompson, who is noted to have overlooked important distinctions among different social sectors of the peasantry, in *The New Cultural History,* ed. Lynne Hunt (Berkeley, 1989), 53–61. George Rudé's study of the French Revolution arguably held less attraction for Latin Americanists than did his *Ideology and Popular Protest,* new ed. (Chapel Hill, 1995), chap. 3, which refers directly to Latin America, exploring the relevance of "inherent" and "derived" ideas for understanding the political consciousness of Andean peasants.

13 Among the more influential studies were Pablo Macera, "Las plantaciones azucareras andinas (1821–1875)," cited in note 4 above; Shane J. Hunt, "La economía de las haciendas y plantaciones de América Latina,"

Historia y Cultura 9 (1975): 7–66; and Solomon Miller, "Hacienda to Plantation in Northern Peru: The Process of Proletarianization of a Tenant Farmer Society," in *Contemporary Change in Traditional Societies of Mexico and Peru,* ed. Charles J. Erasmus, S. Miller, and Louis C. Faron (Urbana, Ill., 1967; reprint 1978), 133–226. Other important sources became known through Douglas E. Horton, *Haciendas and Cooperatives: A Preliminary Study of Latifundist Agriculture and Agrarian Reform in Northern Peru,* University of Wisconsin, Land Tenure Research Paper No. 53 (Madison, 1974), and Klaren, *Modernization, Dislocation and Aprismo.* For the view over the long-term, see Florescano, *Haciendas.*

14 Magnus Mörner, "The Spanish American Hacienda: A Survey of Recent Research and Debate," *Hispanic American Historical Review* 53.2 (1973): 183–216.

15 Pablo Macera, "Feudalismo colonial americano: el caso de las haciendas peruanas, in *Trabajos de historia* 3: 139–227; Eric Hobsbawm, "A Case of Neo-feudalism: La Convención, Peru," *Journal of Latin American Studies* 1 (1969): 31–50.

16 A valuable essay, relying on the Mexican case, insightfully questions past understandings of debt peonage and rural wages in Latin America and beyond: Alan Knight, "Mexican Peonage: What Was It and Why Was It?" *Journal of Latin American Studies* 18.1 (1986): 41–71.

17 See the varieties of labor illustrated in essays by I. Rutledge, P. Klaren, J. Martínez-Alier, and M. Deas, in Duncan and Rutledge, *Land and Labour,* 205–98. Friedrich Katz, "Labor Conditions on Haciendas in Porfirian Mexico: Some Trends and Tendencies," *Hispanic American Historical Review* 44.1 (1974): 14–37, acknowledges differences by region and social sector in Porfirian Mexico.

18 Charles Gibson, *The Aztecs Under Spanish Rule: A History of the Indians of the Valley of Mexico, 1519–1810* (Stanford, Calif., 1964), 245–66, makes a probing assessment, suggesting that the tie between colonial wages and debt was not a strong one; see also Edith Couturier, "The Hacienda of Hueyapan: The History of a Mexican Social and Economic Institution, 1550–1940" (Ph.D. dissertation, Columbia University, New York, 1965), 265–66.

19 Arnold Bauer, "Chilean Rural Labor in the Nineteenth Century," *American Historical Review,* 76.4 (1971): 1059–83; Mario Góngora, *Origen de los inquilinos de Chile central* 2d ed. (Santiago, 1974); Jan Bazant, "Peones, arrendatarios y aparceros en Mexico: 1851–1853," *Historia Mexicana* 23.2 (1973): 330–57. Van Young, *Hacienda and Market,* 243–61, and Richard Salvucci, *Textiles and Capitalism in Mexico* (Princeton, N.J., 1987), 112–20, demonstrate convincingly how difficult it is to pin down the meaning of peonage.

20 Duncan and Rutledge, *Land and Labour,* 229–68. Essays by Martínez Alier and Mörner in the same volume, 145–55, 455–82, bespeak a lack of uniformity in the process. Also see Carlos Samaniego, "Peasant Movements at the Turn of the Century and the Rise of the Independent Farmer," in *Peasant Cooperation and Capitalist Expansion in Central Peru,* ed. Norman Lang and Bryan Roberts (Austin, Tex., 1978), 45–71. Sidney Mintz noted some of the local and global signposts of the transition away from communalism in "Epilogue: The Divided Aftermaths of Freedom," in *Between Slavery and Free Labor: The Spanish-Speaking Caribbean in the Nineteenth Century,* ed. Moreno Fraginals, Frank Moya Pons, and Stanley L. Engerman (Baltimore, 1985), 270–78.

21 William Roseberry, "Rent, Differentiation, and the Development of Capitalism among the Peasants," *American Anthropologist* 78.1 (March 1976): 45–58. At the end Roseberry referred briefly to numerous studies by Sidney Mintz illustrating this process in the Caribbean, to the work of Scott Cook and Martin Diskin on Oaxaca, and to research he would publish later on coffee farming in Venezuela, *Coffee and Capitalism in the Venezuelan Andes* (Austin, Tex., 1983).

22 Florencia E. Mallon, *The Defense of Community in Peru's Central Highlands,* (Princeton, N.J., 1983), 192–213; Gavin Smith, *Livelihood and Resistance: Peasants and the Politics of Land in Peru* (Berkeley, Calif., 1989), 77–111. Equally notable are Norman Long and Bryan R. Roberts, eds., *Peasant Cooperation and Capitalist Expansion in Central Peru* (Austin, 1978) and Long and Roberts, eds., *Miners, Peasants and Entrepreneurs: Regional Development in the Central Highlands of Peru* (Cambridge, England, 1984), studies done in the same period and likewise set in the central highlands. Long and Roberts and their coinvestigators similarly placed emphasis on social differentiation across communities. In the latter work, see especially the essays by Laite, 107–39, and Gavin Alderson-Smith, 217–34. Laite and Alderson-Smith observed patterns that crystallized in the 1960s and 1970s. Contrast intervillage struggles for advantage during the War of the Pacific noted by Nelson Manrique, *Campesinado y nación: las guerrillas indígenas en la guerra con Chile* (Lima, 1981), chaps. 6–7.

23 A number of Hunt's pathbreaking analyses, superseding Levin, have appeared in their most accessible forms as "La economía de las haciendas y plantaciones de América Latina, *Historia y Cultura* 9 (1975): 7–66, and "Guano y crecimiento en el Perú del siglo XIX," *HISLA* 4 (1974): 35–92.

24 Thorp and Bertram, *Growth,* chaps. 3, 8–10.

25 Alberto Flores Galindo, *Arequipa y el sur andino (siglos XVIII–XX)* (Lima, 1977); Paul Gootenberg *Tejidos y harinas, corazones y mentes: el imperialismo norteamericano del libre comercio en el Perú 1825–1840* (Lima, 1989); Nelson Manrique, *Campesinado;* C. Alexander G. de Secada,

"Arms, Guano, and Shipping: The W. R. Grace Interests in Peru, 1865–1885, *Business History Review* 59 (1985): 597–621; Rory Miller, "The Making of the Grace Contract: British Bondholders and the Peruvian Government, 1885–1890," *Journal of Latin American Studies* 8 (1976): 73–100. Alfonso W. Quiroz, *La deuda defraudada* (Lima, 1987), shows how Peruvian merchants and lenders allied with foreign financial houses retained control of the basic financial structure of the state after 1850.

26 Dennis Gilbert, *La oligarquía peruana: historia de tres familias,* trans. Mariana Mould de Pease (Lima, 1982); Michael J. Gonzales, *Plantation Agriculture and Social Control in Northern Peru, 1875–1933* (Austin, Tex., 1985); Burga, *De la encomienda.*

27 José Matos Mar, *La oligarquía en el Perú.* Still the best intimate study of three sample families from the group, including the Aspíllagas, is Gilbert, *La oligarquía peruana.*

28 See, especially, chap. 2 of Klaren, *Modernization, Dislocation, and Aprismo;* José Carlos Mariátegui, *Seven Interpretive Essays on Peruvian Reality,* trans. Marjory Urquidi (Austin, Tex., 1971); and Cotler, "The Mechanics of Domination," 35–71.

29 The term *sur chico* was first used by historian Pablo Macera to suggest the regional unity of the coastal portions of the southeastern departments of Ica, Arequipa, Moquegua, and Tacna in Peru, a region of desert valleys where vineyards, foodstuffs, sugar, and cotton were predominant through much of Peru's colonial and national history.

Chapter 1 Planters, Managers, and Consent

Translations throughout this book are mine.

1 Aspíllaga's reputation and influence rested on his successful part-ownership and management of a sugar plantation, Hacienda Cayaltí, in the north coast Saña valley near the port town of Chiclayo. That side of the Aspíllaga clan's agricultural activities is well examined in the works of Gonzales, *Plantation Agriculture and Social Control;* Dennis Gilbert, *La oligarquía peruana;* and Bill Albert, *An Essay on the Peruvian Sugar Industry, 1880–1920, and the Letters of Ronald Gordon, Administrator of the British Sugar Company in Cañete, 1914–1920* (Norwich, England, 1975).

2 The Aspíllagas were among a few dozen families in Peru who by the end of the nineteenth century had reached an important juncture in their rise to political and social power. The nature, extent, and use of their power continues to be the subject of intense study and debate. To begin, see Matos Mar, *La oligarquía en el Perú;* Manuel Burga and Alberto Flores Galindo, *Apogeo y crisis de la república aristocrática* 4th ed. (Lima, 1987); and François Bourricaud, *La oligarquía en el Perú* 2d ed. (Lima, 1971). Julio Cotler, *Clases, estado y nación en el Perú* (Lima, 1978), provides an incisive sociological analysis of this social sector's power throughout Peru's twentieth century.

3 Debts owed to fellow planters were amortized through low annual payments. Then current market rates of 12 to 18 percent governed interest on the remainder of the elder Ramón's legacy. AFA, Hacienda Palto, *Letterbooks*, Palto to Lima, November 20, 1876.

4 Sidney Mintz and E. R. Wolf made the classic distinction between haciendas and plantations in "Haciendas and Plantations in Middle America and the Antilles," *Social and Economic Studies* 6.3 (1957): 380–412; a hacienda trajectory is outlined in Matos Mar, *Hacienda, comunidad y campesino,* 15–178. Detailed studies followed in Duncan and Rutledge, *Land and Labour.* Failing to see any meaningful difference between the usage of the terms hacienda, plantation, and fundo, I have used these words interchangeably in this work. Pablo Macera's essay in *Trabajos de historia,* 4 vols. (Lima, 1977), 4: 9–307, raised provocative questions on this subject that heavily influenced subsequent works on Peruvian economic history, for example, Burga, *De la encomienda.*

5 On the difference between overseers and stewards, see William K. Scarborough's classic study, *The Overseer: Plantation Management in the Old South,* (Athens, Ga.; reprint 1984), 178–94. On Scarborough's scale of prestige, the plantation administrator in the Pisco valley stood somewhere between the overseer and the steward in the southern antebellum United States. Scarborough did not try to rank power, but on that scale the Peruvian administrator undoubtedly would score higher than his North American counterpart.

6 See AFA, Hacienda Palto, *Letterbooks, 1876–77,* "Orden interior de la hacienda de Palto 12 marzo 1877." Internal references in the correspondence indicate that after the formal end of Asian indenture, and for decades thereafter, the owners apparently issued instructions for good management, along with an inventory of the plantation's goods, to each new administrator. Few of them are known to have survived.

7 This practice was characteristic of inexperienced owners of industry, according to E. P. Thompson, "Time, Work Discipline and Industrialism," *Past and Present* 38 (1967): 56–97. Peruvian plantation owners apparently overlooked differences in labor organization between sugar and cotton when making assessments in this early period. Detailed discussion in a Bolivian setting is in Erick D. Langer, "Labor Strikes and Reciprocity on Chuquisaca haciendas," *Hispanic American Historical Review* 65.2 (1985): 255–78.

8 AFA, Hacienda Palto, *Letterbooks, 1876–77,* "Orden interior de la hacienda de Palto 12 marzo 1877," fol. 3v. Gonzales, "Chinese Plantation Workers and Social Conflict in Peru in the Late Nineteenth Century," *Journal of Latin American Studies* 21 (1989): 385–424.

9 Examples of such instances are in AFA, Hacienda Palto, *Letterbooks,* Palto to Lima, February 8, 1898; cf. *informe* (report), June 12, 1918.

10 AFA, Hacienda Palto, *Letterbooks,* Palto to Lima, July 27, 1886.

11 José Deustua, *La Minería peruana y la iniciación de la república, 1820–1840* (Lima, 1986), 61–66.

12 Ernesto Yepes del Castillo, *Perú, 1820–1920: un siglo de desarrollo capitalista* (Lima, 1972). W. S. Bell, *An Essay on the Peruvian Cotton Industry, 1825–1920,* University of Liverpool, Centre for Latin American Studies, Working Paper No. 6 (Liverpool, England, 1985), summarizes available cotton production and export figures for the nineteenth century. Juan Copello and Luis Petriconi offered a plan for commercial protectionism and "middle-class industrialism" to compensate for the lost trade that would follow. See Paul Gootenberg, *Imagining Development: Economic Ideas in Peru's "Fictitious Prosperity" of Guano, 1840–1880* (Berkeley, Calif., 1993), 164–81.

13 Aurelio García y García, *Derrotero de la costa del Perú* 2d ed. (Lima, 1870), 82–87.

14 Insightful contemporary reports of the invasion of Peru are in a multi-volume publication of the dispatches and journalistic accounts from Chile by Pascual Ahumada Moreno, *Guerra del Pacífico: recopilación completa de todos los documentos oficiales, correspondencias y demás publicaciones referentes a la guerra que ha dado a luz la prensa de Chile, Perú y Bolivia.* 8 vols. in 4 books (Valparaíso, 1884). Detailed recent case studies of Peruvian society during the war are in Percy Cayo Córdoba et al., *En torno a la Guerra del Pacífico* (Lima, 1983), and Wilson Reátegui Chávez et al., *La Guerra del Pacífico,* 2 vols. (Lima, 1979, 1984).

15 Ahumada Moreno, *Guerra del Pacífico,* 4: 142, 219; Mamerto Castillo Negrón, *Monografía de Pisco* (Lima, 1947), 167–70, 204–5. See also many items in AFA, Hacienda Palto, *Letterbooks,* outstanding among them Palto to Lima, April 21, 1879; February 8, March 21, 28, June 13, 1881; February 11, 1882.

16 Ahumada Moreno, *Guerra del Pacífico* 4: 237–41; Rolando Pachas Castilla, "Impacto de la Guerra del Pacífico en las haciendas de Ica, Chincha, Pisco y Cañete," in *La Guerra del Pacífico,* ed. Reátegui Chávez, 2 vols. (Lima, 1979, 1984) 1: 197–220; Pachas Castilla, "Impacto de la Guerra del Pacífico en el Sur Medio: 1860–1900," in *La Guerra del Pacífico,* ed. Reátegui Chávez, 2: 140–95.

17 AFA, Hacienda Palto, *Letterbooks,* Palto to Lima, January 19, 1881.

18 AFA, Hacienda Palto, *Letterbooks,* Palto to Lima, undated letter of late 1880.

19 Pedro Emilio Dancuart, *Anales de la hacienda pública del Perú: leyes, decretos, reglamentos y resoluciones, aranceles, presupuestos, cuentas y contratos que constituyen la legislación e historia fiscal de la República,* 24 vols. (Lima, 1902–26), 15: 55–56.

20 AFA, Hacienda Palto, *Letterbooks, 1882–83,* Palto to Lima, November 19, 1882.

21 AFA, Hacienda Palto, *Letterbooks,* Palto to Lima, September 5, 1882. Apparently, the south Italian region of Calabria was widely reputed to be ruled by banditry and lawlessness.

22 Recent efforts to explain late nineteenth-century peasant resistance have used a "banditry" framework, provoking considerable debate inasmuch as "banditry" is not fully defined by or confined to the peasantry. The debate is in Gilbert M. Joseph, "On the Trail of Latin American Bandits: A Reexamination of Peasant Resistance," *Latin American Research Review* 25.3 (1990): 7–53, and in the responses by Richard W. Slatta, "Bandits and Rural Social History: A Comment on Joseph," *Latin American Research Review* 26.1 (1991), and others, with a reply by Joseph in the "Commentary and Debate" section of the 26.1 (1991) issue, 145–74. For Peru, see Carlos Aguirre and Charles Walker, eds., *Bandoleros, abigeos y montoneros: criminalidad y violencia en el Perú, siglos xviii–xx* (Lima, 1990), where the racial overtones of the identification of bandits by the authorities are highlighted; Benjamin S. Orlove, "The Position of Rustlers in Regional Society: Social Banditry in the Andes," in *Land and Power,* ed. Orlove and Custred (New York, 1980), 179–94; and Lewis Taylor, *Bandits and Politics in Peru: Landlord and Peasant Violence in Hualgayoc, 1900–1930* (Cambridge, 1983).

23 AFA, Hacienda Palto, *Letterbooks,* Palto to Lima, September 21, October 26, 1884; Chincha to Lima (copy), October 25, 1884.

24 AFA, Hacienda Palto, *Letterbooks,* Palto to Lima, November 9, 1884.

25 AFA, Hacienda Palto, *Letterbooks,* Palto to Lima, January 25, February 1, 15, 22, April 26, 1885.

26 On Cáceres's wartime and postwar leadership, see Manrique, *Campesinado,* and Mallon, *Defense of Community,* 80–132.

27 Mark Thurner, " 'Republicanos' and 'la Comunidad de Peruanos': Unimagined Political Communities in Postcolonial Andean Peru," *Journal of Latin American Studies* 27.2 (1995): 291–318.

28 The civil war of 1894 to 1895 has not yet been adequately studied. Jorge Basadre, *Historia de la república del Perú, 1822–1933,* 16 vols., 6th ed. (Lima, 1968), 10: 93–143, gives the general outlines of the rebellion; Cotler, *Clases,* 124–32, frames its social impact within the fallout over the Grace Contract (W. R. Grace & Co.'s assumption of Peru's war debt in exchange for huge mineral, petroleum, and guano mining concessions). Also see the most recent summary and evaluation by Peter Klaren, "The Origins of Modern Peru," in *The Cambridge History of Latin America: ca. 1870–1930,* ed. Leslie Bethel, (Cambridge, England, 1989), 5: 587–640. A detailed study of the Grace Contract is Rory Miller's "The Grace Contract, the Peruvian Corporation, and Peruvian History," *Ibero-Amerikanische Archiv* 9, 3/4 (1983): 319–48.

29 Flores Galindo, *Arequipa;* José Deustua and José Luis Rénique, *Intelectuales, indigenismo y descentralismo en el Perú, 1897–1931* (Cusco, 1984).

30 Richard M. Morse, "Joaquín Capelo: A Lima Archetype," *Journal of Contemporary History* 4.3 (1969): 95–110; see also Joaquín Capelo, "Sociología de Lima," in *Lima en 1900: estudio crítico y antología,* ed Richard M. Morse (Lima, 1973), and Jorge Basadre, *Elecciones y centralismo en el Perú (apuntes para un esquema histórico)* (Lima, 1980), 17.

31 AFA, Hacienda Palto, *Letterbooks, 1894–95;* Cotler, *Clases,* 124–32; Flores Galindo, *Arequipa,* 12–93; Deustua and Rénique, *Intelectuales.* On Vicente del Solar's relationship to Piérola, see Basadre, *Historia,* 10: 102–28, 145–98.

32 Sample nineteenth-century water regulations for the south coast appear in *El Peruano,* October 7, 1863; May 25, May 30, 1870. See also Francisco García Calderón, "Reglamento de aguas de Cerdán extractado por el Dr. Francisco García Calderón y mandado en esa forma," in *Leyes, decretos, resoluciones, reglamentos y circulares vigentes en el ramo de justicia,* comp. Enrique Patron (Lima, 1901). For comparison, a detailed analysis of the politics of water in another locale occurs in the exemplary study by Michael C. Meyer, *Water in the Hispanic Southwest: A Social and Legal History, 1500–1850* (Tucson, Ariz., 1984).

33 The hostilities at the aqueduct from the Aspíllaga side are recounted excitedly in AFA, Hacienda Palto, *Letterbooks,* Palto to Lima, January 8, 13, 15, February 15, 20, 28, March 7, 14, 22, 27, April 9, October 8, 1894. Details of the Aspíllaga purchase of San José are unknown. A smaller fundo, its fields initially served as pastures to feed Palto cattle, which the forty-nine-hectare arrangement called for. Later on, the San José fields would contribute to the total cotton produced by the Aspíllaga operations in the Pisco valley.

34 AFA, Hacienda Palto, *Letterbooks,* Palto to Lima, October 23, 1894.

35 AFA, Hacienda Palto, *Letterbooks,* Palto to Lima, November 13, December 12, 24, 1894.

36 AFA, Hacienda Palto, *Letterbooks,* January 2, 24, February 8, 28, March 7, 8, 12, 30, 1895.

37 This theme, the major point of Mark Thurner, " 'Republicanos' and 'la Comunidad de Peruanos,' " cited in note 27, receives compelling treatment in Mark Thurner, *From Two Republics* (1996).

38 A clear treatment of the politics of fiscal problems in the early stages of oligarchic party dominance is Alfonzo W. Quiroz, "Financial Development in Peru under Agrarian Export Influence, 1884–1950," *The Americas* 47.4 (1990): 447–76; see also Basadre, *Historia* 11: 119–220.

39   AFA, Hacienda Palto, *Letterbooks,* Palto to Lima, February 17, December 14, 1896.

Chapter 2 Indenture, Wages, and Dominance

1   Shane J. Hunt, "Price and Quantum Estimates of Peruvian Exports, 1830–1962," Research Program in Economic Development, Discussion Paper No. 33 (Princeton, N.J., 1973), p. 39, table 14; Bell, *An Essay on the Peruvian Cotton Industry,* 38, appendix, tables 17, 18, 19.
2   Cf. Klaren, *Modernization, Dislocation and Aprismo,* 3–64.
3   The department of Lima encompassed the area that in 1856 became Ica Department, including the valleys of the Chincha, Pisco, and Ica rivers. On manumission, see Christine Hünefeldt, "Relaciones campo-ciudad de los esclavos de Lima, 1790–1854" (paper presented at the American Historical Association annual conference, New York, 1990); Carlos Aguirre, "Cimarronaje," in *Bandoleros, abigeos y montoneras: criminalidad y violencia en el Perú, siglos xviii–xx,* ed. Carlos Aguirre and Charles Walker (Lima, 1990), 137–82; and Aguirre, *Agentes.*
4   Charles Walker, "Montoneras," and Aguirre, "Cimarronaje," both in Aguirre and Walker, 105–36, 162–73. Indispensable studies of nineteenth-century black slavery and abolition are Hünefeldt, *Paying the Price;* Aguirre, *Agentes;* and Blanchard, *Slavery and Abolition.* See also Héctor Centurión Vallejo, *Esclavitud y manumisión en Trujillo* (Trujillo, Peru, 1954); Paz Soldán, "Memoria sobre la esclavitura en el Perú," in Ricardo Aranda, *Constitución del Perú de 1860 con sus reformas hasta 1893; leyes orgánicas, decretos, reglamentos y resoluciones referentes a ellas, coleccionadas y anotadas por Ricardo Aranda* (Lima, 1893); Macera, "Periodización e Interpretacion," in *Latin America: A Guide to Economic History 1830–1930* (Berkeley, Calif., 1977), 547–62; and Dancuart, *Anales,* 3: 19–21, 6: 65–66.
5   Indentured Chinese workers were used to mine guano on the offshore islands and to build the central railway into the Andean highlands. On Chinese indenture in the guano islands, see Humberto Rodríguez Pastor, "El inmigrante chino en el mercado laboral peruano, 1850–1930" *HISLA* 14 (1989): 97–99. Most sources compare Asian indenture in Peru with slavery, and label it "semislavery." The troublesome contradiction between treatment and wages that arose after the end of indenture receives attention in Arnold Meagher, "The Introduction of Chinese Laborers to Latin America: The 'Coolie Trade,' 1847–1874" (Ph.D. dissertation, University of California, Davis, 1974), 254–55. The most detailed study of this labor system is Michael J. Gonzales, "Chinese Plantation Workers," *Journal of Latin American Studies* 12 (1989): 385–424. See also Humberto Rodríguez Pastor, *Hijos*

del celeste imperio en el Perú (1850–1900): migración, agricultura, mentalidad y explotación (Lima, 1989), and Gonzales, *Plantation Agriculture.*

6 Rodríguez Pastor, *Hijos,* 28–29. Prices paid for indentured Asian labor are given in AFA, Hacienda Cayaltí, *Letterbooks,* Accounts, 1859, statements of October 27, 1859, October 27, 1867; Gonzales, *Plantation Agriculture,* 150; and Rodríguez Pastor, *Trabajadores chinos de la Hacienda Palto* (manuscript), Lima, n.d., 6.

7 Bell, *An Essay on the Peruvian Cotton Industry,* 32–33, citing Yepes del Castillo, *Peru 1820–1920,* 110–19. For Palto numbers, see Rodríguez Pastor, *Trabajadores chinos,* 7.

8 Studies of forced Chinese migration to nineteenth-century Peru begin with Watt Stewart, *Chinese Bondage in Peru: A History of the Chinese Coolie in Peru, 1849–1874* (Durham, N.C., 1951); Jean Piel, "L'importation de main d'oeuvre chinoise et le developpement agricole au Pérou au XIXe siècle," *Cahiers d'Amériques Latines* 9/10 (1974): 87–103; Marcelo Segall, "Esclavitud y tráfico de culíes en Chile," *Journal of Inter-American Studies* 10.1 (1968): 117–33; and Denise Helly, *Idéologie et ethnicité: les chinois Macao à Cuba* (Montreal, 1979). For the little-noticed traffic in kidnapped Polynesians, see H. E. Maude, *Slavers in Paradise: The Peruvian Slave Trade in Polynesia, 1862–1864* (Stanford, Calif., 1981). Further insights can be gained from studies of African and South Asian indenture in the Caribbean in Monica Schuler, *"Alas, Alas, Kongo": A Social History of Indentured African Immigration into Jamaica, 1841–1865* (Baltimore, 1980), and Keith O. Lawrence, *Indentured Labor in the British Empire, 1834–1920* (London, 1984).

Indispensable on the social implications of Chinese forced migration to the Western Hemisphere are Lucie Cheng and Edna Bonacich, eds., *Labor Immigration under Capitalism: Asian Workers in the United States before World War II* (Berkeley, Calif., 1984); and several studies by Evelyn Hu-Dehart, including "Immigrants to a Developing Society: The Chinese in Northern Mexico, 1875–1932," *Journal of Arizona History* 21.3 (1980): 275–312; "The Chinese of Baja California Norte, 1910–1934," *Proceedings of the Pacific Coast Council on Latin American Studies,* vol. 12 (1985–86), 9–29; "Coolies, Shopkeepers, Pioneers: The Chinese of Mexico and Peru (1849–1930)," *Amerasia* 15.2 (1989): 91–116; and "Chinese Coolie Labor in Cuba and Peru in the Nineteenth Century: Free Labor or Neoslavery?" (manuscript, Boulder, Colo., n.d.), which the author kindly allowed me to read.

9 The records of individual indentured laborers did not survive. Some confusion arises in discussions of indenture and contractees. The distinction being made here recognizes that "indenture" signified forcible capture in Asia, after which a "contract" was made on a man's labor between an agent and buyer. "Contractee," refers to Asians in Peru who, however much pres-

sured, themselves negotiated the new post-1874 contracts as free farmworkers. See, for example, AFA, Hacienda Palto, *Letterbooks,* Palto to Lima,
December 19, 1886.

10 AFA, Hacienda Palto, *Letterbooks,* Palto to Lima, May 9, 1879. Differences were based on the appearance of good health and relative youth.

11 AFA, Hacienda Palto, *Letterbooks,* Antero to Lima, April 23, 1877. The
Aspíllagas claimed the right to resolve old debts through continued labor,
and Antero's plan met that need. For detailed treatment of the idea, see
Rodríguez Pastor, *Hijos,* 40–50.

12 AFA, Hacienda Palto, *Letterbooks,* Palto to Lima, September 25, October 13, 1881.

13 Rodríguez Pastor, "El inmigrante chino," 93–104.

14 Indispensable studies of mine labor recruitment include Mallon, *Defense
of Community,* 186, 193–98, 223–24; Long and Roberts, *Miners, Peasants
and Entrepreneurs,* 51–52, 115–16, 118–19; Elizabeth Dore, *The Peruvian
Mining Industry: Growth, Stagnation, and Crisis* (Boulder, Colo., and London, 1988), 92–95; and Alberto Flores Galindo, *Los mineros de la Cerro de
Pasco 1900–1930* (Lima, 1974), 34–50. See also Heraclio Bonilla, *El minero
en los Andes: una aproximación a su estudio* (Lima, 1974), 40–46. Discussion of the search for new techniques in labor contracting is in Rodríguez
Pastor, *Hijos,* 113–71.

15 AFA, Hacienda Cayaltí, *Letterbooks, Cayaltí Varios,* Lima to Palto,
March 30, 1882.

16 Much useful information on the Afro-Peruvians after abolition is gathered in Denys Cuche, *Poder blanco y resistencia negra en el Perú* (Lima,
1975).

17 Juan de Arona [pseud., Pedro Paz Soldán y Unánue], *La inmigración en el
Perú* (Lima, 1891; reprint 1971), 99–102; Heraclio Bonilla, "The War of the
Pacific and the National and Colonial Problem in Peru," *Past and Present* 81
(1978): 92–118.

18 AFA, Hacienda Palto, *Letterbooks: Lima Varios, junio 1879–octubre
1880,* Palto to Lima, undated letter, 1880.

19 AFA, Hacienda Palto, *Letterbooks: Lima Varios, junio 1879–octubre
1880,* Lima to Pisco, July 30, 1880. The problem arose again at the close of
the war with Chile.

20 AFA, Hacienda Palto, *Letterbooks, 1882–83,* Ismael Aspíllaga, undated
informe.

21 AFA, Hacienda Palto, *Letterbooks, 1884–85,* Ismael to Lima, informe,
May 5, 1884.

22 For further analysis of the plantation tambo, consult Cross, "Living Standards," 1–19.

23 Fuller biographical treatment is in Rodríguez Pastor, *Hijos,* 181–87; see also Gonzales, "Chinese Plantation Workers," 399. On Ayate's prewar job as barracks overseer and later activities, see AFA, Hacienda Palto, *Letterbooks,* Palto to Lima, October 9, 1881; April 20, 1882.

24 AFA, Hacienda Palto, *Letterbooks,* Palto to Lima, August 23, 1881; Hacienda Cayaltí, *Letterbooks: Cayaltí Varios, abril 1880–noviembre 1882,* Lima to Palto, April 20, 1882.

25 AFA, Hacienda Palto, *Letterbooks,* Palto to Lima, September 9, 12, October 9, 1881; March 30, April 20, April 21, May 4, September 4, 1882.

26 Indenture statistics are based on extrapolation backward from postindenture wage records of Hacienda Palto. See, especially, Rodríguez Pastor, *Hijos,* and Gonzales, "Chinese Plantation Workers."

27 On the cash problem in Peru during the War of the Pacific, consult Dancuart, *Anales,* 13: 39–71; in the Pisco valley, consult AFA, Hacienda Palto, *Letterbooks,* Ismael to Lima, informe, March 2, 1883.

28 AFA, Hacienda Palto, *Letterbooks,* Palto to Lima, October 31, 1882.

29 AFA, Hacienda Cayaltí, *Letterbooks: Cayaltí Varios,* Palto to Lima, August 12, 1881.

30 On changes in the "task," see AFA, Hacienda Palto, *Letterbooks,* Palto to Lima, September 25, 1881; March 19, June 13, 26, July 4, 1882.

31 AFA, Hacienda Cayaltí, *Letterbooks: Cayaltí Varios,* Lima to Palto, October 9, 16, 1882.

32 AFA, Hacienda Palto, *Letterbooks,* Palto to Lima, May 9, 1881.

33 AFA, Hacienda Palto, *Letterbooks,* Palto to Lima, February 14, 1883.

34 AFA, Hacienda Palto, *Letterbooks,* Ismael Aspíllaga informe, March 2, 1883.

35 AFA, Hacienda Palto, *Letterbooks,* Palto to Lima, February 15, 1885. For the local impact of monetary policy, see AFA, Hacienda Palto, *Letterbooks,* Palto to Lima, January 25, April 12, July 5, 1885.

36 AFA, Hacienda Palto, *Letterbooks,* Palto to Lima, July 12, October 31, 1886.

37 Ibid.

38 AFA, Hacienda Palto, *Letterbooks,* Ismael, undated informe, 1886 [?].

39 Dancuart, *Anales* 15: 10–13, 141–43; AFA, Hacienda Palto, *Letterbooks,* Palto to Lima, May 17, 1885; March 15, July 12, 1886; February 6, 1889.

40 Some credit for increasing yields is owing to improved cotton technology. After the owners had begun to plant a second type of cotton, Sea Island, along with *egipto,* in 1888, Hacienda Palto went to two cotton harvests a year, one in January through March, the other in June through August. Egipto bloomed and remained on the plant through the cold months (May–August) but was subject to sudden frost that yellowed and wilted the tuft. Sea Island cotton, more resistant to blight and frost (though shorter in thread) was a preferred second-season varietal. A new blend (styled "Tangüis") would become available in 1911 after Fermín Tangüis conducted successful genetic experiments at Hacienda Urrutia next door to Palto. Tangüis allowed planters to return to a single season. For a full discussion of the biological properties of cotton, see John M. Munro, *Cotton,* 2d ed. (New York, 1987), 22, 25, 47, 55, 40, 236, 248.

41 AFA, Hacienda Palto, *Letterbooks,* Palto to Lima, August 27, September 17, December 12, 29, 1889.

42 AFA, Hacienda Cayaltí, *Letterbooks,* Lima to Palto, January 5, 1889. On cotton prices, 1885–89, see Bell, *An Essay on the Peruvian Cotton Industry,* 37, appendix, tables 19, 20.

43 AFA, Hacienda Palto, *Letterbooks,* Palto to Lima, April 16, May 5, 1889.

44 Biblioteca Nacional, Lima, "Expediente sobre la averiguación practicada por la comisión china, asesorada por funcionarios del gobierno, respecto a la situación de sus connacionales [*sic*] que prestan sus servicios en las haciendas. Lima, mayo 9 de 1887," fols. 126–38. See also the discussion on overwork and the high death rate among indentured Asians in Macera, "Las plantaciones azucareras andinas," *Trabajos de historia,* 4: 190–92, 206–35.

45 Rodríguez Pastor, *Hijos,* 207–52, provides detailed coverage of Sino-Peruvian activities after indenture. Focused on the relative success of Chinese immigrant urbanization are Stephen I. Thompson, "Assimilation and Non-assimilation of Asian-Americans and Asian Peruvians," *Comparative Studies in Society and History* 21.4 (1979): 572–88, and Bernard Wong, "A Comparative Study of the Assimilation of the Chinese in New York City and Lima, Peru," *Comparative Studies in Society and History* 20.3 (1978): 335–57.

46 Aguirre, *Agentes;* Hünefeldt, *Paying the Price.*

47 Rolando Pachas Castilla, "Impacto de la Guerra del Pacífico en las haciendas de Ica, Chincha, Pisco y Cañete," in Wilson Reátegui, *La Guerra del Pacífico,* (2 vols., ed. Wilson Reátegui, Lima, 1979, 1984), 1:197–219; Gonzales, "Chinese Plantation Workers." On the conflicts between the two groups prior to the war, see AFA, Hacienda Palto, *Letterbooks,* Palto to Lima, July 1–10, 1877, and Hacienda Cayaltí. *Letterbooks: Cartas Varias, Lima — Varios, julio 1877–agosto 1878,* Lima to Palto, July 16, 1877.

48 See Bonilla, "The War."

Chapter 3 Stagnation, Recovery, and Peasant Opportunities

1 AFA, Hacienda Palto, *Letterbooks,* Palto to Lima, May 26, July 23, 1882; Hacienda Cayaltí, *Letterbooks: Cayaltí Varios,* Lima to Palto, May 31, 1882. Silverio Rosas died early in the twentieth century and his son, Polo, followed in his footsteps until the 1920s. The Rosas family persevered on the Aspíllaga plantation for more than two generations.

2 It is important to note that although I speak of the plantations — particularly those that grew cotton — in the plural, the evidence for this study comes primarily from the papers of Hacienda Palto. However, it also was the custom of plantation managers and owners to visit neighboring plantations (and to receive neighbors) periodically. The practice helped these neighbors to reaffirm their ties and to keep abreast of new developments. As we have seen, when issues concerning water sharing and borderland use arose, friendly competition quickly descended into hostile warfare. On the cotton plantations in general, see Pablo Macera, "Algodón y comercio exterior peruano en el siglo XIX," *Trabajos de historia,* 3: 275–96.

3 For examples, see the studies in Duncan and Rutledge, *Land and Labour;* Bill Albert, "*Yanaconaje* and Cotton Production on the Peruvian Coast: Sharecropping in the Cañete Valley during World War I," *Bulletin of Latin American Research* 2.2 (May 1983): 107–16; Hobsbawm, "A Case of Neo-Feudalism;" and Langer, "Labor Strikes." Contrast Bauer, "Rural Workers"; Paul E. Durrenberger, "Chayanov and Marx," *Peasant Studies* 9.2 (1982): 119–29; and Martínez-Alier, *Haciendas.*

4 AFA, Hacienda Cayaltí, *Letterbooks: Cayaltí Varios,* Lima to Palto, January 4, March 3, 1882.

5 Gavin Smith, in *Livelihood and Resistance: Peasants and the Politics of land in Peru* (Berkeley, Calif., 1989), stressed the theoretical differences between peasants and farmers. For the view of an economist who emphasized similarities rather than differences, see José María Caballero, "Sharecropping as an Efficient System: Further Answers to an Old Puzzle," *Sharecropping and Sharecroppers,* ed. T. Byres (London, 1983), 107–19. The conventional view of the tenant contract in the late nineteenth century denies the voluntary qualities of it emphasized here but rarely gives labor scarcity central importance. An enormous bibliography on the theory and practice of debt peonage in Latin America was superbly represented by Friedrich Katz, in "Labor Conditions," 1–47, and by Bauer, in "Rural Workers." Works on nineteenth-century Peru include Peter Blanchard, "The Recruitment of Workers in the Peruvian Sierra at the Turn of the Century: The Enganche System," *Inter-American Economic Affairs* 33 (1979): 63–83; Gonzales, "Chinese Plantation Workers"; and Gonzales, "Capitalist Agriculture and Labor Contracting in Northern Peru, 1880–1905," *Journal of Latin American Studies* 12 (1980): 291–315. For another face of credit in the absence of banks in nineteenth-century Latin America, see Erick D. Langer, "Merchants, Peasants, and Credit in Southern Bolivia, 1830–1930" (paper presented at LASA [Latin American Studies Association] conference, Washington, D.C., September 28–30, 1995).

6 AFA, Hacienda Palto, *Letterbooks, 1882–83,* Ismael to Lima, undated informe.

7 AFA, Hacienda Palto, *Letterbooks,* Ismael to Lima, informe, July 23, 1882; February 21, December 6, 1886.

8 AFA, Hacienda Cayaltí, *Letterbooks,* Lima to Palto, undated, 1884, 728–29. Thanks to Humberto Rodríguez Pastor for calling this document to my attention.

9 AFA, Hacienda Palto, *Letterbooks,* Palto to Lima, April 12, 18, May 10, October 10, November 15, 1886; January 2, 1887. On volatile swings in foodstuff prices, see Paul Gootenberg, "Carneros y *Chuño:* Price Levels in Nineteenth-Century Peru," *Hispanic American Historical Review* 70.1 (1990): 1–56, and Quiroz, *La Deuda.* For scant late nineteenth-century prices, see Hunt, "Price and Quantum Estimates," p. 61, table; various issues of *Revista de Agricultura* (Lima), especially 1877; and *El Comercio* (Lima), various issues, but especially dates of 5–6, 10–11, 13–16, July 1877. On money and taxes, see Basadre, *Historia,* 9: 38–44, 139–40; 10: 209–12, 224–28.

10 AFA, Hacienda Palto, *Letterbooks,* Palto to Lima, December 19, 1886.

11 Detailed discussion of the location and condition of new cotton fields appears in AFA, Hacienda Palto, *Letterbooks, 1885–86,* Palto to Lima, August 2, 9, 23, September 27, November 18, December 13, 1885.

12 AFA, Hacienda Palto, *Letterbooks,* Palto to Lima, May 30, 1886; September 20, 1888; September 30, 1889.

13 Scott, *Weapons,* 304–50.

14 Acting out as a form of peasant resistance is the subject of Michael Taussig, *The Devil and Commodity Fetishism in South America* (Chapel Hill, N.C., 1980), chaps. 4–7. Roland Anrup, *El taita y el toro: en torno a la configuración patriarcal del régimen hacendario cuzqueño* (Stockholm, 1990), examines the meanings of symbolic actions in Andean resistance. For a wide-ranging, insightful examination of peasant goals during uprisings in Peruvian history, see Flores Galindo, *Buscando un inca: identidad y utopía en los Andes* (Lima, 1987).

15 Indispensable for the study of peasant resistance to landowner repression are Bill Albert, "*Yanaconaje* and Cotton Production," 107–16; Arroyo, *La hacienda costeña;* Burga, *De la encomienda;* Klaren, *Modernization, Dislocation, and Aprismo;* Martínez-Alier, *Los huacchilleros del Perú* (Paris, 1973); Mallon, *Defense of Community;* Matos Mar, *Yanaconaje y reforma agraria en el Perú: el caso del valle de Chancay* (Lima, 1976); and Carlos Samaniego, "Peasant Movements at the Turn of the Century and the Rise of the Independent Farmer." In *Peasant Cooperation and Capitalistic Expansion in Central Peru,* ed. Norman Long and Bryan Roberts (Austin, Tex., 1978), 45–71.

16 Women headed tenant households in small numbers on cotton plantations. At Hacienda Palto, perhaps 10 to 15 percent of tenant heads of household were women. Agustina Alvarado, a tenant who married another tenant at Palto in 1902, declared to the priest that she had lived on the plantation for the past forty years. AFA, Hacienda Palto, *Letterbooks, 1901,* "Razón de arrendatarios que hay en la Hacienda Palto la extensión de terrenos y entregas por deudas atrasadas en libras de algodón en rama del 1901 al 1902." See also Archivo del Archediócesis de Pisco, *Parish Register of Marriages, 1902,* 186.

17 Other institutions — compadrazgo for one — helped to determine the place and status of an individual and his or her status within the community. A vast scholarly literature on Andean village social relations was ably represented by Giorgio Alberdi and Enrique Mayer, comps., in *Reciprocidad e intercambio en los Andes peruanos* (Lima, 1974), and Catherine J. Allen, *The Hold Life Has* (Washington, D.C., 1988). Andean economic patterns are elucidated in Matos Mar, ed., *Hacienda;* José María Caballero, *Economía agraria de la sierra peruana antes de la reforma agraria de 1969* (Lima, 1981); "Region and Class" in *Modern Peruvian History,* ed. Rory Miller (Liverpool, 1987); Long and Roberts, *Miners, Peasants and Entrepreneurs;* and B. Orlove and G. Custred, "Agrarian Economies and Social Processes in Comparative Perspective: The Agricultural Production Unit," in *Land and Power,* ed. Orlove and Custred (New York, 1980), 13–30. Studies of south coast communities include E. A. Hammel, *Power in Ica: The Structural History of a Peruvian Community* (Boston, 1969); Louis Faron, "The Formation of Two Indigenous Communities in Coastal Peru," *American Anthropologist* 62.3 (1960): 427–53; and Eduardo Arroyo, *La hacienda costeña en el Perú: Mala-Cañete, 1532–1968* (Lima, 1981). Insightful on the social formation of concepts of justice is Barrington Moore Jr., *Injustice: The Social Bases of Obedience and Revolt* (White Plains, N.Y., 1978).

18 Scott, in *Weapons,* 322–30, makes the point that among subaltern groups, what is perceived as inevitable is not necessarily also perceived as just. It seems to me that tenants make this distinction in order to amplify opportunities to harmonize what is inevitable with what is just. See the critiques of Scott's views in *Journal of Peasant Studies* 13.2 (1986).

19 Bell, *An Essay on the Peruvian Cotton Industry,* 38; Thorp and Bertram, *Latin America in the 1930s: The Role of the Periphery in the World Crisis* (New York, 1984), 54–57.

20 AFA, Hacienda Palto, *Letterbooks,* August 28, September 20, October 8, 29, November 13, 1894.

21 AFA, Hacienda Palto, *Letterbooks,* Palto to Lima, March 7, April 2, 1893.

22 AFA, Hacienda Palto, *Letterbooks,* Palto to Lima, December 10, 1893.

Among scholars who have stressed the role of "incentives," in the fixed rent relationship are Cheung, *A Theory;* C. H. H. Rao, "Uncertainty, Entrepreneurship, and Sharecropping in India," *Journal of Political Economy* 79.4 (1971): 578–95; Martínez-Alier, *Haciendas;* and Joseph D. Reid Jr., "Sharecropping as an Understandable Market Response: The Post-bellum South," *Journal of Economic History* 33.3 (1973): 106–30.

23 AFA, Hacienda Palto, *Letterbooks, 1892–94* (copy), 478–85.

24 AFA, Hacienda Palto, *Letterbooks.* Monthly account statements of 1895 and 1896 show half the yield of 1893, the latter a level of production this plantation did not reach again until 1897. Not until the early twentieth century did mixed tenantry yield a consistently high volume of cotton.

25 AFA, Hacienda Palto, *Letterbooks,* August 8, 23, 1894; January 10, 24, 1895.

26 AFA, Hacienda Palto, *Letterbooks,* Palto to Lima, April 2, April 12, May 2, 1893; May 22, 1894.

27 This episode is recorded in AFA, Hacienda Palto, *Letterbooks,* Palto to Lima, February 28, March 12, March 30, 1895; Lima to Palto, March 2, 1895.

28 AFA, Hacienda Palto, *Letterbooks,* Palto to Lima, August 26, 1895.

29 The manager also factored into this figure receipt of another 600 arrobas of cotton from renting oxen to the tenants.

30 AFA, Hacienda Palto, *Letterbooks,* Palto to Lima, September 9, 24, October 14, November 6, 19, 1895.

31 Bauer, in "Rural Workers," 1979, compared the situation to the contemporary search for short-term loans from Household Finance Corporation. See also Hunt, "La economía de las haciendas y plantaciones de América Latina," *Historia y Cultura* 9 (1975): 7–66.

32 On the credit battle, see AFA, Hacienda Palto, *Letterbooks,* Palto to Lima, August 23, 28, 1894; February 8, March 7, 30, April 6, July 24, 1895.

33 See Bauer, "Rural Workers," and Samaniego, "Peasant Movements," 61–62, on sources of agricultural finance. On credit available to planters during the recovery period, see Gianfranco Bardella, *Setenta y cinco años de vida económica de Perú, 1889–1964* (Lima, 1964). The broader picture is lucidly portrayed in Alfonso W. Quiroz, *Domestic and Foreign Finance in Modern Peru, 1850–1950: Financing Visions of Development* (Pittsburgh, Pa., 1993), 44–61.

34 The *libretas* (labor-time booklets) in which tenants recorded cash payments received unfortunately have not survived. See AFA, Hacienda Palto, *Letterbooks,* November 6, 19, December 4, 17, 1895; July 21, 1896; January 4, February 14, October 28, 1898.

35 AFA, Hacienda Palto, *Letterbooks,* Luis Ferreira to Lima, June 21, 1897. Ferreira soon disappeared from the list of Hacienda Palto tenants. See comments of July 1, September 1, 21, 1897, and the letter of July 2, 1897, quoted from in this chapter's epigraph.

36 AFA, Hacienda Palto, *Letterbooks,* February 8, October 28, 1898.

37 See AFA, Hacienda Palto, *Letterbooks,* November 10, December 3, 1905.

38 On advances, a form of credit, see especially the explanations given in AFA, Hacienda Palto, *Letterbooks,* Palto to Lima, December 4, 1895; April 5, 1896; February 14, October 28, 1898. On the opening of new fields, see Palto to Lima, February 17, 1896.

39 This range excludes the forty-nine-hectare contract made between the owners of Palto and a tenant who rented practically all of Hacienda San José, the plantation abutting the Condor irrigation aqueduct to the northeast.

40 AFA, Hacienda Palto, *Letterbooks,* "Razón de los arrendatarios de la Hacienda Palto, la extensión de terreno que ocupan lo que pagan arrendamientos, yuntas, deudas. del 1º de setiembre al 1903," enclosure in Palto to Lima, September 30, 1902.

41 The structure of peasant community labor organization receives detailed examination in Stephen Gudeman, *The Demise of a Rural Economy: From Subsistence to Capitalism in a Latin American Village* (London, 1978), 9–120.

42 AFA, Hacienda Palto, *Letterbooks,* Palto to Lima, October 29, December 3, 1899; August 18, September 19, 1901.

43 AFA, Hacienda Palto, *Letterbooks,* Palto to Lima, June 22, 1902.

44 On this round of conflict, see AFA, Hacienda Palto, *Letterbooks,* Palto to Lima, May 24, 1902; June 8, June 22, November 11, 1902.

45 AFA, Hacienda Palto, *Letterbooks,* Palto to Lima, September 9, 24, 1895.

46 AFA, Hacienda Palto, *Letterbooks,* November 31, December 14, 1903.

47 AFA, Hacienda Palto, *Letterbooks,* Palto to Lima, July 2, 1904.

48 AFA, Hacienda Palto, *Letterbooks,* Palto to Lima, November 6, December 4, 17, 1895; on the manager's earliest activities in this area, see July 25, August 16, September 18, 1903.

49 AFA, Hacienda Palto, *Letterbooks,* Palto to Lima, January [date unknown], 20, 27, September 9, 1906.

50 AFA, Hacienda Palto, *Letterbooks,* Palto to Lima, July 29, 1905.

51 AFA, Hacienda Palto, *Letterbooks,* Palto to Lima, September 2, 1905.

52 AFA, Hacienda Palto, *Letterbooks,* Palto to Lima, January 9, October 24, November 15, 1908.

53 See Thorp and Bertram, *Growth;* Bill Albert, *South America and the First World War* (Cambridge, 1988); and Bell, *An Essay on the Peruvian Cotton Industry.*

Chapter 4 Plantation Growth and Peasant Choices

1 AFA, Hacienda Palto, *Letterbooks,* Palto to Lima, November 7, 28, 1909; January 1, 1910; October 14, 1911.

2　AFA, Hacienda Palto, *Letterbooks,* Palto to Lima, April 21, June 21 informe, August 31, September 8, 1907.

3　The Peruvian term for a sharecropper, *yanacón,* translates roughly as "sharecropper." Ethnohistorians tell us that *yanacona* was a Quechua title reserved for a class of people of indeterminate status and apparently different ethnic backgrounds who provided specialized services to the household of the Inca. The term quite likely was applied in the colonial period to a specific form of peasantry associated with large estates. Both peasants and managers/owners associate the term with contracted labor that goes beyond wages. The system is called *yanaconaje* (technically "sharecroppage"); the sharecropper is a yanacón (plural *yanaconas*). See Sócrates Villar Córdova, "La institución del yanacona en el incanato," *Nueva coronica* 1 (Lima, 1966): 18–23; Ann M. Wightman, *Indigenous Migration and Social Change: The Forasteros of Cuzco, 1520–1720* (Durham, N.C., 1990); and Matos Mar, *Yanaconaje y reforma agraria.*

4　Underutilization is a well-known convention of rationalist economic theories. However, from a conservationist standpoint it can mean that a peasant foresees no return from further inputs of labor and so land is best left idle. At Hacienda Palto such decisions led tenants to use land as pasturage or to sublet it. See Caballero, "Sharecropping"; Rao, "Uncertainty;" and Reid Jr., "Sharecropping and Agricultural Uncertainty," *Economic Development and Cultural Change* 24.4 (1976): 549–76.

5　AFA, Hacienda Palto, *Letterbooks,* arrendatarios and compañeros to Aspíllaga Hermanos, June 4, 1908. Enclosure: "Norberto Luján, Eusebio Córdova, Florenciano Barbera, Vicente de la Cruz, Francisco Luján, Luis Torres, Juan Huamán, Damaso Martínez, Genaro Flores, Pedro Otoya, Palomino ("Lino") Palmares, Demetrio Esquivel (representing his father, Juan), and Pedro Otoya (surrogate)."

6　Scott, *Domination,* 89–90, 139–40, 184–87, discusses triangulation under the topic of "ingratiation." Thus far studies of this phenomenon fall into two camps: some look at labor negotiations between wage hands and planters, and others view the problem as a ritual. For an example of the former, see Philippe I. Bourgois, *Ethnicity at Work: Divided Labor on a Central American Banana Plantation* (Baltimore, 1989); and for the latter, see Roberto da Matta, *Carnivals, Rogues, and Heroes: An Interpretation of the Brazilian Dilemma,* trans. John Drury (Notre Dame, Ind., 1991).

7　This analysis follows the concept of varieties of resistance as developed in Scott, *Weapons,* 289–303. A stimulating discussion of violations of authority is in Moore Jr., *Injustice,* 20–31, and, of course, the incident also calls to mind a well-known feature of popular rebellions in Latin American history if one only recalls the dynamics of the Tupac Amaru uprising in Peru and the Miguel Hidalgo rebellion in Mexico, to mention only the most obvious.

8 AFA, Hacienda Palto, *Letterbooks,* Palto to Lima, October 4, 1908. Three forms of sharecropping were used in the valley at this time. Which predominated on a plantation was largely a function of security arrangements and the confidence an owner could place in the manager. With regard to sharecropping and the need for more pastures, the manager was referring to the fact that arrendatarios often held large herds of animals. The enlargement of pastures would make sharecropping more attractive to them.

9 The links between family networks and labor have received extensive treatment. Harold K. Schneider, *Economic Man: The Anthropology of Economics* (New York and London, 1974) is a paradigmatic work in this area. See also Durrenberger, "Chayanov," and E. Durrenberger and T. Tanenbaum, "A Reassessment of Chayanov and His Recent Critics," *Peasant Studies* 8.1 (1981): 48–63. For the Andes, see Bolton and Mayer, *Andean Kinship;* G. Smith, *Livelihood;* and Mallon, *Defense.*

10 AFA, Hacienda Palto, *Letterbooks,* Palto to Lima, October 18, 1908, lists the arrendatarios with cash savings and creditors.

11 On Gutiérrez, see AFA, Hacienda Palto, *Letterbooks,* Palto to Lima, August 21, October 4, November 20, 1909; November 13, 1910. However, no other record of Gutiérrez's relationship to Aspíllaga has emerged.

12 AFA, Hacienda Palto, *Letterbooks,* Gutiérrez to Ramón Aspíllaga, August 22 [date uncertain], 25, 1912; on the measurement of irrigation ditches, see Palto to Lima, October 26, 1912.

13 AFA, Hacienda Palto, *Letterbooks,* Palto to Lima, January 28, 1900.

14 On the respect for Esquivel among his neighbors, see AFA, Hacienda Palto, *Letterbooks,* Palto to Lima, August 10, 25, 1907; on their debts, see August 31, September 8, 1907. A more succinct account of this model tenant is in my essay, "Juan Esquivel: Cotton Plantation Tenant," in *The Human Tradition in Latin America: The Twentieth Century,* ed. William H. Beezley and Judith Ewell (Wilmington, Del., 1987), 59–73.

15 AFA, Hacienda Palto, *Letterbooks,* Palto to Lima, July 27, September 22, November 7, 1907.

16 On learning of this incident, a group of arrendatarios volunteered that the cattle had been injured when they stumbled into a nearby stone quarry. When Pedro Otoya refused to lie in support of the false accusations against Esquivel, the manager fired the erstwhile shepherd. On the ox-hacking accusation and the stocks, see AFA, Hacienda Palto, *Letterbooks,* Palto to Lima, April 4, June 15, 20, 1908. Years later upon becoming the new manager, Maximiliano Alcántara, a former arrendatario who had witnessed the conflict, confessed that the ox-hacking charge had been trumped up by his predecessor, who tried to bribe other arrendatarios to support his lie. Alcántara, who finally would eject Esquivel from Palto's fields, gave his version in AFA, Hacienda Palto, *Letterbooks,* Palto to Lima, January 24, 1920.

17 On Esquivel's high rent, see AFA, Hacienda Palto, *Letterbooks,* Palto to Lima, August 21, 1909.

18 Both Esquivel and Nicanor Islas had large herds. In the same letter, the manager pointed out that Islas, who was "under my protection," had an attractive, valuable herd of oxen, cows, calves, a mare, ponies, burros, and other animals, an indication that the manager also coveted Islas's holdings. AFA, Hacienda Palto, *Letterbooks,* Palto to Lima, February 15, 1913, 2.

19 AFA, Hacienda Palto, *Letterbooks,* Palto to Lima, April 3, 1910.

20 AFA, Hacienda Palto, *Letterbooks,* Palto to Lima, July 24, October 15, 1910.

21 AFA, Hacienda Palto, *Letterbooks,* Palto to Lima, August 17, 26, 31; September 22, 1912. The other highly successful tenant was Joaquín Gutiérrez, mentioned earlier, who at the same time held a bit over thirteen fanegadas. On Gutiérrez, see Palto to Lima, October 26, 1912; on both see Hacienda Palto, *Letterbooks, planilla* (payroll; work plan) September 7, 1913.

22 AFA, Hacienda Palto, *Letterbooks,* Palto to Lima, August 4, 1911; July 17, 1913.

23 AFA, Hacienda Palto, *Letterbooks,* Juan Esquivel, Hacienda Palto, to Ramón Aspíllaga, Lima, September 8, 1918.

24 See, especially, AFA, Hacienda Palto, *Letterbooks,* Palto to Lima, September 10, 22, 1912.

25 AFA, Hacienda Palto, *Letterbooks,* Palto to Lima, January 20, 1913.

26 AFA, Hacienda Palto, *Letterbooks,* Palto to Lima, February 1, 1913.

27 AFA, Hacienda Palto, *Letterbooks,* Palto to Lima, February 15, 1913.

28 AFA, Hacienda Palto, *Letterbooks,* informe by E. R. Aspíllaga, October 21, 1914; Albert, *South America.*

29 AFA, Hacienda Palto, *Letterbooks,* Palto to Lima, October 31, November 28, 1914.

30 Albert, *South America.* Peons who earned S/1.20 per day in the harvest of 1914 found that daily wages had dropped precipitously at the end of October to S/.80 a day. For comparison with urban wages in the early war years, see Peter Blanchard, *The Origins of the Peruvian Labor Movement, 1883–1919* (Pittsburgh, Pa., 1982).

31 The visits were made by Edmundo R. Aspíllaga Anderson, son of Ramón Aspíllaga Anderson and grandson of the founder of the family business. Edmundo Aspíllaga was a trained engineer whose education his father respected but whose excessive harshness toward peasants thc father found necessary to curb. Further detail is in Gilbert, *La oligarquía peruana.*

32 The cost of pasturing a dozen oxen for one month was six *libras peruanas.* AFA, Hacienda Palto, *Letterbooks,* Palto to Lima, informe, November 11, 1914.

33 AFA, Hacienda Palto, *Letterbooks,* Palto to Lima, informe, May 9, 1914, 4–5. Compañeros had been able to resist entry by alien cattle if they could show that such action would damage newly planted seedlings. Managers watched carefully to prevent peasants from planting cotton seedlings too soon after a harvest of fodder.

34 AFA, Hacienda Palto, *Letterbooks,* Palto to Lima, informe, March 4, 1915.

35 AFA, Hacienda Palto, *Letterbooks,* Palto to Lima, November 26, December 11, 1910.

36 AFA, Hacienda Palto, *Letterbooks,* Palto to Lima, February 8, 1913.

37 AFA, Hacienda Palto, *Letterbooks,* Palto to Lima, February 15, 1913.

38 AFA, Hacienda Palto, *Letterbooks,* Palto to Lima, informe, September 28, 1915, pp. 15–16.

39 AFA, Hacienda Palto, *Letterbooks,* Palto to Lima, November 8, 1913.

40 AFA, Hacienda Palto, *Letterbooks,* Palto to Lima, October 10, 1914.

41 See Albert, *South America,* on the effect of the end of submarine warfare on Latin American international commerce, and Bell, *Essay on the Peruvian Cotton Industry,* on the rise in Peruvian cotton exports.

42 AFA, Hacienda Palto, *Letterbooks,* Palto to Lima, informe, September 15, 1917. These are the regulations set forth for the last contracts prior to the adoption of yanaconaje.

43 AFA, Hacienda Palto, *Letterbooks,* Palto to Lima, informe, November 11, 1915.

44 Bell, *Peruvian Essay on the Peruvian Cotton Industry,* 59–63; Thorp and Bertram, *Growth,* 54.

45 AFA, Hacienda Palto, *Letterbooks,* "Inspección realizada del 1º al 8 de Julio de 1917 por E. R. Aspíllaga N."; Palto to Lima, August 20, September 1, 1917.

46 AFA, Hacienda Palto, *Letterbooks,* Palto to Lima, July 18 informe; September 1, 8, 1917.

47 AFA, Hacienda Palto, *Letterbooks,* Palto to Lima, January 14, 15, 21, February 5, 1917.

48 AFA, Hacienda Palto, *Letterbooks,* Palto to Lima, September 15, 1917. An informe of November 18, 1917, contains a long essay on the new conditions of yanaconaje at Hacienda Palto and a long discussion on cattle. On the latter, see also May 26, June 3, 1917. On yanaconaje in general in the sur chico, see Albert, "*Yanaconaje* and Cotton Production."

49 AFA, Hacienda Palto, *Letterbooks,* Palto to Lima, April 1, August 20, 1917.

50 AFA, Hacienda Palto, *Letterbooks,* Palto to Lima, September 8, 1917; informe, July 13, 1917, pp. 17–21; informe, November 18, 1917, pp. 7–8; on advances and the new arrendatarios, see Palto to Lima, September 15, 1917.

51 AFA, Hacienda Palto, *Letterbooks,* Palto to Lima, informe, July 13, 1917, pp. 15–16.

52 Vague mention of the strike that occurred at Palto can be found in AFA, Hacienda Palto, *Letterbooks,* Palto to Lima, April 4, May 14, 1917.

53 See Klaren, *Modernization, Dislocation, and Aprismo;* Steve Stein, *Populism in Peru: The Emergence of the Masses and the Politics of Social Control* (Madison, Wis., 1980); Blanchard, *Origins,* 120–35. Although Wilfredo Kapsoli overlooked these early demonstrations in the Pisco valley, he pointed accurately to sources of political awareness among peasants, in *Los movimientos campesinos en el Perú, 1879–1965: ensayos* (Lima, 1977), 23–93, 158–69.

54 The first mention of "peones de afuera" occurs in AFA, Hacienda Palto, *Letterbooks,* Palto to Lima, June 16, 1917.

55 AFA, Hacienda Palto, *Letterbooks.* The first references to Tiburcio Muñoz occurs in AFA, Hacienda Palto, *Letterbooks,* Palto to Lima, 1914 and the last in 1927.

56 After brother Ismael died in mid-December, 1901, the Aspíllaga brothers had combined supervision of the two fundos, San José and Palto, entrusting oversight of San José to a well-known arrendatario, who reported to the Palto administrator. But a problem soon arose. Ismael, who owned the plantation, had willed the property to his wife, Damacita, who asserted her wishes regarding its management, a development that evidently caused the brothers some concern when the Palto manager disputed her rulings. Citing the burden of increased security costs, in 1920 the Aspíllaga brothers placed Hacienda San José under the management of Guillermo González Cerdeña, Damacita's nephew, who was skilled in large-scale agriculture. Thereafter, the San José operation no longer appeared in the comments of the Palto manager. With this action, together with a reduction of options available to yanaconas, the owners hoped to reduce tensions on both plantations. See AFA, Hacienda Palto, *Letterbooks,* Palto to Lima, December 20, 1901; January 24, 1920.

57 Figures compiled from charts in AFA, Hacienda Palto, *Letterbooks,* Palto to Lima, February 1, 1898; September 12, 1909; and a chart enclosed with an informe, Palto to Lima, September 8, 1913.

58 On typical conditions of sharecropping, consult above all, Cheung, *A Theory,* 16–29, and Reid, "Sharecropping in History and Theory," 426–40. For Latin America specifically, see Martínez-Alier, "Sharecropping: Some Illustrations," in *Sharecropping and Sharecroppers,* ed. T. J. Byres (London, 1983), 94–106, and José María Caballero, "Sharecropping." For Peru, consult Macera, *Trabajos de Historia,* and José Matos Mar, *Yanaconaje y reforma agraria en el Perú.* On the conventional view of this institution, both Mariátegui and Castro Pozo have been deeply influential. See also Klaren, *Modernization, Dislocation and Aprismo,* for analysis of the views of early twentieth-century Peruvian social critics. These critics undoubtedly contributed — even if only through the arguments of Mariátegui — to the form scholarship took until the 1960s: see Humberto Rodríguez Pastor, "Caqui: hacienda del valle de Chancay" (thesis, Universidad Nacional Mayor de San Marcos, Lima, 1965). Burga, *De la encomienda;* and Albert, "*Yanaconaje and Cotton Production.*" Debate on the appropriate conditions for the emergence of sharecropping under capitalism in Eastern Europe is in Jonathan M. Weiner, "Class Structure and Economic Development in the American South, 1865–1955" (with commentary by R. Higgs and H. Woodman and reply by Weiner) *American Historical Review* 84.4 (1979): 970–1006.

59 A static but useful definition is in Matos Mar, *Yanaconaje y reforma agraria,* a work that concentrates on the post–World War II phenomenon as background for the agrarian reforms of the 1960s.

Chapter 5 Yanaconas, Mechanization, and Migrant Labor

1 Bell, *Essay on the Peruvian Cotton Industry,* 12–13, 33, 38, 55–57, discusses the characteristics of El Niño current and blames it for major cotton decline and stagnation on the far north coast.

2 The most detailed studies of plantations and peasants in this era are Albert, *Yanaconaje and Cotton Production;* Heraclio Bonilla and Alejandro Rabanal, "La Hacienda San Nicolás (Supe) y la Primera Guerra Mundial," *Economía* 2.3 (1979): 3–48; Burga, *De la encomienda;* and Arroyo, *La hacienda costeña.* The detailed work of Nils Jacobsen, *Mirages of Transition: The Peruvian Altiplano, 1780–1930* (Berkeley, Calif., 1993), pertains to the southern highlands.

3 On cotton production in general, see Bell, *Essay on the Peruvian Cotton Industry,* tables 2, 23, and Albert, *South America,* 111. Horacio Pinto, in *Estadísticas históricas del Perú. sector Agrícola: Algodón* (Lima, 1977), 18, showed a brief decline after the first two years of the world war, followed by steady annual yields. Likewise, see Albert, "*Yanaconaje and Cotton Production,*" 110.

4 Archivo del Sub-prefecto de Pisco *Libro de presos, 1904.* For discussion of the character of the wavelike migrations known to have occurred all along the coast, see Henri Favre, "The Dynamics of Indian Peasant Society and Migration to Coastal Plantations in Central Peru," in *Land and Labour in Latin America,* ed. Kenneth Duncan and Ian Rutledge, with Colin Harding (Cambridge, 1977), 253–68. For the north coast see Klaren, *Modernization, Dislocation and Aprismo,* 24–49, which attributes internal migration largely to the "pull" of enganche, and Gonzales, *Plantation Agriculture,* 123–30, which gives greatest weight to the "push" of highland economic decline.

5 AFA, Hacienda Palto, *Letterbooks,* E. R. Aspíllaga to Lima, informe, February 23, 1919, 8.

6 Thorp and Bertram, *Growth,* 52–53; Quiroz, "Financial Development," 457.

7 AFA, Hacienda Palto, *Letterbooks,* Palto to Lima, October 26, 1918; January 3, 1920. The owners of Hacienda Palto purchased their first tractor, a Huber, from a U.S. company in 1919. They followed in the next two years by bringing in a Fordson and then another made by Titan. The three tractors served the plantation's "direct cultivation" fields for many years. A recollection of the purchase of the first Huber in 1918 is in AFA, Hacienda Palto, *Letterbooks,* Palto to Lima, informe, February 23, 1929.

8 The manager of Hacienda Palto discussed aftosa with the owners at length in AFA, Hacienda Palto, *Letterbooks,* Palto to Lima, October 12, 1924.

9 Patrick Husson, "Changement social et insurrection indiennes: la 'révolte du sel' à Huanta, Pérou, en 1896," *Cahiers des Amériques Latines* 23.1 (1981): 102–49, illustrates community infiltration of landowner herds for improvement purposes.

10 On the need for cash, see AFA, Hacienda Palto, *Letterbooks,* Palto to Lima, November 8, 18, 1923; March 8, 1924.

11 A vivid model for detailed examination of Latin American plantations is Manuel Moreno Fraginals, *The Sugarmill: The Socioeconomic Complex of Sugar in Cuba, 1760–1860* (New York, 1976). Klarén, *Modernization, Dislocation and Aprismo,* 15–20, and Burga, *De la encomienda,* illustrate the process in Peru. See also Gonzales, *Plantation Agriculture,* 42–70.

12 AFA, Hacienda Palto, *Letterbooks,* Palto to Lima, October 7, 1923.

13 AFA, Hacienda Palto, *Letterbooks,* Palto to Lima, informe, August 1, 1925.

14 Quiroz, *Domestic and Foreign Finance,* 180.

15 E. E. Davies, *History of Duncan Fox & Co. Limited by E. E. Davies* (manuscript, London, n.d.), unfortunately does not mention the company's activities in the sur chico. Falling cotton prices apparently drove Graham Rowe, the oldest British firm operating on the west coast of South America, out of business. Great Britain, Public Records Office, Foreign Office 371/15109/No. 178, November 9, 1931. See also AFA, Hacienda Palto, *Letterbooks,* Palto to Lima, December 20, 1933. Centralization of ginning and lending in the hands of monopoly merchant houses did not lead to foreign control of cotton production, which remained in local hands to the preference of both sides. Company records in Piura indicate strongly that Duncan Fox and similar foreign houses studiously avoided taking over the management of plantations in default of loans.

16 For much of that time, San José also acted as an experimental station. Cotton varieties were tested in the fields and if they proved to be successful, they were grown at Hacienda Palto. A prominent example of this practice was the introduction of the new "Tangüis" strain of cotton developed at nearby Hacienda Urrutia by the leaseholder, botanist Fermín Tangüis. The Aspíllagas tried the Tangüis strain at San José and when it proved to be hardier and longer stapled than others, they planted it at Palto. Rómulo Ferrero, *El algodón Tangüis y su origen* (Lima, 1935). Macera, *Trabajos de historia*, 4: 434, cites other contemporary studies of Tangüis cotton; see also AFA, Hacienda Palto, *Letterbooks*, Palto to Lima, February 4, 18, 1911, and Munro, *Cotton*, 40, 47, 55, 236, 248.

17 On the new mayordomos, see AFA, Hacienda Palto, *Letterbooks*, Palto to Lima, May 12, 1923; March 8, 1924.

18 AFA, Hacienda Palto, *Letterbooks*, Palto to Lima, May 12, 1923. On the axiom of maintaining social distance, see Eugene D. Genovese, *The World the Slaveholders Made: Two Essays in Interpretation* (New York, 1969), and Scarborough, *The Overseer*.

19 Recently, economic anthropologists have framed the issue of plantation security within the discussion of incentives to plant versus guarantees of a basic return on rent. With the use of incentives, plantation owners left the choice of paying for security to the renter, guessing that security was as great a concern to the tenant, who would just as likely pay for it. By assuming the cost of security unto him- or herself, on the other hand, the landowner could be assured of a steadier rent but also a lower profit. Then follows: The evidence here appears to favor the judgment of those such as Martínez-Alier, *Haciendas*, Caballero, "Sharecropping," and Reid, "Sharecropping in History and Theory"—each of which argues that plantation owners reaped higher returns by reducing security costs to a minimum and placing the proper incentives in tenant contracts.

20 On the Ley Vial of 1925, see Karno, (Ph.D. dissertation, UCLA, 1970); Herbold, (Ph.D. dissertation, Yale University, 1973); Thomas A. Davies Jr., *Indian Integration in Peru: A Century of Experience* (Lincoln, Nebr., 1975); Baltasar Caravedo Molinari, *Burguesía e industria en el Perú (1933–1945)* (Lima, 1976); and Wilfredo Kapsoli, "El campesinado rural y la ley vial," *Campesino*, 1.2 (1969): 1–17. On migration coastward from the Andes after World War I, see Gonzales, *Plantation Agriculture*, 117–46; and Olinda Celestino, *Migración y cambio structural: la comunidad de Lampián* (Lima, 1972). Claude Collin Delavaud, *Les régions côtières du Pérou septentrional: occupation du sol, aménagement régional* (Lima, 1968), 122–25, though focused on the 1940s, is useful.

21 On soil exhaustion and the rise of modern commercial farming see Edward Hyams, *Soil and Civilization* (New York, 1952). A very detailed study of the history of government efforts to direct the exploitation of natural fertilizer—guano—for national export agriculture is Pablo Macera, "El guano y la agricultura peruana de exportación (1909–1945)," in *Trabajos de historia,* ed. Pablo Macera (Lima, 1977), 4: 309–499.

22 On the recommended pattern of guano use at Hacienda Palto and its practical application in the period under scrutiny, see AFA, Hacienda Palto, *Letterbooks,* November 25, 1923; April 12, 1924; informe, May 15, 1925, p. 5; informe, April 4, 1929, p. 15.

23 Fernando López Aliaga, an agronomic engineer, wrote a series of important technical articles, "El algodón en el valle de Cañete," in *El agricultor peruano,* May 1–July 15, 1909, that carried the admonitions just mentioned and others, noting strongly the author's amazement that the coastal landowners had for decades considered the valley lands sufficiently rich to make fertilization worthless.

24 On guano de las islas, see AFA, Hacienda Palto, *Letterbooks,* Palto to Lima, September 13, 1919; December 11, 1920; December 24, 1921. In the last letter the manager of Palto reported that all over the valley, fertilizer was helping to increase yields. In the highly important survey cited in note 21 above, Macera analyzed the relationship among guano, the major agrarian exports, and the state in the early twentieth century, and in the process he also commented on the impact of this relationship on rural society.

25 On the tambo, consult Cross, "Living Standards," 1–19. Gonzales, *Plantation Agriculture,* 152–54; Bauer, "Rural Workers in Spanish America: Problems of Peonage and Oppression," *Hispanic American Historical Review* 59.1 (1979): 34–63, refers to the tambo as a plantation store. Debate between Arnold Bauer and and Brian Loveman "Critique of Arnold J. Bauer's 'Rural Workers in Spanish America: Problems of Peonage and Oppression,'" *Hispanic American Historical Review* 59.3 (1979): 478–85; and "Arnold J. Bauer's Reply," *Hispanic American Historical Review* 59.3 (1979): 486–89 on the nature of sharecropper debt and sharecropper culture focuses on the relative freedom and power afforded to peasants by sharecropping arrangements. U.S. historians have added heat to these discussions. Harold D. Woodman surveyed the problem in "Sequel to Slavery: The New History Views the Postbellum South, *Journal of Southern History* 34.4 (1977): 523–54; see also Jonathan Weiner, "Class Structure," 970–1006, and the accompanying comments. Both referred to conceptions of peasant freedom and coercion presented in Reid, "Sharecropping as an Understandable Response," *Journal of Economic History* 33 (1973): 106–30, and to the same author's "Sharecropping and Agricultural Uncertainty," 549–76; "Sharecropping in History and Theory," 426–40; and other works. A theoretically informed Latin Americanist's perspective on these questions is Alan Knight, "Mexican Peonage: What Was It and Why Was It?" *Journal of Latin American Studies* 18.1 (1986): 41–74.

26 On Joaquín Capelo, see Morse, "Joaquín Capelo," 95–110, and Morse, ed., *Lima en 1900* (Lima, 1973). Prominent contemporary dissections of enganche are given attention by Klaren, who rested a careful analysis on these sources, in *Modernization, Dislocation and Aprismo,* 26–37, and by Macera, *Trabajos de historia* 4: 410–16. Haya and the Apristas considered enganche as part of the timeless oppressive social relations between landlords and peasants. In *Seven Interpretive Essays,* 63–68, social critic José Carlos Mariátegui argued that this form of labor contracting "prolonged feudalism into our capitalistic age."

27 AFA, Hacienda Palto, *Letterbooks,* Palto to Lima, May 3, 1919; February 23, 1919, p. 7; see also Palto to Lima, December 1, 1923; February 27, April 3, October 9, 1927; May 20, 1928; May 9, 1929; March 29, 1931.

28 In one case negotiations centered on the reluctance of the tambero to assume the former tenant's debts. On the range of goods carried at the tambos of Hacienda Palto, including *limas* (files), sugar, kerosene, and so on, see AFA, Hacienda Palto, *Letterbooks,* Palto to Lima, December 1, 1923; April 23, 1927. On the argument that tambos throughout the valley carried very limited inventories, see the complaints expressed in Hacienda Palto, *Letterbooks,* Palto to Lima, May 9, 1929; March 2, 1931.

29 The term "agreement" is used advisedly. There is no evidence that contractual arrangements between tenants and subtenants were made on paper in accordance with law; enforcement in these cases was a product of the moral sanctions of the community plus familiarity or kinship between tenant and subtenant. See Caballero, "Sharecropping as an Efficient System," and David Lehman, "Dos vías de desarrollo capitalista en la agricultura o Crítica de la razón chayanoviano-marxizante,'" *Revista Andina* 3.2 (1985): 343–78.

30 Michael J. Gonzales, "The Rise of Cotton Tenant Farming in Peru, 1890–1920: The Condor Valley," *Agricultural History* 65.1 (1991): 64, 66. Analysis of subrent is in Roseberry, "Rent." Eduardo Fioravanti, *Latifundio y sindicalismo agrario en el Perú* (Lima, 1974), 114–42, analyzes conditions in the 1950s that promoted political consciousness and conflict between renters and subrenters.

31 Tenant conditions are summarized in AFA, Hacienda Palto, *Letterbooks,* Palto to Lima, informe, August 1, 1925, pp. 14–15.

32 AFA, Hacienda Palto, *Letterbooks,* Palto to Lima, informe, August 1, 1925, pp. 14–15.

33 AFA, Hacienda Palto, *Letterbooks,* Palto to Lima, January 20, 22, May 20, July 18, 1923.

34 AFA, Hacienda Palto, *Letterbooks,* Palto to Lima, May 20, 23, 1923.

35 AFA, Hacienda Palto, *Letterbooks,* July 22, September 16, October 14, 1923.

36 The pattern becomes clear in Lyman L. Johnson, "Changing Criminal Patterns in Buenos Aires, 1890–1914," *Journal of Latin American Studies* (1982): 359–80.

37 AFA, Hacienda Palto, *Letterbooks.* On cattle theft, see Palto to Lima,

October 11, 1921; on cotton theft, see Palto to Lima, March 8, September 7, 1924.

38 AFA, Hacienda Palto, *Letterbooks,* Palto to Lima, October 29, November 8, 1923.

39 On the disaster, see AFA, Hacienda Palto, *Letterbooks,* August 3, 1927.

40 AFA, Hacienda Palto, *Letterbooks,* Palto to Lima, informe, August 1, 1925, p. 8.

41 Discussion of compañeros and yanaconas is in AFA, Hacienda Palto, *Letterbooks,* Palto to Lima, informe, April 4, 1927, pp. 10–12.

42 Julian Laite, "Processes of Industrial and Social Change," in *Peasant Cooperation and Capitalist Expansion in Central Peru,* ed. Norman Long and Bryan R. Roberts (Austin, 1978), 72–98. Household strategies by highlanders that were designed to amplify sources of income are discussed in detail in Alderson-Smith, "Confederations of Households: Extended Domestic Enterprises in City and Country," in *Peasants, Miners and Entrepreneurs: Regional Development in the Central Highlands of Peru,* ed. Norman Long and Bryan R. Roberts (Cambridge, England, 1984), 217–34.

43 Again see appendices of AFA, Hacienda Palto, *Letterbooks,* Palto to Lima, informe, April 4, 1927.

44 Recent anthropological studies suggest that return migration benefited highland communities. Refer to Long and Roberts, *Peasant Cooperation,* and G. Smith, *Livelihood.* But among peasants previously settled in the valley, the arrival of migrants often contributed to cultural and racial conflicts, and problems arose when plantations neglected children's education. For treatment of this issue, see Rupert V. Vance, *Human Factors in Cotton Culture* (Chapel Hill, N.C., 1929), 252–319.

45 Albert, in *South America,* 287–305, devoted the bulk of his analysis of rising labor consciousness to the urban scene. See also Bergquist, *Labor in Latin America: Comparative Essays on Chile, Argentina, Venezuela and Colombia* (Stanford, Calif., 1986). Ruth Berins Collier and David Collier, *Shaping the Political Arena: Critical Junctures, the Labor Movement, and Regime Dynamics in Latin America* (Princeton, N.J., 1991), 59–91, present a framework for understanding the growing political consciousness by workers; Blanchard, *Origins,* 126–35, recognizes the rural context of political consciousness in the twentieth-century labor movement.

Chapter 6 Yanaconas, Migrants, and Political Consciousness

1 Franco the elder's activities are detailed in AFA, Hacienda Palto, *Letterbooks,* Palto to Lima, November 8, 15, 1908. On the stabbing incident, see May 23, September 19, 1909; on his loan tactics, see May 29, June 21,

June 25, July 11, August 21, 1909; on his repeated drinking, September 12, October 2, 1909; and on the manager's assessment of him, Palto to Lima, January 1, 1910.

2 For the effect of the world depression on the mining regions see Mallon, *Defense,* 270–76, and Dore, *Peruvian Mining,* 44–61, 103–19. Baltasar Caravedo Molinari, *Burguesía e industria,* 49–56, outlines the creation of a domestic market in Lima and the provinces; also consult Thorp and Bertram, *Growth,* 145–201.

3 Thorp and Bertram, *Growth,* 170–72. On the changes that overcame the Peruvian sugar industry see Albert, *An Essay.*

4 The observer was the Italian exile scholar Antonello Gerbi. See Thorp and Bertram, *Growth,* 173–74.

5 Thorp and Bertram, *Growth,* 175.

6 Thorp and Bertram, *Growth,* 175. For details on the domestic impact of cotton export earnings, see Quiroz, *Domestic and Foreign Finance,* 83–85.

7 This did not include the fourteen-fanegada section the "Huarangal," which had been leased to Luis Albizuri, the former cotton broker of Pisco. See AFA, Hacienda Palto, *Letterbooks,* Palto to Lima, informe, May 15, 1931, p. 5. On Antero Aspíllaga Anderson, see Gilbert, *La oligarquía peruana.*

8 Aníbal Quijano, "Perú en los años treinta," in *América Latina en los años treinta,* ed. Pablo Gonzáles Casanova (Mexico City, 1977), 239–304. Cotler, *Clases,* 227–72, concentrates on urban politics but effectively sets the scene for growing popular political awareness in the hinterlands.

9 Useful studies of the APRA, Communist, and Socialist movements in the critical early 1930s are Carmen Rosa Balbi, *El Partido Comunista y el APRA en la crisis revolucionaria de los años treinta* (Lima, 1980), and Carmen R. Balbi and Laura Madalengoitia, *Parlamento y lucha política, Perú, 1932* (Lima, 1980). See also Heraclio Bonilla and Paul Drake, eds., *El APRA, de la ideología a la praxis* (Lima: Centro Latinoamericano de Historia Económica y Social, 1989). Studies of Mariátegui's efforts to link society, nation, and socialist thought include Jesús Chavarría, "La desaparición del Perú colonial (1870–1919)," *Aportes* (Paris) 23 (1972): 120–53, and Chavarría's biography of the same intellectual, *José Carlos Mariátegui and the Rise of Modern Peru, 1890–1930* (Albuquerque, N. Mex., 1979); Carlos Franco, "Mariátegui-Haya: surgimiento de la izquierda nacional," *Socialismo y Participación* 8 (1979): 11–44; Harry E. Vanden, *Nationalist Marxism in Latin America: José Carlos Mariátegui's Thought and Politics* (Boulder, Colo., 1986); and John Womack Jr., "Mariátegui, Marxism, and Nationalism," *Marxist Perspectives* (Summer 1980): 170–74. Also hear the voice of a peasant–turned–political leader in Teresa Oré, ed., with Nelly Plaza, René Antezana, and Jaime Luna, *Memorias de un viejo luchador campesino: Juan H. Pévez* (Lima, 1993).

10 Pinto, *Estadísticas históricas,* registers rising national production in mid-decade, and in Ica Department Pinto's figures show the trend continuing to the end of the decade, pp. 5, 13; see also Pablo Macera, *Palto: hacendados y yanaconas del algodonal peruano (documentos, 1877–1943)* (Lima, 1976), 129, 138–40.

11 The total land rented to yanaconas included the fourteen-fanegada pasture leased to former Pisco cotton speculator Luis Albizuri. AFA, Hacienda Palto, *Letterbooks,* Palto to Lima, informe, May 15, 1935.

12 The SNA propaganda booklet issued in 1936, *Como se produce el algodón en el Perú* (Lima, 1936), features the small independent peasant as the backbone of cotton production. Evidently produced to lobby the National Congress in protest against the duties levied on raw cotton exports, the booklet argues essentially that the duty undercut the small independent cotton farmer. See also Macera, *Trabajos de historia,* 4: 475–82.

13 AFA, Hacienda Palto, *Letterbooks,* Palto to Lima, November 4, 1934. On the effect of mining on the villages, consult Dore, *Peruvian Mining,* 111–21.

14 Klaren, *Modernization, Dislocation and Aprismo,* 99–100; AFA, Hacienda Palto, *Letterbooks,* Palto to Lima, September 28, 1931; informe, December 22, 1934.

15 After a peak Palto harvest of 530,295 pounds of raw cotton in 1933, volume remained at a high plateau until the end of the decade. AFA, Hacienda Palto, *Letterbooks,* Palto to Lima, annual report, July 12, 1933; Macera, *Palto,* 150. Statistics in Pinto, *Estadísticas históricas,* 13, show that overall Ica departmental production departed somewhat from this pattern, reaching a peak in 1938 then declining during World War II.

16 AFA, Hacienda Palto, *Letterbooks,* Palto to Lima, July 12; October 8, 1933.

17 AFA, Hacienda Palto, *Letterbooks,* Palto to Lima, December 9, 1933.

18 Aníbal Quijano, "Perú en los años treinta," 239–304. Thorp and Bertram, *Growth,* 174, attributes the change in labor policy to both growing peasant political strength and the new government-sponsored credit system. See also Rosemary Thorp, *Latin America in the 1930s: The Role of the Periphery in the World Crisis* (New York, 1984).

19 A fuller description of this process in an Andean setting is Mallon, *Defense of Community,* 254–63; see also the discussion in Durrenberger, "Chayanov."

20 On migration, see George Kubler, *The Indian Caste of Peru, 1795–1940: A Population Study Based upon Tax Records and Census Reports* (Washington, D.C., 1952); Dore, *Peruvian Mining;* Long and Roberts, *Peasant Cooperation.*

21 AFA, Hacienda Palto, *Letterbooks,* Palto to Lima, November 11, 1934. See pay discussions in *Letterbooks,* Palto to Lima, informe, May 15, 1935.

22 Oré, *Memorias.*

23 Bank preferences, private and public, were largely driven by the need for control. Thorp and Bertram in *Growth,* 173–74, provided the example of the activities of the Partido Socialista (Socialist Party) in the far northern Piura valley, which organized the yanaconas into unions and negotiated contracts. Exhibiting remarkable similarity with their cohorts in the Pisco valley, Piura landowners then abandoned yanaconaje and turned to wage labor or "cash tenants." A prominent congressman and social critic of yanaconaje in northern Peru is Hildebrando Castro Pozo, ed., *El Yanaconaje en las haciendas piuranas* (Lima, 1947). See also his *Del ayllu al cooperativismo socialista* (Lima, 1936), 215–22; 242–46, in which he argued that yanaconaje could lead to cooperative landholding. On Benavides regime policies that favored agrarian investors, see David Werlich, *Peru: A Short History* (Carbondale, Ill., 1978), pp. 212–19. Caravedo Molinari, in *Burguesía,* 56–62, agreed that pay remained low through the decade while cotton prices were high. He also found the possibilities for technological change limited.

24 A model for this process is offered in John K. Hatch, "The Corn Farmers of Motupe: A Study of Traditional Farming Practices in Northern Coastal Peru" (Ph.D. dissertation, University of Wisconsin, Madison, Wis., 1974). Peasants always felt cheated by the plantation manager, whom they accused of rigging the scales. Conversely, yanaconas often were accused of weighing down the cotton with debris before it reached the scales.

25 AFA, Hacienda Palto, *Letterbooks,* Palto to Lima, April 16, 1933; informe, May 15, 1935, chart following p. 5.

26 Fioravanti, *Latifundio y sindicalismo,* 67–74.

27 On how subrent worked in the highland region of La Convención-Lares between the 1930s and the 1960s, see Wesley W. Craig Jr., "Peru: The Peasant Movement in La Convención," in *Latin American Peasant Movements,* ed H. A. Landsberger (Ithaca, N.Y., 1969), 274–96.

28 See the discussion of the literature on compadrazgo in Bolton and Mayer, *Andean Kinship,* and in R. E. Smith, *Kinship Ideology.* See also the discussion of variations in reciprocal arrangements in Michael J. Sallnow, "Cooperation and Contradiction: The Dialectics of Everyday Practice," *Dialectical Anthropology* 14 (1989): 241–57.

29 Macera, *Palto,* 143–44.

30 Ibid., appendix.

31 AFA, Hacienda Palto, *Letterbooks,* informe, January 1938, in Macera, *Palto,* 137–41, appendix: "Campaña algodonera de 1940. Hacienda Palto, 31 de Enero"; "Examen de la campaña algodonera. 1941–1942," 145–150.

32 On the new law, see T. A. Davies, *Indian Integration,* and commentary by Castro Pozo, in *El yanaconaje.*

Conclusion: Plantation Society and Peruvian Culture

1 See the recent plantation studies in Brij. V. Lal, Doug Munro, and Edward D. Beechert, *Plantation Workers: Resistance and Accommodation* (Honolulu, 1993), especially the essays on Guatemalan coffee plantations by David McCreery, "Hegemony and Repression in Rural Guatemala, 1871–1940" 217–40, and on sugar plantations in Peru by Michael Gonzales, "Planter Control and Worker Resistance in Northern Peru, 1880–1921: The Condor Valley" 297–316.

2 Notable statements of fear that Peruvian "culture" was in danger of "mongrelization" and "weakening" are Arona, *La inmigración* (Lima, 1891); Carlos Paz Soldán, "El vicio amarillo en Lima," *La Crónica*, April 23, 1916: 13; and surprisingly Felipe M. Boisset, *El problema racial en el Perú (o el peligro de la raza amarilla); sus causas y sus efectos. Necesidad de seleccionar la raza por medio de una corriente inmigratoria científicamente encauzada. Puntos de mira socialista; maximalismo y terrorismo* (Lima, 1919), cast a quick sidelong glance at Afro Peruvians before raking over the Asian population. On the ideological sources of this line of thinking, see Nancy Leys Stepan, *"The Hour of Eugenics": Race, Gender, and Nation in Latin America* (Ithaca, N.Y., 1991).

3 Rebecca J. Scott, "Defining the Boundaries of Freedom in the World of Cane: Cuba, Brazil and Louisiana after Emancipation," *American Historical Review*, 99.1 (1994): 70–102.

4 Several plantation managers at Hacienda Palto who were former tenants on the plantation may have been of African or Asian descent, although the documents reveal nothing on this point.

5 Sallnow, "Cooperation and Contradiction." A cautionary note is sounded in Sherry B. Ortner, "Resistance and the Problem of Ethnographic Refusal," *Comparative Studies in Society and History* 37.1 (1995): 173–93.

6 On the centrality of credit, see Bauer, "Rural Workers."

7 It is a curiosity that it was precisely in this period that Peruvian intellectuals began formulating some of the heaviest early criticism of yanaconaje. Klaren, *Modernization, Dislocation, and Aprismo,* 25–33, entwines the contemporary critique with a discussion of enganche.

8 The "least costly" approach is discussed critically, with commentary, in Lehmann, "Dos vías."

9 Guha, "Dominance."

10 T. J. Jackson Lears, "Making Fun of Popular Culture," *American Historical Review* 97.5 (1992): 1417–26. See also Anderson, "Antinomies"; and Lears, "Concept of Cultural Hegemony." The latest useful discussion of Gramsci's concept of hegemony is in William Roseberry, "Hegemony and the Language of Contention," in Joseph and Nugent, *Everyday Forms of State*

Formation: Revolution and the Negotiation of Rule in Modern Mexico, ed. G. Joseph and D. Nugent (Durham, N.C., 1995), 355–66.

11 Cf. Derek Sayer, "Everyday Forms of State Formation: Some Dissident Remarks on 'Hegemony,' " in Joseph and Nugent, *Everyday Forms of State Formation,* 367–78.

12 See the discussion of creole nationalism in Benedict Anderson, *Imagined Communities* (rev. ed. London, 1991), 47–66, 144–54. See also Gilbert, *La oligarquía peruana,* and Cotler, *Clases.*

13 Raymond Williams, *Resources of Hope: Culture, Democracy, Socialism* (London, 1989), 74–76; see also Williams, *Keywords: A Vocabulary of Culture and Society* (New York, 1976), 117–18.

GLOSSARY

Sources: Martín Alonso, *Encyclopedia del idioma: diccionario histórico y moderno de la lengua española (siglos XI al XX) etimológica, tecnológico, regional e hispanoamericano* (Madrid, 1982). Héctor B. Bustamante Tarrillo, "Formas de trabajo — remuneraciones — balances de Pago en la Hacienda 'Palto' en los años 1946–1947 (manuscript, Universidad de San Marcos, October 4, 1974); José Antonio de Lavalle y García, *El guano en la agricultura nacional* (Lima, 1913); Fernando López Aliaga, "El algodón en el valle de Cañete," *El Agricultor Peruano,* May 1–July 15, 1909; José de la Puente, *Diccionario de la legislación de aguas y agricultura del Perú, con inserción de muchos datos y noticias históricas* (Lima: 1885).

abonar: to fertilize; credit; indebt self to a service

acarreo: transport of cotton to port or of crops, etc., from fields

acequia: irrigation channel

adobero: tanner, pickler

adobón: adobe brick; unit of measure equal to 1.2 meters X 70 centimeters

aguardiente: sugar cane whiskey

alcantarilla: drain, culvert

allegadía: rent of part of a tenant's land to another tenant (sub-rent) [see also yanacón-patrón]

almud: unit of measure equal to 1,152 square varas, 0.25 hectare (1/12 fanegada) [see also fanegada]

aparcero: sharecropper

apolcar: see aporcar

aporcar: to dig earth up around the plant

arada: first step in cultivation of cleared fields involving turning over the earth

(h)arar: to rake and furrow

area: unit of measure equal to 100 square meters or 119 square yards

arrastrar: harrow; drag

arrendamiento: relatively low-risk, long-term, fixed-rent tenantry in the south coast valleys of Peru before the 1920s

arrendatario: fixed rent tenant

arriero: muleteer (occupation)

arroba: unit of weight equal to 25 pounds

barbecho: fallow

barchilón: caretaker of animals

boca toma: inlet pipe

caballada: herd of horses

caballería: unit of measure equal to 111 acres

caballerizo: groom

caporal: field foreman

carga: measure of unginned cotton equal to 14 arrobas and 14 pounds (364 pounds)

carreta: wagon

cáscara: husk of rice, etc.

cauce: riverbed; irrigation channel

cerco: enclosure; small, defined area

colca: cotton despository

collo: unit of measure equal to 1,207 square meters (by Ica standards)

comisario: police official, commissioner

compañero: sharecropper (term unique to the south coast valleys) [see also chacarero, sembrador, yanacón]

compañía: a specific form of short-term, relatively high-risk share-cropping in the south coast valleys of Peru before the 1920s; a local term

compuerta: sluice, floodgate, hatch

cordel: standard irrigation measure equal to 20.35 meters (by Cuban standards)

cosecha: harvest

cuadrilla: labor gang on cotton plantations

cuspar: ill-defined field operation; cultivation of the plants with a lampa by hand

chacarero: gardener; tenant [see also sembrador, compañero]

chacarero: general term for small-holder, peasant engaged in foodstuff farming, campesino

chacarilla: garden

chac(a)ra: plot of land sown in foodstuffs, truck garden

champ(e)ar: to sod

champeo (champería): preparation of soil after burning off old bushes; sodding

chamuscar: to scorch

chancaca: molasses

chapodo: pruning; pruned plant of second-year cotton

delgado: thin, exhausted (refers to soil conditions)

desaguador: one who drains water from fields; temporary job

desagüe: final drain outlet

desahijar: to prune twigs, winnow young plants

desgramar: to pull field grass; thresh; shell

despa(o)jar: to strip; winnow; re-move straw, chaff, etc., from grain

despaje: eliminate weeds harvested with cotton

despancar: to husk corn

desparramar: to scatter, spread

despepitar: to deseed

destapar: to unplug, tap

destrancador: one who manipulates irrigation gates; temporary job

destroncar: to uproot; lop off in order to level

drenaje: drainage

encajonar: to crate, box in; buttress with a wall

enganchador: labor agent, contractor

enganche: contractural labor ar-rangement based on an advance on future pay; literally a hook or hanger

entresacar: to cull, thin out

espino: thorn bush; dry bush left behind in the field after a cotton harvest

estera: reed mat for sleeping issued to indentured Asians by the plantation

eventual: temporary, contingent; applied to migrant labor on plantations

faena: debt labor

fanega: unit of measure equal to 156 pounds, 1 fardo, or 1 paca

fanegada: unit of measure equal to 2.9034 hectares or 41,472 square varas (by Pisco standards)

fanegada: unit of measure equal to 6,439 square meters or 6.439 hectares (by Arequipa-Puno standards)

fanegada común: unit of measure equal to 28.978 square meters, 2.8978 hectares, or 7.16 acres

fanegada (Cañete): unit of measure equal to 31,403 square meters or 3.1403 hectares (by Cañete standards)

fanegada (norte): unit of measure equal to 29,696 square meters or 2.9696 hectares (by Northwest standards)

fardo: cotton bale measure equal to about 70 kilograms, or alternately, 156 pounds

fiador: guarantor of a field worker, pledges to replace the worker if he or she breaks the contract

fundo: hacienda, rural landed property: also plantation

gamonales: bosses

gañón (plural, gañanes): plowman

garúa: extremely light, misty rain

gente de afuera: migrant, nonresident, plantation labor [see also nómada]

gramadal: specified area of plantation fallow land

gramalote: forage grassland

guano de las islas: pelican waste from the islands off the coast of Peru; a protein-rich natural fertilizer

habilitación: short-term loan, advance of cash or credit to begin cultivation of fields

hectare: unit of measure equal to 2.47 acres, 10,000 square meters, or approximately 6,393 varas

helado: frost

hijo del país: local farm laborer/ peasant; a cultural designation suggesting non-creole racial/ ethnic, humble origins

hocear: to loosen and pile dirt

hoz: sickle

huerta: vegetable garden; orchard; irrigated land

jornal: daily wage

jornalero: day laborer; field worker paid at a daily, hourly, or job rate

juez de primera instancia: justice of the peace

lampa: a type of hoe with a straight neck and a half-moon blade

libreta: booklet issued by a plantation to field workers and used to keep track of their labor time

libra peruana: Peruvian pound, a monetary value of the early twentieth century, valued against the British pound

lima: file (tool)

machacar: to grind up, loosen soil by dampening, light plowing prior to planting

majuelo: new plant [see also chapodo]

maleza: thicket; a grassy weed

mancarrón: small dam

manzana: unit of measure equal to 1.7266 acres or 698,737 areas; city block

mataje: related to sowing and crumbling earth

mayordomo: overseer

mayordomo de campo: field captain

melasa: treacle; cotton disease; a fungus

melg(e)ar: to build proportioned rows

meter: unit of measure equal to 39.37 inches; a square meter is equal to 1.43 square varas

mita: river water ration (see also riego; turno)

mita, algodón: pound, thresh cotton; separate good from bad; gossip time

nómada: nomad; migrant worker in plantation areas [see also gente de afuera]

paca: unit of measure equal to approximately 70 kilograms (see also fardo)

paila: unit of measure equal to between 80 and 100 liters

paja: straw; thatch

pajeo: weeds removed from between cotton plants; useless cotton branches

pallar: any of several pulses, vegetables grown for human consumption in Peru, including peas, beans

palmar: oasis; a vacation hideaway

paña: movement of harvest workers through a field

partidario: compañero [see also yanacón]

peón: unskilled farmhand, field laborer

peso: 8 reales

pilador: rice husker

planilla: payroll; work plan

podar: to prune

posada: crude, fragile, temporary plantation building erected to house the labor force

predio rural: real estate tax levied by local government

prestamista: money lender (speculator?)

quema: burned thicket left from clearing land

quincha: fencing or housing made of reed; bamboo-like

quintal: unit of measure equal to 100 pounds

ranchería: housing for field hands on plantations in the coastal region of Peru

raspar: to weed

real: 25 céntimos, 1/4 peseta, or 1/8 peso

réditos: interest; revenue; yields

regador: irrigation worker

reja: ploughshare

rejar: to plow; grate

retajar: to castrate, geld

riego: measured flow of water

rodeador: cattle hand

ronda: security duty

roturar: to plow, till

rozar: to clear land of stones, stumps, etc., before plowing

saladar: salt marsh

salitrero: one who throws salitre on furrows to give nutriment to soil

sangradera: bleeder (secondary) ditch

sangradores: drainage workers

sasa: light earth; almost sand

segar (cegar): to harvest; mow

sembrador: gardener, tenant, field hand [see also chacarero, compañero]

sementera: general term for a food or fodder grain

sequiero: irrigation inlet from river

serrano: a person who resides in or is raised in the highland regions of the country

subdelegado de aguas: rural water commissioner

surco: furrow

surquear: to make furrows

tajo: dike; cliff; cutting edge

tajo común: breastworks labor done along a river

tambero: plantation store keeper

tambo: plantation store

tapia: section of adobe wall

tapial: mold for wall bricks

tapiar: to wall in, stop up

tapiero: fence (wall) worker

tajo: row

tarea: piecework, chore

tarea suelta: odd job, chore

toma: tap, inlet

topo: unit of measure equivalent to approximately 1 English acre (ca. 1861); equivalent to approximately 3,493 meters (Arequipa standard)

trozo de tierra: bit of land (refers to farm land, a garden plot)

turno: one's turn; refers to diversion of river flow into irrigation system for a specified period of time by a plantation

vara: 31 to 34 inches; 75 centimeters; 218 varas squared = 1/10 hectare

yanacón (plural, yanaconas): tenant; sharecropper (see also compañero)

yanaconaje: the practice of renting a parcel of land on a plantation for the purpose of commercial farming; implies several forms of credit and land use

yanacón-patrón: tenant who rents land to a sub-tenant (see allegadía)

yunta fletada: rented pair of oxen

zapatear: tap down with feet; treat badly

BIBLIOGRAPHY

Archival and Library Sources

Archive of the Church of Latter-Day Saints, Salt Lake City, Utah
Archivo Arzobispal, Lima
Archivo del Archediócesis de Pisco
Archivo de la Cámara de Diputados, Lima
Archivo de la Sociedad Nacional Agraria
Archivo del Fuero Agrario, Lima
Hacienda Cayaltí. *Correspondencia y cuentas,* 1859, 1867, 1878–82, 1884
Hacienda Palto. *Correspondencia y cuentas,* 1867–1940
Archivo del Sub-Prefecto de Pisco
Archivo General de la Nación, Lima
Archivo Municipal de Ica
Biblioteca Félix Denegri Luna, Lima
Biblioteca Nacional, Lima
  Sala de Investigaciones
British Museum Library, London
Duncan-Fox Archive, Piura, Peru
Great Britain, Public Records Office, Foreign Office
Library of Congress
  Hispanic Division Pamphlet Collection
  Law Division
  Manuscript Division
  Periodicals Division
  Rare Book Division
United States National Agricultural Library

Books, Articles, Pamphlets, and Other Materials
El Agricultor Peruano, 1905–1938

Aguirre, Carlos. "The Lima Penitentiary and the Modernization of Criminal
  Justice in Nineteenth-Century Peru." In *The Birth of the Penitentiary in Latin
  America,* ed. Ricardo Salvatore and Carlos Aguirre. Austin, Tex., 1996.

Aguirre, Carlos. *Agentes de su propia libertad: Los esclavos de Lima y la desintegración de la esclavitud, 1821–1854*. Lima, 1993.

Aguirre, Carlos. "Cimarronaje." In *Bandoleros, abigeos y montoneras: criminalidad y violencia en el Perú, siglos xviii–xx*, ed. Carlos Aguirre and Charles Walker. Lima, 1990, 137–182.

Aguirre, Carlos and Charles Walker, eds. *Bandoleros, abigeos y montoneros: criminalidad y violencia en el Perú, siglos xviii–xx*. Lima, 1990.

Ahumada Moreno, Pascual. *Guerra del Pacífico: recopilación completa de todos los documentos oficiales, correspondencias y demás publicaciones referentes a la guerra que ha dado a luz la prensa de Chile, Perú y Bolivia*. 8 vols. in 4 books. Valparaíso, 1884.

Alavi, Hamza. "Peasant Classes and Primordial Loyalties." *Journal of Peasant Studies* 1.1 (1973): 23–62.

Alberdi, Giorgio, and Enrique Mayer, comps. *Reciprocidad e intercambio en los Andes peruanos*. Lima, 1974.

Albert, Bill. *An Essay on the Peruvian Sugar Industry, 1880–1920, and the Letters of Ronald Gordon, Administrator of the British Sugar Company in Cañete, 1914–1920*. Norwich, 1976.

———. *South America and the First World War*. Cambridge, U.K., 1988.

———. "*Yanaconaje* and Cotton Production on the Peruvian Coast: Sharecropping in the Cañete Valley during World War I." *Bulletin of Latin American Research* 2.2 (May 1983): 107–16.

Alderson-Smith, Gavin. "Confederations of Households: Extended Domestic Enterprises in City and Country." In *Peasants, Miners and Entrepreneurs: Regional Development in the Central Highlands of Peru*, ed. Norman Long and Bryan R. Roberts. Cambridge, England, 1984, 217–34.

Allen, Catherine J. *The Hold Life Has: Coca and Cultural Identity in an Andean Community*. Washington, D.C., 1988.

Alonso, Ana María. "Gender, Power, and Historical Memory: Discourses of *Serrano* Resistance." In *Feminists Theorize the Political*, ed. Judith Butler and Joan W. Scott. London, 1992, 404–25.

Alonso, Martín. *Enciclopedia del idioma: diccionario histórico y moderno de la lengua española (siglos XI al XX) etimológica, tecnológico, regional e hispanoamericano* (Madrid, 1982).

Alston, Lee J., and Robert Higgs. "Contractual Mix in Southern Agriculture since the Civil War: Facts, Hypotheses, and Tests." *Journal of Economic History* 42.2 (1982): 327–54.

Anderson, Benedict. *Imagined Communities*. Rev. ed. London, 1991.

Anderson, Perry. "The Antinomies of Antonio Gramsci." *New Left Review* 100 (November 1976–January 1977): 5–80.

Andrews, George Reid. *The Afro-Argentines of Buenos Aires, 1800–1900*. Madison, Wis., 1980.

———. "Spanish American Independence: A Structural Analysis." *Latin American Perspectives* 12.1 (1985): 105–32.

Aranda, Ricardo. *Constitución del Perú de 1860 con sus reformas hasta 1893: leyes orgánicas, decretos, reglamentos y resoluciones referentes a ellas, coleccionadas y anotadas por Ricardo Aranda.* Lima, 1893.

Archer, Léonie J., ed. *Slavery and Other Forms of Unfree Labour.* London, 1988.

Argumániz, Manuel de. *Memoria.* 4 parts. Typescript, Biblioteca Félix Denegri Luna, Lima, n.d.

Arona, Juan de. [pseud., Pedro Paz Soldán y Unánue]. *La inmigración en el Perú.* Lima, 1891. Reprint 1971.

Arroyo, Eduardo. *La hacienda costeña en el Perú: Mala-Cañete, 1532–1968.* Lima, 1981.

Astiz, Carlos A. *Pressure Groups and Power Elites in Peruvian Politics.* Ithaca, N.Y., 1969.

Aston, T. H., and C. H. E. Philpin, eds. *The Brenner Debate.* Cambridge, 1985.

Balbi, Carmen Rosa. *El partido comunista y el APRA en la crisis revolucionaria de los años treinta.* Lima, 1980.

——. *Parlamento y lucha política, Perú, 1932.* Lima, 1980.

Banaji, Jairus. "Illusions about the Peasantry: Karl Kautsky and the Agrarian Question." *Journal of Peasant Studies* 17.2 (1990): 288–307.

Baran, Paul A. *The Political Economy of Growth.* New York, 1957.

Barber, Bernard. *The Logic and Limits of Trust.* New Brunswick, N.J., 1983.

Bardella, Gianfranco. *Setenta y cinco años de vida económica del Perú, 1889–1964.* Lima, 1964.

Barlow, F. D. *Cotton in South America.* National Cotton Council. Memphis, Tenn., 1952.

Basadre, Jorge. *Elecciones y centralismo en el Perú. (apuntes para un esquema histórico).* Lima, 1980.

——. *Historia de la república del Perú, 1822–1933.* 16 vols. 6th ed. Lima, 1968.

Basave K., Jorge, and Enrique Semo. "Implementos agrícolas en las haciendas mexicanas (1750–1880)." Manuscript. Mexico City, n.d.

Baskes, Jeremy. "Coerced or Voluntary? The *Repartimiento* and Market Participation of Peasants in Late Colonial Oaxaca." *Journal of Latin American Studies* 28.1 (1996): 1–28.

Bauer, Arnold J. "Chilean Rural Labor in the Nineteenth Century," *American Historical Review* 76.4 (1971): 1059–83.

——. *Chilean Rural Society from the Spanish Conquest to 1930.* New York, 1975.

——. "The Hacienda El Huique in the Agrarian Structure of Nineteenth-Century Chile." *Agricultural History* 46.4 (1972): 455–70.

——. "Jesuit Enterprise in Colonial Latin America: A Review Essay." *Agricultural History* 57.1 (1983): 95–103.

——. "Rural Workers in Spanish America: Problems of Peonage and Oppression." *Hispanic American Historical Review* 59.1 (1979): 34–63.

Bazant, Jan. "Landlord, Labourer, and Tenant in San Luis Potosí, Northern Mexico, 1822–1910." In K. Duncan and I. Rutledge with C. Harding, *Land and Labour in Latin America,* ed. K. Duncan and I. Rutledge, with C. Harding. Cambridge, 1977, 59–82.

——. "Peones, arrendatarios y aparceros en Mexico: 1851–1853." *Historia Mexicana* 23.2 (1973): 330–57.

Beckford, George. *Persistent Poverty: Underdevelopment in Plantation Economies of the Third World.* New York, 1972.

Beechey, Veronica. "On Patriarchy." *Feminist Review* 3 (1979): 66–82.

Beeching, Jack. *The Chinese Opium Wars.* New York, 1975.

Bell, W. S. *An Essay on the Peruvian Cotton Industry, 1825–1920.* University of Liverpool, Centre for Latin American Studies, Working Paper No. 6, Liverpool, 1985.

Bennet, Tony, Graham Martin, Colin Mercer, and Janet Woolcott, eds. *Culture, Ideology and Social Process: A Reader.* London, 1981.

Bennett, Wendell, and J. Bird. *Andean Culture History.* New York, 1949.

Bergad, Laird. "On Comparative History: A Reply to Tom Brass." *Journal of Latin American Studies* 16.1 (1984): 153–56.

Bergquist, Charles W. *Coffee and Conflict in Colombia, 1886–1910.* Durham, N.C., 1978.

——. *Labor in Latin America: Comparative Essays on Chile, Argentina, Venezuela and Colombia.* Stanford, Calif., 1986.

Bermüdez, Oscar. *Historia del salitre desde sus orígenes hasta la Guerra del Pacífico.* Santiago, 1963.

Birbeck, Christopher. "Latin American Banditry as Peasant Resistance: A Dead-End Trail?" *Latin American Research Review* 26.1 (1991): 156–60.

Blanchard, Peter. *The Origins of the Peruvian Labor Movement, 1883–1919.* Pittsburgh, Pa., 1982.

——. "The Recruitment of Workers in the Peruvian Sierra at the Turn of the Century: The Enganche System." *Inter-American Economic Affairs* 33 (1979): 63–83.

——. *Slavery and Abolition in Early Republican Peru.* Wilmington, Del., 1992.

Boissett, Felipe M. *El problema racial en el Perú (o el peligro de la raza amarilla): sus causas y sus efectos. Necesidad de seleccionar la raza por medio de una corriente immigratoria científicamente encauzada. Puntos de mira socialista; maximalismo y terrorismo.* Lima, 1919.

Bolton, Ralph, and Enrique Mayer, eds. *Andean Kinship and Marriage.* Washington, D.C., 1977.

Bonilla, Heraclio. "Comercio libre y crisis de la economía andina: el caso del Cuzco" *Histórica,* 21.1 (1978): 1–25.

——. "La coyuntura del comercio internacional del Perú en el siglo XIX." *Desarrollo Económico* 12.46 (1972): 305–31.

——. *La emergencia del control norteamericano sobre la economía peruana, 1850–1930.* Lima, 1975.

————. *Gran Bretaña y el Perú, 1826–1919: los mecanismos de un control económico* 5 vols. Lima, 1975–1977.

————. *Guano y burguesía en el Perú.* Lima, 1974.

————. "Islay y la economía del sur peruano en el siglo xix." *Apuntes: Revista Semestral de Ciencias Sociales* 2 (1974): 31–47.

————. *El minero en los Andes: una aproximación a su estudio.* Lima, 1974.

————. *Un siglo a la deriva: ensayos sobre el Peru, Bolivia y la Guerra.* Lima, 1980.

————. "The War of the Pacific and the National and Colonial Problem in Peru." *Past and Present* 81 (1978): 92–118.

Bonilla, Heraclio, and Alejandro Rabanal. "La Hacienda San Nicolás (Supe) y la Primera Guerra Mundial." *Economía* 2.3 (1979): 3–48.

Bonilla, Heraclio, and Karen Spalding. "La independencia en el Perú: las palabras y los hechos." In *La independencia en el Perú,* ed. H. Bonilla and Pierre Chaunu, 2d ed. Lima, 1981, 15–65.

Bonilla, Heraclio, and Paul Drake, eds. *El APRA, de la ideología a la praxis.* Lima, 1989.

Boserup, Esther. *The Conditions of Agricultural Growth.* London, 1965.

Bourgois, Philippe. *Ethnicity at Work: Divided Labor on a Central American Banana Plantation.* Baltimore, 1989.

Bourricaud, François, Jorge Bravo Bresani, Henri Favre, and Jean Piel. *La oligarquía en el Perú. 3 essays y una polémica.* 2d ed. Lima, 1971.

————, trans. Paul Stevenson. *Power and Society in Contemporary Peru.* Paris, 1967.

Brading, David A. *Caudillo and Peasant in the Mexican Revolution.* Cambridge, U.K., 1980.

————. *Haciendas and Ranchos in the Mexican Bajío, León, 1700–1860.* Cambridge, U.K., 1978.

————. *Miners and Merchants in Bourbon Mexico, 1763–1810.* Cambridge, U.K., 1971.

Brass, Tom. "Coffee and Rural Proletarianization: A Comment on Bergad." *Journal of Latin American Studies* 16.1 (1984): 143–52.

Brenner, Robert. "The Origins of Capitalist Development: A Critique of Neo-Smithian Marxism." *New Left Review* 104 (1977): 25–93.

Brown, Kendall. *Bourbons and Brandy: Imperial Reform in Eighteenth-Century Arequipa.* Albuquerque, N. Mex., 1986.

————. "Jesuit Wealth and Economic Activity within the Peruvian Economy: The Case of Colonial Southern Peru." *Americas* 44.1 (1987): 23–44.

Brush, Stephen B. "The Myth of the Idle Peasant: Employment in a Subsistence Economy." In *Peasant Livelihood,* ed. R. Halperin and J. Dow. New York, 1977, 60–78.

Burga, Manuel. *De la encomienda a la hacienda capitalista.* Lima, 1976.

————. "La hacienda en el Perú, 1850–1930: evidencias y método." *Tierra y Sociedad: Revista del Archivo del Fuero Agrario* 1.1 (1978): 1–38.

——. *Nacimiento de una utopía: muerte y resurrección de los incas.* Lima, 1988.

Burga, Manuel, and A. Flores Galindo. *Apogeo y crisis de la república aristocrática.* 4th ed. Lima, 1987.

Butler, Judith, and Joan W. Scott. *Feminists Theorize the Political.* New York, 1992.

Byres, T. J., ed. *Sharecropping and Sharecroppers.* London, 1983.

Caballero, José María. *Economía agraria de la sierra peruana antes de la reforma agraria de 1969.* Lima, 1981.

——. "Sharecropping as an Efficient System: Further Answers to an Old Puzzle." In *Sharecropping and Sharecroppers,* ed. T. J. Byres. London, 1983, 107–19.

——. "Sharecropping: A Survey of the Issues." Wolfson College, Centre of Latin American Studies, Cambridge University, Manuscript, 1982.

Cambranes, J. C. *Coffee and Peasants in Guatemala: The Origins of the Modern Plantation Economy in Guatemala, 1853–1897.* Stockholm, 1985.

Camprubí Alcázar, Carlos. *Historia de los bancos en el Perú (1860–1879).* Lima, 1957.

Caravedo Molinari, Baltasar. *Burguesía e industria en el Perú (1933–1945).* Lima, 1976.

Cardoso, Fernando Henrique, and Enzo Faletto. *Dependency and Development in Latin America,* trans. Marjory M. Urquidi. Berkeley, Calif., 1979.

Carter, William E. *Aymara Communities and the Bolivian Agrarian Reform.* Gainesville, Fla., 1964.

Casanova, Juan Norberto. *Ensayo económico-político sobre el porvenir de la industria algodonera fabril del Perú.* Lima, 1849.

Castañón, Emilio. "Esquema de nuestra historia económica en el siglo xix." *El Comercio* (supplement), July 28, 1957.

Castillo Negrón, Mamerto. *Monografía de Pisco.* Lima, 1947.

Castro Pozo, Hildebrando. *El yanaconaje en las haciendas piuranas.* Lima, 1947.

Cayo Córdoba, Percy, et al. *En torno a la Guerra del Pacífico.* Lima, 1983.

Celestino, Olinda. *Migración y cambio structural: la comunidad de Lampián.* Lima, 1972.

Centurión Vallejo, Héctor. *Esclavitud y manumisión en Trujillo.* Trujillo, Peru, 1954.

Chacón, Ramón. "John Kenneth Turner, *Barbarous Mexico,* and the Debate about Debt Peonage in Yucatán during the Porfiriato." *Peasant Studies* 13.2 (1986): 97–119.

Chang-Rodríguez, Eugenio. "Chinese Labor Migration into Latin America in the Nineteenth Century." *Revista de Historia de América* 46 (1958): 357–97.

——. "El indigenismo peruano y Mariátegui." *Revista Iberoamericana* 50.127 (April–June 1984): 367–93.

——. *La literatura política de González Prada.* Mexico, 1957.

Chaplin, David. *The Peruvian Industrial Labor Force.* Princeton, N.J., 1967.

Chatterjee, Partha. "More on Modes of Power and the Peasantry." *Subaltern Studies: Writings on South Asian History and Society* 3 (1983): 311–49.

Chavarría, Jesús. "La desaparición del Perú colonial (1870–1919)." *Aportes* (Paris) 23 (1972): 120–53.

———. *José Carlos Mariátegui and the Rise of Modern Peru, 1890–1930.* Albuquerque, N. Mex., 1979.

Chávez Orozco, Luis. *Agricultura e industria textil de Veracruz: siglo xix.* Xalapa, Mexico, 1965.

Chayanov, A. V. *The Theory of Peasant Economy.* Trans. and ed. D. Thorner, B. Kerblay, and R.E.F. Smith. Homewood, Ill., 1966.

Cheng, Lucie, and Edna Bonacich, eds. *Labor Immigration under Capitalism: Asian Workers in the United States before World War II.* Berkeley, Calif., 1984.

Cheung, Steven N. S. *The Theory of Share Tenancy.* Chicago, 1969.

Chevalier, François. *Land and Society in Colonial Mexico.* Trans. Alvin Eustis. Berkeley, Calif., 1970.

———. "Témoignages littéraires et disparités de croissance: l'expansion de la grande propriété dans le Haut-Pérou aux XXe siècle." *Annales: Economies, Sociétés, Civilisations* 21.4 (1966): 815–31.

Chevalier, J. M. *Civilization and the Stolen Gift: Capital, Kin, and Cult in Eastern Peru.* Toronto, 1982.

———. "There is Nothing Simple about Simple Commodity Production." *Journal of Peasant Studies* 10.4 (1983): 153–86.

Clendinnen, Inga. *Ambivalent Conquests: Maya and Spaniard in Yucatán, 1517–1570.* Cambridge, England, 1987.

Coatsworth, John H. "Patterns of Rural Rebellion in Latin America: Mexico in Comparative Perspective." In *Riot, Rebellion, and Revolution: Rural Social Conflict in Mexico.* Princeton, 1988, 21–64.

Colburn, Forrest D., ed. *Everyday Forms of Peasant Resistance.* Armonk, N.Y., and London, 1989.

Coleman, Kenneth, ed. "How to Run a Middle Georgia Plantation in 1885: A Document." *Agricultural History* 42.1 (1968): 55–60.

Collier, Ruth Berins, and David Collier. *Shaping the Political Arena: Critical Junctures, the Labor Movement, and Regime Dynamics in Latin America.* Princeton, 1991.

Collin Delavaud, Claude. *Les régions côtières du Pérou septentrional: occupation du sol, aménagement régional.* Lima, 1968.

El Comercio (Lima), 1839–1879, 1884–1915.

Como se produce el algodón en el Perú: la pequeña agricultura y el algodón. Lima, 1936.

Conrad, Robert. "The Planter Class and the Debate on Chinese Immigration to Brazil, 1850–1953." *International Migration Review* 9.1 (1975): 41–55.

Contreras, Carlos. *Mineros y campesinos en las Andes.* Lima, 1992.

Copello, Juan, and Luis Petriconi. *Estudio sobre la independencia económica del Perú (1876).* Lima, 1877. Reprint 1971.

Córdova y Urrutia, José María. *Estadística histórica, geográfica, industrial y comercial de los pueblos que componen las provincias del departamento de Lima.* Lima, 1839.

Correa Elías, Alejandro. *Resultado de la selección del algodón tangüis en el valle de Cañete.* Lima, 1936.

Costa Villavicencio, Lázaro. *Monografía del departamento de Ica.* Lima, 1954.

Cortes Conde, Roberto, and Stanley J. Stein, eds. *Latin America: A Guide to Economic History 1830–1930.* Berkeley, Calif., 1977.

Cotler, Julio. *Clases, estado y nación en el Perú.* Lima, 1978.

——. "The Mechanics of Internal Domination and Social Change in Peru." In *Peruvian Nationalism: A Corporatist Revolution,* ed. David Chaplin. New Brunswick, N.J., 1976, 35–71.

Courtenay, Philip P. *Plantation Agriculture.* New York, 1965.

Couturier, Edith. "The Hacienda of Hueyapan: The History of a Mexican Social and Economic Institution, 1550–1940." Ph.D. dissertation, Columbia University, 1965.

Craig, Jr., Wesley W. "Peru: The Peasant Movement of La Convención." In *Latin American Peasant Movements,* ed. H. A. Landsberger. Ithaca, N.Y., 1969, 274–96.

Cross, Harry E. "Living Standards in Rural Nineteenth-Century Mexico: Zacatecas, 1820–1880." *Journal of Latin American Studies* 10.1 (1978): 1–19.

Cuche, Denys. *Poder blanco y resistencia negra en el Parú.* Lima, 1975.

Curtin, Philip D. *The Rise and Fall of the Plantation Complex: Essays in Atlantic History.* Cambridge, 1990.

Cushner, Nicholas P. *Farm and Factory: The Jesuits and the Development of Agrarian Capitalism in Colonial Quito, 1600–1767.* Albany, N.Y., 1982.

——. *Lords of the Land: Sugar, Wine and Jesuit Estates of Coastal Peru, 1600–1767.* Albany, N.Y., 1980.

Dalton, George. "How Exactly Are Peasants Exploited?" *American Anthropologist* 76.3 (1974): 553–61.

——. "Peasantries in Anthropology and History." *Current Anthropology* 13.3–4 (1972): 385–414.

da Matta, Roberto. *Carnivals, Rogues, and Heroes: An Interpretation of the Brazilian Dilemma,* trans. John Drury. Notre Dame, Ind., 1991.

Dancuart, Pedro Emilio. *Anales de la hacienda pública del Perú: leyes, decretos, reglamentos y resoluciones, aranceles, presupuestos, cuentas y contratos que constituyen la legislación e historia fiscal de la República.* 24 vols. Lima, 1902–1926.

Davies, E. E. *History of Duncan Fox & Co. Limited by E. E. Davies.* Manuscript, London, n.d.

Davies, Keith A. *Landowners in Colonial Peru.* Austin, Tex., 1984.

Davies, Thomas M. Jr. *Indian Integration in Peru: A Half Century of Experience, 1900–1948.* Lincoln, Neb., 1974.

Deere, Carmen Diana. "Changing Social Relations of Production and Peruvian Peasant Women's Work." *Latin American Perspectives* 4.1–2 (winter and spring 1977): 48–69.

Denegri, Marco Aurelio. *La crisis del enganche.* Lima, 1911.

Derpich Gallo, Wilma. "Estudios históricos sobre los chinos en el Perú." *Apuntes* 13 (1983): 97–101.

Deustua, José. "Comercio de arriería, rutas y caminos en Cerro de Pasco, Perú, 1820–1870: Algunas proposiciones y evidencias." Paper presented at the 46th International Congress of Americanists, Amsterdam, July 1988.

———. *La minería peruana y la iniciación de la república, 1820–1840.* Lima, 1986.

———. "Mining Markets, Peasants and Power in Nineteenth-Century Peru." *Latin American Research Review* 29.1 (1994): 29–54.

Deustua, José, and José Luis Rénique. *Intelectuales, indigenismo y descentralismo en el Perú, 1897–1931.* Cuzco, 1984.

Dew, Edward. *Politics in the Altiplano: The Dynamics of Change in Rural Peru.* Austin, 1969.

Dore, Elizabeth. *The Peruvian Mining Industry: Growth, Stagnation, and Crisis.* Boulder, Colo., 1988.

Duggett, Michael. "Marx on Peasants." *Journal of Peasant Studies* 2.2 (1975): 159–82.

Duncan, Kenneth, and Ian Rutledge, eds., with Colin Harding. *Land and Labour in Latin America.* Cambridge, U.K., 1977.

Dunn, W. E. *Peru: A Commercial and Industrial Handbook.* United States Department of Commerce, Trade Promotion Series, No. 25. Washington, D.C., 1927.

Durrenberger, E. Paul. "Chayanov and Marx." *Peasant Studies* 9.2 (1982): 119–29.

Durrenberger, E., and T. Tanenbaum. "A Reassessment of Chayanov and His Recent Critics." *Peasant Studies* 8.1 (1981): 48–63.

Duval, Alfredo. "Memoria sobre el cultivo del algodón en el Perú, presentada a la Sociedad Algodonera de Manchester." *La Revista de Lima* 3 (1861): 425–34; 4 (1861): 91–94, 129–36.

Eisenberg, Peter. *The Sugar Industry in Pernambuco.* Berkeley, Calif., 1974.

Eley, Geoff. "Nations, Publics, and Political Cultures: Placing Habermas in the Nineteenth Century." In *Culture/Power/History: A Reader in Contemporary Social Theory,* ed. Nicholas B. Dirks, Geoff Eley, and Sherry B. Ortner. Princeton, N.J., 1994, 297–335.

Engelsen, Juan R. "Social Aspects of Agricultural Expansion in Coastal Peru, 1825–1878." Ph.D. dissertation, University of California, Los Angeles, 1977.

Erasmus, Charles J. "Land Reform and Social Revolution in Southern Bolivia: The Valleys of Chuquisaca and Tarija." In *Land Reform and Social Revolu-*

tion in Bolivia, ed. Dwight B. Heath, Charles J. Erasmus, and Hans C. Buech-
ler, New York, 1969, 63–165.

Espinoza, C. "Los barones del algodón en Piura." In *El problema agrario en el
valle de Chira (Piura),* ed. B. Ramírez. Lima, 1982, 1–61.

Fariss, Nancy M. *Maya Society under Colonial Rule: The Collective Enterprise
of Survival.* Princeton, N.J., 1984.

Farmer, C. *El cultivo del algodón.* Paris, 1904.

Faron, Louis. "The Formation of Two Indigenous Communities in Coastal
Peru." *American Anthropologist* 62.3 (1960): 437–53.

——. "A History of Agricultural Production and Local Organization in the
Chancay Valley, Peru." In *Contemporary Change in Traditional Societies of
Mexico and Peru,* ed. Charles J. Erasmus, S. Miller, and Louis C. Faron.

Favre, Henri. "The Dynamics of Indian Peasant Society and Migration to
Coastal Plantations in Central Peru." In *Land and Labour in Latin America,*
ed. Kenneth Duncan and Ian Rutledge, with Colin Harding, Cambridge, U.K.
253–68.

Feder, Ernst. *The Rape of the Peasantry: Latin America's Landholding System.*
New York, 1971.

Fegan, Brian. "Tenants' Non-Violent Resistance to Landowner Claims in Central Luzon." *Journal of Peasant Studies* 13.2 (1986): 87–106.

Fernández Montagne, Ernesto and Germán Granda Alva. *Apuntes socioeco-
nómicos de la inmigración china en el Perú (1848–1874).* Thesis, Universidad
del Pacífico, Lima, 1977.

Ferrero, Rómulo. *El algodón Tangüis y su origen.* Lima, 1935.

Figueroa, Alberto. *Capitalist Development and the Peasant Economy in Peru.*
Cambridge, U.K., 1984.

Fioravanti, Eduardo. *Latifundio y sindicalismo agrario en el Perú.* Lima, 1974.

Firth, Raymond, and B. Young, eds. *Capital, Savings and Credit in Peasant
Societies.* Chicago, 1964.

Florescano, Enrique, ed. *Haciendas, latifundios y plantaciones en América Latina.* Mexico, 1975.

Flores Galindo, Albert. *Arequipa y el sur andino (siglos XVIII–XX).* Lima, 1977.

——. *Buscando un inca: identidad y utopía en los Andes.* Lima, 1987.

——. *Los mineros de la Cerro de Pasco 1900–1930.* Lima, 1974.

——. "Los rostros de la plebe." *Revista Andina* 1.2 (1983): 315–52.

——. *Tiempo de plagas.* Lima, 1988.

Franco, Carlos. "Mariátegui-Haya: surgimiento de la izquierda nacional," *Socialismo y Participación* 8 (1979): 22–44.

Frank, Andre Gunder. *Capitalism and Underdevelopment in Latin America:
Historical Studies of Chile and Brazil.* New York, 1967.

Fried, Morton, ed. *Colloquium on the Overseas Chinese.* New York, 1958.

Fuentes, Manuel Atanasio. *Estadística general de Lima.* Lima, 1858.

Galenson, David. "The Rise and Fall of Indentured Servitude in the Americas:
An Economic Analysis." *Journal of Economic History* 44.1 (1984): 1–26.

G. de Secada, C. Alexander. "Arms, Guano, and Shipping: The W. R. Grace Interests in Peru, 1865–1885." *Business History Review* 59 (1985): 597–621.

García Calderón, Francisco. *Diccionario de la legislación peruana.* 2 vols., Paris, 1879.

García y García, Aurelio. *Derrotero de la costa del Perú.* 2d ed. Lima, 1870.

Garland, Alejandro. *Peru in 1906, with a Brief Historical and Geographical Sketch.* Lima, 1907.

Geertz, Clifford. *Agricultural Involution: The Processes of Ecological Change in Indonesia.* Berkeley, Calif., 1971.

———. *The Interpretation of Cultures.* New York, 1973.

Genovese, Eugene D. *The Political Economy of Slavery.* New York, 1967.

———. *Roll, Jordan, Roll: The World the Slaves Made.* New York, 1976.

———. *The World the Slaveholders Made: Two Essays in Interpretation.* New York, 1969.

Gibson, Charles. *The Aztecs under Spanish Rule: A History of the Indians of the Valley of Mexico, 1519–1810.* Stanford, Calif., 1964.

Gilbert, Dennis. "Cognatic Descent Groups in Upper-Class Lima (Peru)." *American Ethnologist* 8.4 (1971): 739–57.

———. *La oligarquiá peruana: historia de tres familias.* Trans. Mariana Mould de Pease. Lima, 1982

Ginzburg, Carlo. *The Cheese and the Worms: The Cosmos of a Sixteenth-Century Miller.* Trans. John and Anne Tedeschi. Baltimore, Md., 1980.

Girao Fajardo de Marín, T. E. Luz. *Monografía del distrito de Ica.* Thesis, Instituto Nacional de Perfeccionamiento y Capacitación Magisterial, Lima, 1965.

Godelier, Maurice. *Rationality and Irrationality in Economics.* Trans. Brian Pearce. New York, 1972.

Golte, Jürgen. *La racionalidad de la organización andina.* 2d ed. Lima, 1987.

Gómez Cumpa, José, and Inés Bazán Alfaro. *Capitalismo y región en Lambayeque, 1870–1930.* Chiclayo, Peru, 1981.

Góngora, Mario. *Origen de los inquilinos de Chile central.* 2d ed. Santiago, 1974.

Gonzales, Michael J. "Capitalist Agriculture and Labor Contracting in Northern Peru, 1880–1905." *Journal of Latin American Studies* 12 (1980): 291–315.

———. "Chinese Plantation Workers and Social Conflict in Peru in the Late Nineteenth Century." *Journal of Latin American Studies* 21 (1989): 385–424.

———. *Plantation Agriculture and Social Control in Northern Peru, 1875–1933.* Austin, Tex., 1985.

———. "Planter Control and Worker Resistance in Northern Peru, 1880–1921." In *Plantation Workers: Resistance and Accommodation,* ed. Brij V. Lal, Doug Munro, and Edward D. Beechart, Honolulu, 1993, 297–316.

——. "Planters and Politics in Peru, 1885–1919." *Journal of Latin American Studies* 23 (1991): 515–42.

——. "The Rise of Cotton Tenant Farming in Peru, 1890–1920: The Condor Valley." *Agricultural History* 65.1 (1991): 51–71.

Goodsell, Charles F. *American Corporations and Peruvian Politics*. Cambridge, Mass., 1974.

Gootenberg, Paul. *Between Silver and Guano: Commercial Policy and the State in Postindependence Peru*. Princeton, N.J., 1989.

——. "Carneros y *Chuño*: Price Levels in Nineteenth-Century Peru." *Hispanic American Historical Review* 70.1 (1990): 1–56.

——. *Imagining Development: Economic Ideas in Peru's "Fictitious Prosperity" of Guano, 1840–1880*. Berkeley, Calif., 1993.

——. "The Social Origins of Protectionism and Free Trade in Nineteenth-Century Lima." *Journal of Latin American Studies* 14 (1982): 329–58.

——. *Tejidos y harinas, corazones y mentes: el imperialismo norteamericano del libre comercio en el Perú 1825–1840*. Lima, 1989.

Gorman, Stephen. "The State, Elite, and Export in Nineteenth-Century Peru: Toward an Alternative Reinterpretation of Political Change." *Journal of Inter-American Studies and World Affairs* 21 (1979): 395–419.

Gould, Jeffrey L. *To Lead as Equals: Rural Protest and Political Consciousness in Chinandega, Nicaragua, 1912–1979*. Chapel Hill, N.C., 1990.

Graham, Richard. *Patronage and Politics in Nineteenth-Century Brazil*. Stanford, Calif., 1990.

Gramsci, Antonio. "Notes on Italian History." In *Selections from the Prison Notebooks of Antonio Gramsci*, ed. and trans. Quintin Hoare and G. N. Smith. New York, 1971, 44–122.

Grieshaber, Erwin P. "Hacienda-Community Relations and Indian Acculturation: An Historiographical Essay." *Latin American Research Review* 14.2 (1979): 107–128.

Griffin, Keith. *Underdevelopment in Spanish America*. London, 1969.

Gudeman, Stephen. *The Demise of a Rural Economy: From Subsistence to Capitalism in a Latin American Village*. London, 1978.

——. *Economics as Culture: Models and Metaphors of Livelihood*. London, 1986.

Guha, Ranajit. "Dominance without Hegemony and Its Historiography." *Subaltern Studies: Writings on South Asian History and Society* 6 (1989): 210–309.

——. "The Prose of Counter-Insurgency." In Nicholas B. Dirks, Geoff Eley, and Sherry B. Ortner, eds. *Culture/Power/History: A Reader in Contemporary Social Theory*, ed. Nicholas B. Dirks, Geoff Eley, and Sherry B. Ortner, Princeton, N.J., 1994, 336–71.

Guillet, David. *Agrarian Reform and Peasant Economy in Southern Peru*. Columbia, Mo., 1979.

Haitin, Marcel. "Prices, the Lima Market and the Agricultural Crisis of the Late

Eighteenth Century in Peru." *Journal of Latin American Studies* 22 (1985): 167–98.

Halperín-Donghi, Tulio. "Dependency Theory and Latin American Historiography." *Latin American Research Review* 17 (1982): 115–50.

Hammel, E. A. *Power in Ica: The Structural History of a Peruvian Community.* Boston, 1969.

Hanagan, Michael, and Charles Stephenson, eds. *Proletarians and Protest: The Roots of Class Formation in an Industrializing World.* New York: Greenwood, 1986.

Handelman, Howard. *Struggle in the Andes: Peasant Political Mobilization in Peru.* Austin, Tex., 1975.

Harding, Colin. "Land Reform and Social Conflict in Peru." In *The Peruvian Experiment: Continuity and Change under Military Rule,* ed. Abraham Lowenthal. Princeton, N.J., 1975, 220–53.

Harris, Charles, III. *A Mexican Family Empire: The Latifundios of the Sánchez Navarros, 1765–1867.* Austin, Tex., 1975.

Hart, John M. *Revolutionary Mexico: the Coming and Process of the Mexican Revolution.* Berkeley, Calif., 1987.

Hatch, John K. "The Corn Farmers of Motupe: A Study of Traditional Farming Practices in Northern Coastal Peru." Ph.D. dissertation, University of Wisconsin, Madison, Wis., 1974.

Heilbroner, Robert. *The Act of Work.* Washington, D.C., 1985.

Helly, Denise. *Idéologie et ethnicité: les chinois Macao à Cuba.* Montreal, 1979.

Herbold, Carl F. Jr. "Developments in the Peruvian Administrative System, 1919–1939: Modern and Traditional Qualities of Government under Authoritarian Regimes." Ph. D. Dissertation, University of California at Los Angeles, 1973.

Herring, Ronald J. "Share Tenancy and Economic Efficiency: The South Asian Case." *Peasant Studies* 7.4 (1978): 225–49.

Hirschman, Albert O. *Exit, Voice and Loyalty.* Cambridge, Mass., 1970.

———. *Journeys toward Progress.* New York, 1968 Reprint.

La historia económica en América Latina. 2 vols. Mexico City, 1972.

Hobsbawm, Eric J. *The Age of Capital 1848–1875.* New York, 1975.

———. "A Case of Neo-feudalism: La Convención, Peru." *Journal of Latin American Studies* 1 (1969): 31–50.

———. *Labouring Men: Studies in the History of Labour.* New York, 1964.

———. "Peasant Land Occupations." *Past and Present* 62 (February 1974): 120–52.

———. "Peasants and Politics." *Journal of Peasant Studies* 1.1 (1973): 3–22.

———. "Peasants and Rural Migrants in Politics." In *The Politics of Conformity in Latin America,* ed. Claudio Véliz. London, 1967, 43–65.

Hobsbawm, Eric J., Witold Kula, Ashok Mitra, K. N. Raj, and Ignacy Sachs, eds. *Peasants in History: Essays in Honour of Daniel Thorner.* Calcutta, 1980.

Hollis, Martin, and Edward J. Nell. *Rational Economic Man: A Philosophical Critique of Neo-Classical Economics.* London, 1975.

Horton, Douglas E. *Hacienda and Cooperatives: A Preliminary Study of Latifundist Agriculture and Agrarian Reform in Northern Peru.* University of Wisconsin, Land Tenure Research Paper No. 53, Madison, 1973.

Hu-Dehart, Evelyn. "The Chinese of Baja California Norte, 1910–1934." *Proceedings of the Pacific Coast Council of Latin American Studies.* Vol. 12 (1985–86), 9–29.

——. "Chinese Coolie Labor in Cuba and Peru in the Nineteenth Century: Free Labor or Neoslavery?" Manuscript, Boulder, Colo., n.d.

——. "Coolies, Shopkeepers, Pioneers: The Chinese of Mexico and Peru (1849–1930)." *Amerasia* 15.2 (1989): 91–116.

——. "Immigrants to a Developing Society: The Chinese in Northern Mexico, 1875–1932." *Journal of Arizona History* 21.3 (1980): 275–312.

Huizer, Gerrit. *The Revolutionary Potential of Peasants in Latin America.* Lexington, Mass., 1972.

Hünefeldt, Christine. "Jornales y esclavitud: Lima en la primera mitad del siglo XIX." *Economía* 10.19 (1987): 35–57.

——. *Lucha por la tierra y protesta indígena.* Bonn, 1982.

——. *Paying the Price of Freedom: Family and Labor among Lima's Slaves, 1800–1854.* Berkeley, Calif., 1994.

Hunt, Lynn, ed. *The New Cultural History.* Berkeley, Calif., 1989.

Hunt, Shane J. "La economía de las haciendas y plantaciones de América Latina." *Historia y Cultura* 9 (1975): 7–66.

——. "Evolución de los salarios reales en el Perú: 1900–1940." *Economía* 3.5 (1980): 83–124.

——. "Guano y crecimiento en el Perú del siglo XIX." *HISLA* 4 (1974): 35–92.

——. "Price and Quantum Estimates of Peruvian Exports, 1830–1962." Research Program in Economic Development, Discussion Paper No. 33, Princeton, N.J., 1973.

Husson, Patrick. "Changement social et insurrection indiennes: la 'révolte du sel' à Huanta, Pérou, en 1896." *Cahiers des Amériques Latines* 23.1 (1981): 102–49.

Hyams, Edward. *Soil and Civilization.* New York, 1976.

Iñigo Carera, Nicolás. "Génesis de un semiproletariado rural: la incorporación de los indígenas a la producción algodonera chaqueña." *Cuadernos de CISCO.* Universidad de Buenos Aires, Serie Estudios 4. Buenos Aires, 1975 (mimeo).

Instituto Geográfico Militar, Peru.

Jacobsen, Nils. "Cycles and Booms in Latin American Export Agriculture: The Example of Southern Peru's Livestock Economy, 1855–1920." *Review* 7.3 (1984): 443–507.

——. "The Development of Peru's Slave Population and Its Significance for Coastal Agriculture, 1792–1854." Manuscript.

————. *Mirages of Transition: The Peruvian Altiplano, 1780–1930.* Berkeley, Calif., 1993.

————. "Taxation in Early Republican Peru, 1821–1851: Policy Making between Reform and Tradition." In *Las economías de los países bolivarianos,* ed. Reinhard Liehr. Berlin, 1989, 311–39.

Jacobsen, Nils, and Hans-Jürgen Puhle, eds. *The Economies of Mexico and Peru during the Late Colonial Period, 1760–1810.* Berlin, 1986.

Jiménez, Michael. "Traveling Far in Grandfather's Car: The Life Cycle of Central Colombia Coffee Estates." *Hispanic American Historical Review* 69.2 (1989): 185–219.

Johnson, Lyman L. "Changing Criminal Patterns in Buenos Aires, 1890–1914." *Journal of Latin American Studies* (1982): 359–80.

Joseph, Gilbert. "Resocializing Latin American Banditry: A Reply." *Latin American Research Review* 26.1 (1990): 161–74.

————. "On the Trail of Latin American Bandits: A Reexamination of Peasant Resistance." *Latin American Research Review* 25.3 (1990): 7–54.

Joseph, Gilbert, and D. Nugent, eds. *Everyday Forms of State Formation: Revolution and the Negotiation of Rule in Modern Mexico.* Durham, N.C., 1995.

Journal of Peasant Studies 13.2 (1986) (issue devoted to the theme of "everyday forms of resistance" by peasants).

Kaerger, Karl. *Condiciones agrarias de la sierra sur peruana (1899).* Trans. Christine Hünefeldt. Lima, 1979.

Kapsoli, Wilfredo. "El campesino rural y la ley vial." *Campesino* 1.2 (1969): 1–17.

————. *Los movimientos campesinos en el Perú, 1879–1965: ensayos.* Lima, 1977.

Karno, Howard L. "Augusto B. Leguía: the Oligarchy and the Modernization of Peru, 1870–1930." Ph.D. Dissertation, University of California at Los Angeles, 1970.

Katz, Friedrich. "Labor Conditions on Haciendas in Porfirian Mexico: Some Trends and Tendencies." *Hispanic American Historical Review* 44.1 (1974): 1–47.

————, ed. *Riot, Rebellion, and Revolution: Rural Social Conflict in Mexico.* Princeton, N.J., 1988.

Keith, Robert G. *Conquest and Agrarian Change: The Emergence of the Hacienda System on the Peruvian Coast.* Cambridge, U.K., 1976.

Keremetsis, Dawn. *La industria textil mexicana.* Mexico City, 1973.

Klaren, Peter F. *Modernization, Dislocation and Aprismo: Origins of the Peruvian Aprista Party, 1870–1932.* Austin, Tex., 1973.

————. "The Origins of Modern Peru." In vol. 5, *The Cambridge History of Latin America: ca. 1870–1930,* Leslie Bethel. Cambridge, U.K., 1989, 587–640.

————. "The Social and Economic Consequences of Modernization in the Peruvian Sugar Industry, 1870–1930." In *Land and Labour in Latin America,* ed. Kenneth Duncan and Ian Rutledge, Cambridge, U.K., 1977, 229–52.

Klaren, Peter F., and Thomas J. Bossert, eds. *Promise of Development: Theories of Change in Latin America.* Boulder, Colo., 1986.

Klein, Herbert S. *Bolivia: The Evolution of a Multi-Ethnic Society.* New York, 1982.

Knight, Alan. "Interview: Latin America in History and Historiography." *History Workshop* 34 (1992): 159–76.

——. "Mexican Peonage: What Was It and Why Was It." *Journal of Latin American Studies* 18.1 (1986): 41–74.

——. *The Mexican Revolution.* 2 vols. Lincoln, Nebr., 1986.

——. "Weapons and Arches in the Mexican Revolutionary Landscape." In *Everyday Forms of State Formation: Revolution and the Negotiation of Rule in Modern Mexico,* ed. G. Joseph and D. Nugent. Durham, N.C., 24–68.

Kubler, George. *The Indian Caste of Peru, 1795–1940: A Population Study Based upon Tax Records and Census Reports.* Washington, D.C., 1952.

Kula, Witold. *An Economic Theory of the Feudal System: Towards a Model of the Polish Economy, 1500–1800.* Trans. Lawrence Garner. London, 1976.

Kwong, Alice Jo. "The Chinese in Peru." In *Colloquium on Overseas Chinese,* ed. Morton Fried. New York, 1958, 41–48.

Laclau, Ernesto. "Feudalism and Capitalism in Latin America." *New Left Review* 67 (May–June 1971): 19–38.

——. *Politics and Ideology in Marxist Theory.* London, 1977.

Ladurie, Emmanuel Le Roy. *Montaillou: The Promised Land of Error.* Trans. Barbara Bray. New York, 1978.

Laite, Julian. "Processes of Industrial and Social Change." In *Peasant Cooperation and Capitalist Expansion in Central Peru.* Austin, 1978, 72–98.

Lal, Brij. V., Doug Munro, and Edward D. Beechert, eds. *Plantation Workers: Resistance and Accommodation.* Honolulu, 1993.

Landsberger, Henry A., ed. *Latin American Peasant Movements.* Ithaca, N.Y., 1969.

——, ed. *Rural Protest: Peasant Movements and Social Change.* London, 1974.

Langer, Erick D. "Andean Banditry and Peasant Community Organization 1882–1930." In *Bandidos: The Varieties of Latin American Banditry,* ed. Richard Slatta. New York, 1987, 113–30.

——. "Debt Peonage and Paternalism in Latin America." *Peasant Studies* 13.2 (1986): 121–27.

——. *Economic Change and Rural Resistance in Southern Bolivia, 1880–1920.* Stanford, Calif., 1989.

——. "Labor Strikes and Reciprocity on Chuquisaca Haciendas." *Hispanic American Historical Review* 65.2 (1985): 255–78.

Lavalle y García, José Antonio. *El guano y la agricultura nacional.* Lima, 1913.

——. *Los carácteres agrolígicos de las tierras cultivadas en la costa del Perú.* Lima, 1918.

Lawrence, Keith O. *Indentured Labor in the British Empire, 1834–1920.* London, 1984.

Lears, T. J. Jackson. "The Concept of Cultural Hegemony: Problems and Possibilities." *American Historical Review* 90.3 (1985): 567–93.

———. "Making Fun of Popular Culture." *American Historical Review*. 97.5 (1992): 1417–26.

Legrand, Catherine. *Frontier Expansion and Peasant Protest in Colombia*. Albuquerque, N. Mex., 1986.

Lehman, David, ed. *Agrarian Reform and Agrarian Reformism: Studies of Peru, Chile, China and India*. London, 1974.

———. "Dos vías de desarrollo capitalista en la agricultura o 'Crítica de la razón chayanoviano-marxizante.'" *Revista Andina* 3.2 (1985): 343–78.

Levin, Jonathan V. *The Export Economies*. Cambridge, Mass., 1960.

Long, Norman. "From Paradigm Lost to Paradigm Regained? The Case for an Actor-Oriented Sociology of Development." In *Battlefields of Knowledge: The Interlocking of Theory and Practice in Social Research and Development*, ed. Norman Long and Ann Long. New York, 1992.

Long, Norman, and Jan Douwe Van de Ploeg. "New Challenges in the Sociology of Rural Development." *Sociologia Ruralis* 38.1 (1988): 30–41.

Long, Norman, and Bryan R. Roberts, eds. *Miners, Peasants and Entrepreneurs: Regional Development in the Central Highlands of Peru*. Cambridge, 1984.

López Aliaga, Fernando. "El algodón en el valle de Cañete." *El Agricultor Peruano*, May 1–July 15, 1909.

Love, Joseph L. "The Origins of Dependency Analysis." *Journal of Latin American Studies* 22.1 (1990): 143–68.

Love, Joseph L., and Nils Jacobsen, eds. *Guiding the Invisible Hand: Economic Liberalism and the State in Latin American History*. New York, 1988.

Loveman, Brian. "Critique of Arnold J. Bauer's 'Rural Workers in Spanish America: Problems of Peonage and Oppression,'" *Hispanic American Historical Review* 59.3 (1979): 478–85.

Ly-Tio-Fane Pineo, Huguette. *La diaspora chinoise dans l'Océan Indien Occidental*. Aix-En-Provence, 1979.

Macera, Pablo. "Algodón y comercio exterior peruano en el siglo XIX. *Trabajos de historia* 3 (1977): 275–96.

———. *Crisis de 1929 y las economías de Chile y el Perú*. Lima, 1974.

———. "El guano en la agricultural peruana de exportación (1919–1945)." *Trabajos de historia* 4, Lima, 1977, 309–499.

———. "Feudalismo colonial americano: el caso de las haciendas peruanas." In *Trabajos de historia* 3, Lima, 139–227.

———. *Palto: hacendados y yanaconas del algodonal peruano (documentos, 1877–1943)*. Lima, 1976.

———. "Las plantaciones azucareras andinas (1821–1875)." In *Trabajos de historia* 4, Lima, 1977, 9–308.

———. "Periodización e Interpretación," in *Latin America. A Guide to Economic History, 1830–1930*, ed. Roberto Cortés Conde and Stanley J. Stein. Berkeley, Calif., 1977.

———. *Trabajos de historia.* 4 vols. Lima, 1977.

MacLeod, Murdo J. *Spanish Central America: A Socioeconomic History, 1520–1720.* Berkeley, Los Angeles, 1973.

Malinouski, Ernesto. *La moneda en el Perú.* Lima, 1859.

Mallon, Florencia E. *The Defense of Community in Peru's Central Highlands.* Princeton, N.J., 1983.

———. "Gender and Class in the Transition to Capitalism: Household and Mode of Production in Central Peru." *Latin American Perspectives* 13.1 (1986): 147–74.

———. *Peasant and Nation: The Making of Postcolonial Mexico and Peru.* Berkeley, Calif., 1995.

———. "The Promise and Dilemma of Subaltern Studies: Perspectives from Latin American History." *American Historical Review* 99.5 (1994): 1491–1515.

Manrique, Nelson. *Campesinado y nación: Las guerrillas indígenas en la guerra con Chile.* Lima, 1981.

Marie, Víctor. *El algodón.* Lima, 1918.

Mariátegui, José Carlos. *Seven Interpretive Essays on Peruvian Reality.* Trans. Marjory Urquidi. Austin, Tex., 1971.

Markham, Clements R. *Peru.* London, 1880.

Martinet, J. B. H. *La agricultura en el Perú.* Lima. Reprint, 1977.

Martínez-Alier, Juan. *Haciendas, Plantations and Collective Farms.* London, 1977.

———. *Los huacchilleros del Perú.* Paris, 1973.

———. "Relations of Production in Andean *Haciendas*: Peru." In *Land and Labour in Latin America,* ed. Kenneth Duncan and Ian Rutledge. Cambridge, England, 1977, 141–64.

———. "Sharecropping: Some Illustrations." In *Sharecropping and Sharecroppers,* ed. T. J. Byres. London, 1983, 94–106.

Mathew, William M. "The First Anglo-Peruvian Debt and Its Settlement, 1822–1849." *Journal of Latin American Studies* 2 (1968): 562–86.

———. *The House of Gibbs and the Peruvian Guano Monopoly.* London, 1981.

Matos Mar, José, comp. *Dominación y cambio en el Perú rural.* Lima, 1969.

———, comp. *Hacienda, comunidad y campesino en el Perú.* 2d ed. Lima, 1976.

———, comp. *La oligarquía en el Perú: 3 ensayos y una polémica.* 2d ed. Lima, 1971.

———. *Yanaconaje y reforma agraria en el Perú: el caso del valle de Chancay.* Lima, 1976.

Matos Mar, José, and Jorge A. Carbajal H. *Erasmo: yanacón del valle de Chancay.* Lima, 1974.

Maude, H. E. *Slavers in Paradise: The Peruvian Slave Trade in Polynesia, 1862–1864.* Stanford, Calif., 1981.

Mayer, Enrique, comp. *La chacra de papa. Economía y ecología.* Lima, 1992.

———. *A Tribute to the Household: Domestic Economy and the Encomienda in Colonial Peru.* Austin, Tex., 1982.

McClintock, Cynthia, and Abraham Lowenthal, eds., *The Peruvian Experiment Reconsidered*. Princeton, N.J., 1983.

McCreery, David. "Coffee and Class: The Structure of Development in Liberal Guatemala." *Hispanic American Historical Review* 56.3 (1976): 438–60.

———. "Debt Servitude in Rural Guatemala, 1876–1936." *Hispanic American Historical Review* 63.4 (1983): 735–59.

———. "Hegemony and Repression in Rural Guatemala, 1871–1940." In *Plantation Workers*, ed. Lal, Munro, and Beechert (Honolulu, 1993, 217–40).

McMicken, K. B. *Memoria sobre el cultivo del algodón en el valle de Cañete*. Lima, 1929.

Meagher, Arnold J. "The Introduction of Chinese Laborers to Latin America: The 'Coolie Trade,' 1847–1874." Ph.D. dissertation, University of California, Davis, 1974.

Meek, Ronald L. *Studies in the Labor Theory of Value*. 2d ed. New York, 1956.

Meillassoux, Claude. "The Social Organization of the Peasantry: The Economic Basis of Kinship." *Journal of Peasant Studies* 1.1 (1973): 81–90.

Méndez, Cecilia. "La otra historia del guano: Perú 1840–1870." *Revista Andina* 5.1 (1987): 7–46.

Menzel, Dorothy. *Pottery Style and Society in Ancient Peru: Art as a Mirror of History in the Ica Valley, 1350–1570*. Berkeley, Calif., 1976.

Meyer, Michael C. *Water in the Hispanic Southwest: a Social and Legal History, 1500–1850*. Tucson, Ariz., 1984.

Middendorf, Ernst W. *Perú: observaciones y estudios del país y sus habitantes durante una permanencia de 25 años*. Trans. Ernesto More. 2 vols. Lima, 1973–1974.

Migdal, Joel S. *Peasants, Politics and Revolutions: Pressures Toward Political and Social Change in the Third World*. Princeton, N.J., 1974.

Miller, Rory. "The Coastal Elite and Peruvian Politics, 1895–1919. *Journal of Latin American Studies* 14.1 (1982): 97–120.

———. "The Grace Contract, the Peruvian Corporation, and Peruvian History." *Ibero-Amerikanische Archiv* 9.3/4 (1983): 319–48.

———. "The Making of the Grace Contract: British Bondholders and the Peruvian Government, 1885–1890." *Journal of Latin American Studies* 8 (1976): 73–100.

———, ed. *Region and Class in Modern Peruvian History*. Liverpool, 1987.

Miller, Simon. "The Mexican Hacienda between the Insurgency and the Revolution: Maize Production and Commercial Triumph on the *Temporal*." *Journal of Latin American Studies* 16 (1984): 309–36.

Miller, Solomon. "Hacienda to Plantation in Northern Peru: The Processes of Proletarianization of a Tenant Farmer Society." In *Contemporary Change in Traditional Societies of Mexico and Peru*, ed. Solomon Miller, Charles J. Erasmus, and Louis C. Faron, Urbana, Ill., 1967. Reprint 1978, 133–226.

Mintz, Sidney W. "Epilogue: The Divided Aftermaths of Freedom." In *Between Slavery and Free Labor: The Spanish-Speaking Caribbean in the Nineteenth*

Century, ed. M. Moreno Fraginals, Frank Moya Pons, and Stanley L. Engerman. Baltimore, 1985, 270–78.

——. *From Plantations to Peasantries in the Caribbean.* Washington, D.C., 1984.

——. "A Note on the Definition of Peasantries." *Journal of Peasant Studies* 1.1 (1973): 91–106.

——. "The Rural Proletariat and the Problem of Rural Proletarian Consciousness." *Journal of Peasant Studies* 1.3 (1974): 291–325.

——. *Sweetness and Power: The Place of Sugar in Modern History.* New York, 1985.

Mintz, Sidney, and E. R. Wolf. "Haciendas and Plantations in Middle America and the Antilles." *Social and Economic Studies* 6.3 (1957): 380–412.

Mires, Fernando. "Los indios y la tierra, o como concibió Mariátegui la revolución en el Perú." *Ibero-America: Nordic Journal of Latin American Studies* 8.2/9.1–2 (1980): 68–99.

Moore, Barrington, Jr. *Injustice: The Social Bases of Obedience and Revolt.* White Plains, N.Y., 1978.

——. *Political Power and Social Theory: Six Studies.* Cambridge, 1958.

——. *Social Origins of Dictatorship and Democracy; lord and peasant in the making of the modern world.* Boston, 1966.

Moore, Sally F. "Epilogue: Uncertainties in Situations, Indeterminacies in Culture." In *Symbol and Politics in Communal Ideology: Cases and Questions,* ed. Sally Falk Moore and Barbara G. Meyerhoff. Ithaca, N.Y., 1975.

Moreno Fraginals, Manuel. *The Sugar Mill. The Socio-economic Complex of Sugar in Cuba, 1760–1860.* New York, 1976.

Moreno Fraginals, Manuel, Frank Moya Pons, and Stanley L. Engerman, eds. *Between Slavery and Free Labor: The Spanish-Speaking Caribbean in the Nineteenth Century.* Baltimore, Md., 1985.

Moreyra y Paz Soldán, Carlos. *Bibliografía regional peruana (colección particular).* Lima, 1967.

Mörner, Magnus. *Adventurers and Proletarians.* Pittsburgh, Pa., 1985.

——. *The Andean Past: Land, Societies, and Conflicts.* New York, 1985.

——. "A Comparative Study of Tenant Labor in Parts of Europe, Africa and Latin America, 1700–1900." *Latin American Research Review* 5.2 (1970): 3–15.

——. "Latin American 'Landlords' and 'Peasants' and the Outer World during the National Period." In *Land and Labour in Latin America,* ed. Kenneth Duncan and Ian Rutledge, with Colin Harding. Cambridge, England, 1977, 455–82.

——. "Slavery and Race in the Evolution of Latin American Societies: Some Recent Contributions to the Debate." *Journal of Latin American Studies* 8.1 (1976): 127–35.

——. The Spanish American Hacienda: A Survey of Recent Research and Debate." *Hispanic American Historical Review* 53.2 (1973): 183–216.

———. *Tenant Labor in Andean South America since the Eighteenth Century: A Preliminary Report.* Moscow, 1970.

Morse, Richard M. "Joaquín Capelo: A Lima Archetype." *Journal of Contemporary History* 4.3 (1969): 95–110.

———, ed. *Lima en 1900: estudio crítico y antología.* Lima, 1973.

Mouffe, Chantal. "Hegemony and Ideology in Gramsci." In *Gramsci and Marxist Theory,* ed. Mouffe, Chantal. London, 1979, 168–204.

Munro, John M. *Cotton.* 2d ed. New York, 1987.

Normano, João F. *The Japanese in South America: An Introductory Survey with Special Reference to Peru.* New York, 1943.

Norris, Glen Lang. "Tradition and Transformation in the Industrialization of an Ecuadorian Sugar Plantation." Ph.D. dissertation, University of Illinois, 1969.

Núñez, Estuardo. *Relaciones de viajeros.* Lima, 1971.

O'Brien, Jay, and William Roseberry, eds. *Golden Ages, Dark Ages: Imagining the Past in Anthropology and History.* Berkeley, Calif., 1991.

O'Brien, Thomas F. "Chilean Elites and Foreign Investors: Chilean Nitrate Policy, 1880–1882." *Journal of Latin American Studies* 11.1 (1979): 101–20.

Odriozola, Manuel de. *Colección de documentos literarios del Perú.* 11 vols. Lima, 1863–1877.

O'Phelan Godoy, Scarlett. *Rebellions and Revolts in Eighteenth-Century Peru and Upper Peru.* Cologne, 1985.

Oré, Teresa, ed., with Nelly Plaza, René Antezana, and Jaime Luna. *Memorias de un luchador campesino: Juan H. Pévez.* Lima, 1983.

Orlove, Benjamin. "Against a Definition of Peasantries: Agricultural Production in Andean Peru. "In *Peasant Livelihood: Studies in Economic Anthropology and Cultural Ecology,* ed. Rhoda Halperin and James Dow. New York, 1977, 22–35.

———. "The Position of Rustlers in Regional Society: Social Banditry in the Andes." In *Land and Power in Latin America,* ed. B. Orlove and G. Custred. New York, 1980, 179–94.

Orlove, Benjamin, and Glynn Custred. "Agrarian Economies and Social Processes in Comparative Perspective: The Agricultural Production Unit." In *Land and Power in Latin America,* ed. B. Orlove and G. Custred. New York, 1980, 13–30.

———, eds. *Land and Power in Latin America.* New York, 1980.

Ortner, Sherry B. "Resistance and the Problem of Ethnographic Refusal." *Comparative Studies in Society and History* 37.1 (1995): 173–93.

———. "Theory in Anthropology since the Sixties." In *Culture/Power/History. A Reader in Contemporary Social Theory,* ed. Nicholas B. Dirks, Geoff Eley, and Sherry B. Ortner. Princeton, N.J., 1994, 372–411.

Oviedo, Juan de. *Colección de leyes, decretos y órdenes publicados en el Perú desde el año 1821 hasta 31 de diciembre de 1859.* 16 vols. Lima, 1861–72.

Pachas Castilla, Rolando. "Impacto de la Guerra del Pacífico en las haciendas de

Ica, Chincha, Pisco y Cañete." In Wilson Reátegui, *La Guerra del Pacífica*, 2 vols., ed. Wilson Reátegui. Lima, 1979, 1984.

———. "Impacto de la Guerra del Pacífico en el Sur Medio: 1860–1900." In *La Guerra del Pacífico* 2, ed. Wilson Reátegui Chávez. Lima, 1984, 140–95.

Paige, Jeffrey M. *Agrarian Revolution: Social Movements and Export Agriculture in the Underdeveloped World*. New York, 1975.

Palmer, David Scott. *Peru: The Authoritarian Tradition*. New York, 1980.

Pan, Lynn. *Sons of the Yellow Emperor: A History of the Chinese Diaspora*. (Boston, 1990).

Parel, Anthony, and Thomas Flanagan. *Theories of Property*. Waterloo, Canada, 1979.

Parodi Medina, Rafael. *Monografía histórica de Palpa*. Huancayo, Peru, 1947.

Patrón, Enrique. *Leyes, decretos, resoluciones, reglamentos y circulares vigentes en el ramo de justicia*. Lima, 1901.

Paz Soldán, Carlos Enrique. "El vicio amarillo en Lima." *La Crónica* (Lima), April 23, 1916: 13.

Paz Soldán, Pedro. "Memoria sobre la esclavitura en el Perú." In Ricardo Aranda, *Constitución del Perú de 1860 con sus reformas hasta 1893; leyes orgánicas, decretos, reglamentos y resoluciones referentes a ellas, coleccionadas y anotadas por Ricardo Aranda*. Lima, 1893.

Pearse, Andrew. *The Latin American Peasant*. London, 1975.

Peloso, Vincent C. "Cotton Planters, the State, and Rural Labor Policy: Ideological Origins of the Peruvian *República Aristocrática*," *The Americas: A Quarterly Review of Inter-American Cultural History* 40.2 (1983): 209–28.

———. "Development Theory and Recent Peasant Politics in Latin America." *Peasant Studies* 5.4 (October 1976): 25–30.

———. "Forms of Rural Social Change in Twentieth Century Peru." *Peasant Studies* 4.2 (April 1975): 21–25.

———. "Juan Esquivel: Cotton Plantation Tenant." *The Human Tradition in Latin America: The Twentieth Century*, ed. William H. Beezley and Judith Ewell. Wilmington, Del., 1987, 59–73.

———. "Succulence and Sustenance: Regional Class and Diet in Nineteenth-Century Peru." In *Food, Politics, and Society in Latin America*, ed. John Super and Thomas C. Wright. Lincoln, Nebr., 1985, 46–64.

———. "Transformación de la sociedad campesina, articulación y subdesarrollo en las haciendas algodoneras peruanas: el valle de Pisco, 1883–1925." *Allpanchis* 18.21 (1983): 175–94.

Peloso, Vincent C., and Barbara A. Tenenbaum, eds. *Liberals, Politics, and Power: State Formation in Nineteenth-Century Latin America*. Athens, Ga., 1996.

Pérez, Louis A., Jr. *Lords of the Mountain: Social Banditry and Peasant Protest in Cuba, 1878–1918*. Pittsburgh, Pa., 1989.

———. "Vagrants, Beggars, and Bandits: The Social Origins of Cuban Separatism, 1878–1895." *American Historical Review* 90 (1985): 1092–1121.

Perú. *Censo general de la república del Perú, 1876.* 7 vols. Lima, 1878.

El Peruano. Lima, 1863, 1870.

Piel, Jean. *Capitalisme agraire au Pérou: l'essor du neo-latifundisme dans le Pérou républicain.* Pari, 1983.

———. *Crise agraire et conscience creole au Pérou.* Paris, 1982.

———. "L'importation de main d'oeuvre chinoise et la developpement agricole au pérou au XIXe siècle," *Cahiers d'Amériques Latines* 9/10 (1974): 87–103.

———. "The Place of the Peasantry in the National Life of Peru in the Nineteenth Century." *Past and Present* 46 (1970): 108–33.

Pike, Frederick B. *The Modern History of Peru.* New York, 1967.

———. *The United States and the Andean Republics: Peru, Bolivia, and Ecuador.* Cambridge, Mass., 1977.

Pinto, Horacio. *Estadísticas históricas del Perú. Sector agrícola: algodón.* Lima, 1977.

Platt, D. C. M. *Latin America and British Trade, 1806–1914.* New York, 1973.

Platt, Tristan. "Conciencia andina y conciencia proletaria: Qhuyaruna y allyu en el norte de Potosí." *HISLA: Revista latinoamericana de historia económica y social* 2 (1983): 47–73.

———. "Liberalism and Ethnocide in the Southern Andes." *History Workshop* 17 (1984): 3–18.

Popkin, Samuel. *The Rational Peasant: The Political Economy of Rural Society in Vietnam.* Berkeley, Calif., 1979.

Prakash, Gyan. *Bonded Histories.* Cambridge, U.K., 1989.

Puente, José de la. *Diccionario de la legislacion de aguas y agricultura del Perú, con inserción de muchos datos y noticias históricas* (Lima, 1885).

Quijano, Aníbal. "Contemporary Peasant Movements." In *Elites in Latin America,* ed. Seymour M. Lipset and A. Solari. New York, 1967, 301–42.

———. "Perú en los años treinta." In *América Latina en los años treinta,* ed. Pablo González Casanova. Mexico City, 1977, 239–304.

Quiroz, Alfonso W. *La deuda defraudada.* Lima, 1987.

———. *Domestic and Foreign Finance in Modern Peru, 1850–1950: Financing Visions of Development.* Pittsburgh, Pa., 1993.

———. "Estructura económica y desarrollos regionales de la clase dominante, 1821–1850." In *Independencia y revolución, 1780–1840,* ed. Alberto Flores Galindo. 2 vols. Lima, 1987, 201–65.

———. "Financial Development in Peru under Agrarian Export Influence, 1884–1950." *Americas* 47.4 (1990): 447–76.

Raimondi, Antonio. *Notas de viajes para su obra "El Perú"* 4 vols. Lima, 1942.

———. *El Perú.* 5 vols. Lima, 1965–66.

Ramírez, Susan. *Provincial Patriarchs: Land Tenure and the Economics of Power in Colonial Peru.* Albuquerque, N. Mex., 1986.

Ramírez Gaston, José M. *150 años, economía y finanzas en el Perú, 1821–1971 y en el virreinato, 1544–1824.* Lima, 1974.

Ransom, Roger, and Richard Sutch. *One Kind of Freedom: The Economic Consequences of Emancipation.* Cambridge, 1977.

Rao, C. H. H. "Uncertainty, Entrepreneurship, and Sharecropping in India." *Journal of Political Economy* 79.4 (1971): 578–95.

Reátegui Chávez, Wilson. *La Guerra del Pacífico.* 2 vols. Lima, 1979, 1984.

———. "Movimientos campesinos en La Mar e Ica." *Campesino* 1.2 (1969): 18–30.

Reid, Joseph D., Jr., "Sharecropping and Agricultural Uncertainty." *Economic Development and Cultural Change* 24.4 (1976): 549–76.

———. "Sharecropping in History and Theory." *Agricultural History* 49.2 (1975): 426–40.

———. "Sharecropping as an Understandable Market Response: The Post-bellum South." *Journal of Economic History* 33.3 (1973): 106–130.

Revista de Agricultura. Lima.

Riley, James D. "Crown Law and Rural Labor in New Spain: The Status of *Gañanes* during the Eighteenth Century." *Hispanic American Historical Review* 64.2 (1984): 259–86.

Rivero, Francisco de. *Memoria o sean apuntamientos sobre la industria agrícola del Perú y sobre algunos medios que pudieran adoptarse para remediar su decadencia.* Lima, 1845.

Rodríguez Dulanto, A. M. *Agricultura nacional: primera conferencia dada en la Sociedad Nacional de Agricultura.* Lima, 1904.

Rodríguez Pastor, Humberto. "Asiáticos en el agro y en pueblos costeños peruanos." *Debate agrario* 12 (1991): 11–39.

———. "Caqui: hacienda del valle de Chancay." Thesis, Universidad Nacional Mayor de San Marcos, Lima, 1965.

———. *Hijos del celeste imperio en el Perú (1850–1900). migración, agricultura, mentalidad y explotación.* Lima, 1989.

———. "El inmigrante chino en el mercado laboral peruano, 1850–1930." *HISLA* 13–14 (1989): 93–147.

———. *La rebelión de los rostros pintados.* Lima, 1977.

———. *Trabajadores chinos de la Hacienda Palto.* Manuscript, Lima, n.d.

Romero, Emilio. *Historia económica del Perú.* Buenos Aires, 1949.

Rosdolsky, Roman. *The Making of Marx's Capital.* Trans. Pete Burgess. London, 1980.

Roseberry, William. "Beyond the Agrarian Question in Latin America" in *Confronting Historical Paradigms: Peasants, Labor, and the Capitalist World System in Africa and Latin America,* ed. Steve Stern et al. Madison, 1993.

———. *Coffee and Capitalism in the Venezuelan Andes.* Austin, Tex., 1983.

———. "La Falta de Brazos: Land and Labor in the Coffee Economies of Nineteenth-Century Latin America." *Theory and Society*" 20.3 (1991): 351–82.

———. "Hegemony and the Language of Contention." In *Everyday Forms of State Formation: Revolution and the Negotiation of Rule in Modern Mexico,* ed. G. Joseph and D. Nugent. Durham, N.C., 1995, 355–66.

——. "Images of the Peasant in the Consciousness of the Venezuelan Proletariat." In *Proletarians and Protest. The Roots of Class Formation in an Industrializing World,* ed. Michael Hanagan and Charles Stephanson. New York, 1986, 149–69.

——. "Rent, Differentiation, and the Development of Capitalism among Peasants." *American Anthropologist* 78.1 (March 1976): 45–58.

Rose Jibaja, Jorge. "El algodón en el Perú." *Revista de la Facultad de Ciencias Económicas y Comerciales* 31 (1944): 144–70.

Rosenfeld, A. H., and C. F. Jones. "The Cotton Industry of Peru." *Economic Geography* 4 (1927): 507–23.

Rossell Castro, Alberto. *Historia regional de Ica: época colonial.* Lima, 1964.

Rudé, George. *Ideology and Popular Protest.* New ed. Chapel Hill, N.C., 1995.

Saha, Panchanan. *Emigration of Indian Labour, 1834–1900.* Delhi, 1970.

Salas, Miriam. "Los obrajes huamanguinos y sus interconexiones con otros sectores económicos en el centro-sur peruano a fines del siglo xviii." In *The Economies of Mexico and Peru during the Late Colonial Period, 1760–1810,* ed. Nils Jacobsen and Hans-Jürgen Puhle. Berlin, 1986, 203–33.

Sallnow, Michael J. "Cooperation and Contradiction: The Dialectics of Everyday Practice." *Dialectical Anthropology* 14 (1989): 241–57.

Salvucci, Richard J. *Textiles and Capitalism in Mexico.* Princeton, N.J., 1987.

Samaniego, Carlos. "Peasant Movements at the Turn of the Century and the Rise of the Independent Famer." In *Peasant Cooperation and Capitalist Expansion in Central Peru,* ed. Norman Long and Bryan Roberts. Austin, Tex., 1978, 45–71.

Santos de Quiroz, Mariano. *Colección de leyes, decretos y órdenes publicados en el Perú desde su independencia en el año 1821 hasta 1851.* 12 vols. Lima, 1831–1853.

Saulniers, Alfred, and Julio Revilla. "The Economic Role of the Peruvian State: 1821–1919." Paper presented at the Latin American Studies Association conference, Mexico City, September 1983.

Sayer, Derek. "Everyday Forms of State Formation: Some Dissident Remarks on 'Hegemony.'" In *Everyday Forms of State Formation,* ed. G. Joseph and D. Nugent. 366–78.

Scarborough, William K. *The Overseer: Plantation Management in the Old South.* Athens, Ga. Reprint 1984.

Schneider, Harold K. *Economic Man: The Anthropology of Economics.* New York, 1974.

Schuler, Monica. *"Alas, Alas, Kongo": A Social History of Indentured African Immigration into Jamaica, 1841–1865.* Baltimore, Md., 1980.

Schultz, Theodore W. *Transforming Traditional Agriculture.* New Haven, Conn., 1964.

Scott, James C. *Domination and the Arts of Resistance: Hidden Transcripts.* New Haven, Conn., 1990.

——. "Everyday Forms of Resistance." *Journal of Peasant Studies* 13.2 (1986): 5–35.

———. "Hegemony and the Peasantry." *Politics and Society* 7.3 (1977): 262–96.

———. *The Moral Economy of the Peasant: Rebellion and Subsistence in Southeast Asia.* New Haven, Conn., 1976.

———. "Revolution in the Revolution: Peasants and Consciousness." *Theory and Society* 7.1–2 (1979): 97–134.

———. *Weapons of the Weak.* New Haven, Conn., 1985.

Scott, Joan W. "Gender: A Useful Category of Historical Analysis." *American Historical Review* 91.5 (1986): 1053–75.

Scott, Rebecca J. "Defining the Boundaries of Freedom in the World of Cane: Cuba, Brazil and Louisiana after Emancipation." *American Historical Review* 99.1 (1994): 70–102.

Segall, Marcelo. "Esclavitud y tráfico de culíes en Chile." *Journal of Inter-American Studies* 10.1 (1968): 117–33.

Sen, Amartya K. *Behaviour and the Concept of Preference.* London, 1971.

———. *Inequality Reexamined.* Cambridge, Mass., 1992.

———. *The Standard of Living.* New York, 1987.

Sennett, Richard. *Authority.* New York, 1980.

Shanin, Teodor. "Defining Peasants: Conceptualizations and De-Conceptualizations Old and New in a Marxist Debate." *Peasant Studies* 8.4 (1979): 38–60.

———. *Defining Peasants: Essays Concerning Rural Societies, Expolary Economies, and Learning from Them in the Contemporary World.* Oxford, 1990.

———. "The Nature and Logic of the Peasant Economy: A Generalization." *Journal of Peasant Studies* 1.1 (1973): 63–80.

———. "Peasantry: Delineation of a Sociological Concept and A Field of Study." *European Journal of Sociology* 12 (1971): 289–300.

———, ed. *Peasants and Peasant Societies: Selected Readings.* Harmondsworth, U.K., 1971.

———, ed. *The Rules of the Game: Cross-Disciplinary Essays on Models in Scholarly Thought.* London, 1972.

Silva Santisteban, Fernando. *Los obrajes en el virreinato del Perú.* Lima, 1964.

Silverman, Sydel. "The Peasant Concept in Anthropology." *Journal of Peasant Studies* 7.1 (1979): 49–69.

Singelman, Peter. "The Closing Triangle: Critical Notes on a Model for Peasant Mobilization in Latin America." *Comparative Studies in Society and History* 17.4 (1975): 389–409.

———. "Establishing a Trail in the Labyrinth." *Latin American Research Review* 26.1 (1991): 152–55.

Skocpol, Theda. "What Makes Peasants Revolutionary?" In *Power and Protest in the Countryside: Studies of Rural Unrest in Asia, Europe, and Latin America,* ed. R. P. Weller and S. E. Guggenheim. Durham, N.C., 1982, 157–79.

Slatta, Richard W. *Bandidos: The Varieties of Latin American Banditry.* New York, 1987.

———. "Bandits and Rural Social History: A Comment on Joseph." *Latin American Research Review* 26.1 (1991): 145–51.

Smith, Gavin. *Livelihood and Resistance: Peasants and the Politics of Land in Peru.* Berkeley, Calif., 1989.

———. "Socio-economic Differentiation and Relations of Production among Rural-Based Petty Producers in Central Peru, 1880–1970." *Journal of Peasant Studies* 6.3 (1979): 286–310.

Smith, Raymond E. *Kinship Ideology and Practice in Latin America.* Chapel Hill, N.C., 1984.

Sociedad Nacional Agraria. *Como se produce el algodón en el Perú.* Lima, 1936.

Spalding, Karen. "Class Structure in the Southern Peruvian Highlands." In *Land and Power in Latin America,* ed. Benjamin Orlove and Glynn Custred. New York, 1980, 79–98.

———. *Huarochirí: An Andean Society under Inca and Spanish Rule.* Stanford, Calif., 1984.

———. "*Kurakas* and Commerce: A Chapter in the Evolution of Andean Society." *Hispanic American Historical Review* 53.4 (1973): 581–99.

Stavenhagen, Rodolfo. *Social Classes in Agrarian Societies.* Garden City, N.J., 1975.

Stein, Stanley J. *The Brazilian Cotton Manufacture: Textile Enterprise in an Underdeveloped Area, 1850–1950.* Cambridge, Mass., 1975.

———. *Vassouras: A Brazilian Coffee County, 1850–1900.* Cambridge, Mass., 1957.

Stein, Stanley J., and Barbara H. Stein. *The Colonial Heritage of Latin America: Essays on Economic Dependence in Perspective.* New York, 1970.

Stein, Steve. *La crisis del estado patrimonial.* Lima, 1988.

———. *Lima obrera, 1900–1930.* Vol. 1. Lima, 1986.

———. *Populism in Peru.* Madison, Wis., 1980.

Stepan, Nancy Leys. *The "Hour of Eugenics": Race, Gender, and Nation in Latin America.* Ithaca, N.Y., 1991.

Stern, Steve J. "Feudalism, Capitalism, and the World-System in the Perspective of Latin America and the Caribbean." *American Historical Review* 93.4 (1988): 829–72.

———. *Peru's Indian Peoples and the Challenge of Spanish Conquest: Huamanga to 1640.* Madison, Wis., 1982.

———. "Reply: 'Ever More Solitary.'" *American Historical Review* 93.4 (1988): 886–97.

———, ed. *Resistance, Rebellion, and Consciousness in the Andean Peasant World, 18th to 20th Centuries.* Madison, Wis., 1987.

Stewart, Watt. *Chinese Bondage in Peru: A History of the Chinese Coolie in Peru, 1849–1874.* Durham, N.C. 1951.

Stiglich, Germán. *Diccionario geográfico del Perú.* Lima, 1922.

Stinchcombe, Arthur L. "Agricultural Enterprise and Rural Class Relations." *American Journal of Sociology* 67.2 (1961): 65–76.

Street, James H. "Mechanizing the Cotton Harvest." *Annual Report of the*

Board of Regents, the Smithsonian Institution. Publication No. 43, Washington, D.C., 1958, 413–27.

Tandeter, Enrique. "Forced and Free Labor in Late Colonial Potosí." *Past and Present* 93 (1981): 98–136.

Tantaleán Arbulú, Javier "Política, técnicas e instrumentos económicos del Estado, Perú, 1821–1879." *Economía* 11–12 (1983): 47–112.

Tarrillo, Héctor B. Bustamante. "Formas de trabajo—remuneraciones—balances de Pago en la Hacienda 'Palto' en los años 1946–1947" (manuscript, Universidad de San Marcos, October 4, 1974).

Taylor, Lewis. *Bandits and Politics in Peru: Landlord and Peasant Violence in Hualgayoc 1900–1930.* Cambridge, U.K., 1983.

——. *Cambios capitalistas en las haciendas cajamarquinas, 1900–1935.* Centre of Latin American Studies, University of Cambridge, Working Paper No. 39, July 1983.

Taylor, William B. *Drinking, Homicide and Rebellion in Colonial Mexican Villages.* Stanford, Calif., 1979.

——. *Landlord and Peasant in Colonial Oaxaca.* Stanford, Calif., 1972.

Taussig, Michael. *The Devil and Commodity Fetishism in South America.* Chapel Hill, N.C., 1980.

Tenenbaum, Barbara A. *The Politics of Penury: Debt and Taxes in Mexico, 1821–1856.* Albuquerque, N. Mex., 1986.

Tepaske, John Jay. "La crisis financiera del virreinato de Nueva España a fines de la colonia." *Secuencia. Revista de Historia y Ciencias Sociales* 19 (January–April 1991): 123–40.

——. "General Tendencies and Secular Trends in the Economies of Mexico and Peru, 1750–1810: The View from the *Cajas* of Mexico and Lima." In *The Economies of Mexico and Peru during the Late Colonial Period, 1760–1810,* ed. Nils Jacobsen and Hans-Jürgen Puhle. Berlin, 1986, 316–39.

——, ed. *Research Guide to Andean History: Bolivia, Chile, Ecuador, and Peru.* Durham, N.C., 1981.

——. *The Royal Treasuries of the Spanish Empire in America.* Vol. 1: *Peru.* Durham, N.C., 1982.

Thompson, E. P. "Eighteenth-Century English Society: Class Struggle without Class?" *Social History* 3.2 (1978): 133–65.

——. *The Making of the English Working Class.* New York, 1966.

——. "The Moral Economy of the English Crowd in the Eighteenth Century." *Past and Present* 50 (1971): 76–136.

——. "Patrician Society, Plebeian Culture." *Journal of Social History* 8.1 (1974): 382–405.

——. "Time, Work Discipline and Industrialism." *Past and Present* 38 (1967): 56–97.

——. *Whigs and Hunters: The Origin of the Black Act.* London, 1977.

Thompson, Stephen I. "Assimilation and Non-assimilation of Asian-Americans and Asian Peruvians." *Comparative Studies in Society and History* 21.4 (1979): 572–88.

Thorp, Rosemary. *Latin America in the 1930s: The Role of the Periphery in the World Crisis.* New York, 1984.

Thorp, Rosemary, and Geoff Bertram. *Growth and Policy in an Open Economy: Peru, 1890–1977.* New York, 1977.

Thurner, Mark. *From Two Republics to One Divided: Contradictions of Postcolonial Nationmaking in Andean Peru.* Durham, N.C., 1997.

———. "'Republicanos' and 'la Comunidad de Peruanos': Unimagined Political Communities in Postcolonial Andean Peru." *Journal of Latin American Studies* 27.2 (1995): 291–318.

Tilly, Charles. "Talking Modern." *Peasant Studies* 6.2 (1977): 66–67.

Tolmos, Marcos, Luis. *Síntesis monográfica de la provincia de Chincha.* Chincha Alta, Peru, 1963.

Tullis, F. Lamond. *Lord and Peasant in Peru: A Paradigm of Political and Social Change.* Cambridge, Mass., 1970.

Tutino, John. *From Insurrection to Revolution in Mexico: Social Bases of Agrarian Violence, 1750–1940.* Princeton, N.J., 1986.

Ugarte, César Antonio. *Historia económica del Perú.* Lima, 1926.

Vance, Rupert V. *Human Factors in Cotton Culture.* Chapel Hill, N.C., 1929.

Vanden, Harry E. *Nationalist Marxism in Latin America: José Carlos Mariátegui's Thought and Politics.* Boulder, Colo., 1986.

van den Berghe, Pierre L., ed. *Class and Ethnicity in Peru.* Leiden, 1974.

———. "The Use of Ethnic Terms in the Peruvian Social Sciences Literature." *International Journal of Comparative Sociology* 3–4 (1974): 132–42.

van den Berghe, Pierre L., and George P. Primov. *Inequality in the Peruvian Andes: Classes and Ethnicity in Cuzco.* Columbia, Mo., 1977.

Vandergeest, Peter. "Commercialization and Commoditization: A Dialogue between Perspectives." *Sociologia Ruralis* 38.1 (1988): 7–29.

Vanderghem, Jorge. *Memorias presentadas al Ministerio de Fomento del Perú sobre diversos viajes emprendidos en varias regiones de la República.* Lima, 1902.

Van Young, Eric. *Hacienda and Market in Eighteenth-Century Mexico: The Rural Economy of the Guadalajara Region, 1675–1820.* Berkeley, Calif., 1981.

———. "Quetzalcóatl, King Ferdinand, and Ignacio Allende Go to the Seashore; or Messianism and Mystical Kingship in Mexico, 1800–1821." In *The Independence of Mexico and the Creation of the New Nation,* ed. Jaime E. Rodríguez O. Los Angeles, 1989, 109–28.

Villar Córdova, Sócrates. "La institución del yanacona en el incanato." *Nueva crónica* 1 (Lima, 1966): 18–23.

Vince, John N. T. *Old Farm Tools.* Aylesbury, England, 1974.

Viotti da Costa, Emilia. *The Brazilian Empire: Myths and Histories.* Chicago, 1985.

———. "Experiences vs. Structures: New Tendencies in the History of Labor and the Working Class in Latin America — What Do We Gain? What Do We Lose?" *International Labor and Working Class History* 36 (1989): 3–24.

Wachtel, Nathan. *The Vision of the Vanquished: The Spanish Conquest through Indian Eyes, 1530–1570.* Trans. Ben and Sian Reynolds. New York, 1983.

Walker, Charles. "El estudio del campesinado en las ciencias sociales peruanas: avances, limitaciones y nuevas perspectivas." *Allpanchis* 21.33 (1989): 161–208.

———. "Montoneras, bandoleros, malhechores: criminalidad y politica en las primeras décadas republicanas." In *Bandoleros, abigeos y montoneras: criminalidad y violencia en el Perú, siglos xviii–xx,* ed. Carlos Aguirre and Charles Walker. Lima, 1990, 105–36.

Wallerstein, Immanuel. "Comments on Stern's Critical Tests." *American Historical Review* 93.4 (1988): 873–85.

———. *Mercantilism and the Consolidation of the European World-Economy, 1600–1750.* New York, 1980.

———. *The Modern World System: Capitalist Agriculture and the Origins of the European World-Economy in the Sixteenth Century.* New York, 1974.

———. *The Second Era of Great Expansion of the Capitalist World-Economy, 1730–1840s.* San Diego, Calif., 1989.

Warman, Arturo. *"We Come to Object": The Peasants of Morelos and the National State.* Trans. Stephen K. Ault. Baltimore, Md., 1980.

Weiner, Jonathan M. "Class Structure and Economic Development in the American South, 1865–1955" (with commentary by R. Higgs and H. Woodman and reply by Weiner). *American Historical Review* 84.4 (1979): 970–1006.

Weller, Robert P., and Scott E. Guggenheim, eds. *Power and Protest in the Countryside: Rural Unrest in Asia, Europe, and Latin America.* Durham, N.C., 1982.

Wells, Allen, and Gilbert M. Joseph. "Structure of Domination and Forms of Resistance on Yucatecan Estates during the Late Porfiriato, ca 1880–1915." In *Plantation Workers,* ed. Brij Lal, Doug Munro, and Edward D. Beechert. Honolulu, 1993, 241–96.

Werlich, David. *Peru: A Short History.* Carbondale, Ill., 1978.

Wightman, Ann M. *Indigenous Migration and Social Change: The Forasteros of Cuzco, 1520–1720.* Durham, N.C., 1990.

Whiteford, Scott. *Workers from the North: Plantations, Bolivian Labor, and the City in Northwest Argentina.* Austin, Tex., 1981.

Williams, Raymond. *The Country and the City.* London, 1973.

———. *Keywords: A Vocabulary of Culture and Society.* New York, 1976.

Winn, Peter. *Weavers of Revolution: The Yarur Workers and Chile's Road to Socialism.* New York, 1986.

Witt, Heinrich. *Diario y observaciones sobre el Perú (1824–1890).* Trans. Kika Garland de Montero. Lima, 1987.

Wolf, Eric R. *Europe and the People without History.* Berkeley, Calif., 1982.

———. *Peasants.* Englewood Cliffs, N.J., 1966.

———. *Peasant Wars of the Twentieth Century.* New York, 1969.

———. "Types of Latin American Peasantry: A Preliminary Discussion." *American Anthropologist.* 57.3 (1955): 452–71.

Womack, Jr., John. "Mariátegui, Marxism, and Nationalism." *Marxist Perspectives* (summer 1980): 170–74.

———. *Zapata and the Mexican Revolution.* New York, 1968.

Wong, Bernard. "A Comparative Study of the Assimilation of the Chinese in New York City and Lima, Peru." *Comparative Studies in Society and History* 20.3 (1978): 335–57.

Woodman, Harold D. "Sequel to Slavery: The New History Views the Postbellum South." *Journal of Southern History* 34.4 (1977): 523–54.

Wright, Gavin. "Cheap Labor and Southern Textiles before 1880." *Journal of Economic History* 39.3 (1979): 655–80.

Wright, Thomas C. *Landowners and Reform in Chile: The Sociedad Nacional de Agricultura, 1919–1940.* Urbana, Ill., 1982.

Yen, Ching-huang. *Coolies and Mandarins.* Singapore, 1985.

Yepes del Castillo, Ernesto. *Perú 1820–1920: un siglo de desarrollo capitalista.* Lima, 1972.

Zaldívar, Ramón [pseud.]. "Agrarian Reform and Military Reformism in Peru." In *Agrarian Reform and Agrarian Reformism: Studies of Peru, Chile, China, and India.* London, 1974, 25–70.

Zapatero Puch, C. "Informe relativo a las provincias de Chincha y Pisco." *Boletín del Ministerio de Fomento* 3.3 (1905): 47–57.

INDEX

Absentee landowners, xiv–xv, 1, 14–15, 18–20, 22, 23, 42–43, 97, 102, 157; and plantation security, 115–17. *See also* Planters
Acevedo, Tomás, 19, 81, 83, 85–86, 89, 106
Administrators. *See* Managers
Advance. *See* Credit
Advíncula, Gerardo, 81, 82, 89, 106
Afro-Peruvians, 13, 16, 34, 35, 40–43, 48, 50, 51, 53, 55, 157. *See also* Compañeros; Journaleros; Yanaconas
Albizuri, Luis, 71, 204 n.11
Alcántara, Maximillano, 118, 147, 193 n.16
APRA (Alianza Popular Revolucionaria Americana). *See* Political protest
Arrendatarios, 30, 61–64, 86–87, 97, 101, 104; distinguished from compañeros, 74–77, 105–8; rebellion, 83–84. *See also* Fixed-rent tenants; Rent; Tenants; Yanaconas
Aspíllaga Anderson, Antero, 136–37
Aspíllaga Anderson, Edmundo R., 194 n.31
Aspíllaga family, xii, 67, 128–29, 177–78 n.2; business holdings, 17, 18–20; Antero, 29–30, 32, 38; Ismael, 19, 42–43, 196 n.56; Ramón, 17, 18, 89, 178 n.3
Ayate, 45–46. *See also* Enganche; Labor agents

Banco Agrícola, 115, 148
Bandits, 5, 26–28, 36, 47, 180 n.22
Bauer, Arnold, 12, 171 n.8, 200 n.25

Blanchard, Peter, 116, 172 n.2, 182 n.4
Bringas, José, 71, 102
Buteler, Gustavo, 64, 67, 106

Caballero, José María, xiv, 169 n.4, 196 n.58, 199 n.19, 201 n.29
Cáceres, Andrés, 28
Campesinos, 5–7. *See also* Arrendatarios; Compañeros; Fixed-rent tenants; Jornaleros; Peasants; Rural labor; Sharecroppers; Tenants; Yanaconas
Capelo, Joaquín, 29
Capitalist world economy, xvi
Castro Pozo, Hildebrando, 166, 196 n.58, 205 n.23
Castrovirreyna province, 61, 112
Cattle, 30, 65–66, 83, 90–91, 102, 118, 120, 139, 150, 193 n.8, 194 n.18, 198 n.8; as form of savings, 88, 95–97; vs. machines, 113–14
Caucato, Hacienda, 38
Cayaltí, Hacienda, 18
Census data, Peru, 13
Centralization. *See* Ginning
Cerdeña, Nestor, 9, 65–66
Chacra, 85, 86
Child labor, 89, 118, 128, 133, 142–43, 146–47, 156
Civil War of 1894–1895, 32–33, 163, 180 n.28; Nicolás de Piérola and, 28, 29
Coercion, xv, 16, 53, 55, 67, 161
Comisario, 24, 28
Communists. *See* Political protest
Compadrazgo. *See* Kinship

Compañeros (compañía), 65, 85–86, 96–97, 101, 105, 107, 113, 116, 126, 127, 128, 159; hired by arrendatarios, 74–76; rights and responsibilities, 57; and wage labor, 59–60; as partners of the manager, 122; as yanaconas, 111–12. *See also* Sharecroppers; Tenants; Yanaconas

Contractees, 26, 35–40, 48–49; and day laborers, 40–44; resistance by, 50, 52

Contracts, 8, 10–11, 16, 34–35, 37–39, 43–45, 50–51, 57–58, 63–66, 85–86, 99–101, 127, 160, 166–67, 187 n.5. *See also* Tenants

Correspondence: managers and owners, 22

Cotton, xi, xiii, 14–19, 22–23, 25–26, 31–41, 47, 51, 54–60, 66, 69, 72, 82, 85–91, 94–95, 113–16, 117, 120–21, 123–24, 125, 134–36, 138, 143, 149–50, 153, 163–64, 178 n.7, 181 n.33, 185–86 n.40, 187 n.2, 198 n.15; boom periods, 15, 41–43; and cost of labor, 127–30; and double-cropping, 97, 99, 102, 110–11

Couturier, Edith, 12

Credit (habilitación), xvi, 8, 58, 68–73, 85, 88, 93–95, 100–103, 105, 114–15, 118–21, 124–25, 139, 142, 149, 160–61, 190 n.32; Banco Agrícola and, 115; debt peonage and, 151–52; tambo and, 188–21; *See also* Esquivel, Juan

Creole culture, 155, 156, 172 n.2, 206 n.2

Customary rights, 96–97

Debt peonage, 9–10, 15, 59, 66, 70, 73, 80, 85, 93–94, 110, 120, 139, 142, 149, 151, 153, 160–62, 187 n.5

Del Solar, Vicente, 22, 29, 30

Díaz, Agapito, 116

Drainage problem, 67, 79, 82, 93, 98, 100, 123, 144–45, 150; arrendatario view of, 87–88

Duncan, Kenneth, 11, 172 n.2, 176 n.20

Duncan Fox Ltd., 115

Education: on the plantations, 142–43

Enganchador. *See* Labor agents

Enganche, 101–2, 119, 145–46, 160, 162, 201 n.26; and debt, 45–46; Ismael Aspíllaga on, 42–43

Enticements. *See* Rent

Esquivel, Juan, 89–92, 97, 104, 105, 106, 146, 163, 193 n.16, 194 n.18, 196 n.56

Ferreira, Luis, 72

Fertilizer, 118–19, 199 n.21, 200 nn.22–24; and soil quality, 117

Field labor, 17, 138–39, 145. *See also* Jornaleros; Migrant laborers; Rural labor; Wages

Fixed-rent tenants, 70, 71, 73, 76–77, 79, 82, 83; contracts of 1894, 62–66; manager opposed to, 85–86, 88–89. *See also* Arrendatarios; Rent; Tenants

Floods, 76–77, 82; in 1907, 81; in 1910, 91; in 1925, 126–27

Franco, Daniel: the elder, 67, 68, 106, 156, 202 n.1; the younger, 133

Freehold peasantry, 7–8

Freyre, Gilberto, 1

Gamonales, 13

Gañanes, 61

García, Adrián, 64, 79

García y García, Aurelio, 25

Gibson, Charles, 12

Gilbert, Dennis, 14

Ginning, 114–16, 198 n.15

Golden age of cotton, 138

Gómez, Máximo, 116

Gonzales, Michael, 14, 23

Guerrero, Flavio, 67, 68, 106

Guha, Ranajit, xvi, 171 n.10–11

Gutiérrez, Joaquín, 89, 92, 156, 193 n.11

Hegemony, xvi, 14, 18, 25, 32, 157, 164, 165, 167, 170 n.6, 206–7 n.10; and resistance, 158, 164–66, 167, 170 n.6, 206–7 n.10
Hobsbawm, Eric, 9
Horton, Douglas, 9
Hunt, Shane, 9, 14, 174–75 n.13

Ica, 28
Inca: currency, 47, 48, 50, 51
Indenture, xiii, 23–24, 36, 37, 182–83 n.5, 183 nn.8–9, 186 nn.44–45
Islas, Nicanor, 64, 68, 106

Jornaleros, 7, 37, 40–42, 44–49, 52–54. *See also* Afro-Peruvians; Campesinos; Field Labor; Migrant Laborers; Rural labor; Tenants; Wages
Joseph, Gilbert M., 180 n.22
Juez de primera instancia, 24
Justice, 58; and peasant resistance, 62

Kinship, xiv, 21, 87–88, 107–8, 189 n.17, 193 n.9, 201 n.29, 205 n.28
Klaren, Peter, 9, 12, 116, 197 n.58
Knight, Alan, xvi, 158, 171 n.9, 200 n.25

Labor agents (enganchadores), 44
Landowners. *See* Absentee landowners; Planters
Lears, T. J. Jackson, 165, 170 n.6
Leguía, Augusto, 117
Loans. *See* Credit
López Aliaga, Fernando, 118
Luján, Francisco, 81, 106

Macera, Pablo, 9, 174–75 n.13, 178 n.4, 187 n.2
Mallon, Florencia, 13, 170 n.7, 176 n.22
Managers, 1, 6, 11, 15–25, 73, 83, 94, 98; Acevedo, Tomás, 19, 81, 83, 85–86, 89, 106; Alcántara, Maximiliano, 118, 147, 193 n.16; Cerdeña, Nestor, 9, 65–66; favor

compañeros, 85–86; on mechanization, 113
Manrique, Hacienda, 49
Mariátegui, José C., 166, 196 n.58; and criticism of feudalism of yanaconaje, 201 n.26, 203 n.9
Matos Mar, José, 196 n.58, 197 n.59
Mechanization: of cotton agriculture, 112. *See also* Tractors
Mendoza, Dionisio, 67, 68, 107
Migrant laborers, 113, 116–17, 123, 132, 127, 176 n.22, 197 n.4; Chinese, 182–84 nn.5–9; from the highlands, 112; resistance by, 153; wages of, 122
Mintz, Sidney, 170 n.4, 176 n.21, 178 n.4
Mörner, Magnus, 9, 169–70 n.4

National Agrarian Society, 112, 113, 153, 204 n.12

Oligarchy, 14–15, 29, 30–33, 177–78 n.2
Otoya, Pedro, 64, 68, 97, 107

Palmar, xii, 23
Palto (San Francisco Solano de), Hacienda, xi, xvii, 18, 23, 138
Partido Civilista (Civilian Party), 28, 29
Pastures, 65, 69, 86, 96–99, 114
Paternalism, 156, 170–71 n.7
Patron-client trope, xv
Peasants, 7–8, 11–14, 70, 103, 109, 137; resistance of, 158, 160, 165–66, 169–70 n.4, 171 n.8, 173 n.5, 173–74 nn.10–11, 187 n.5; wages of, 148. *See also* Arrendatarios; Campesinos; Compañeros; Fixed-rent tenants; Jornaleros; Migrant laborers; Sharecroppers, Tenants; Yanaconas
Peons de afuera, 104, 112, 125, 196 n.54. *See also* Migrant laborers
Peru, 94, 99, 165; agrarian reform in, xi–xii

Piecework: vs. day labor, xvi, 48, 49. *See also* Wages

Piérola, Nicolás de, 28–30, 163. *See also* Civil War of 1894–1895

Pisco, xi, xvii, 14–21, 24–26, 27, 32, 111; water dispute, 28–30

Planters, 20, 21, 22, 38, 49, 86, 99, 100, 110–11, 149, 154–56, 187 n.2; factions, 26–30; labor strategy, 143–45

Political protest, 103, 137, 142–43, 203 n.9, 205 n.23; and wages, 148, 151, 153, 164–65

Racism, 35, 40, 155, 206 n.2

Ramos, Juan, 67, 68, 107

Rebellion, 26, 165; of 1908, 83–84

Reid, Joseph D., Jr., xiv, 169 n.4, 196 n.58, 199 n.19, 200 n.25

Rent, 8, 11, 44–46, 59, 62–66, 74–77, 86–87, 105–8, 189–90 n.22. *See also* Arrendatarios; Fixed-rent tenants

República aristocrática, 33

Resident labor force, 34, 38–39, 44–45, 52, 80, 108, 123, 130, 162–63

Resistance, xvi, 49–51, 59–62, 158–60, 164, 166–67, 170 n.4, 171 n.9, 188 nn.14–15, 189 n.18; banditry and, 180 n.22

Rodríguez Pastor, Humberto, 182 n.5, 183 n.6, 186 n.45, 197 n.58

Rosas, Polo, 64

Rosas, Silverio, 55

Roseberry, William, 12, 170 n.4, 171 n.9

Rudé, George, 9, 174 n.12

Rural labor, 6–7, 37, 40–41, 99, 173 n.6. *See also* Arrendatarios; Campesinos; Compañeros; Fixed-rent tenants; Jornaleros; Migrant labores; Sharecroppers; Tenants; yanaconas

Rural society, xv, xiii, 5; divisions within, 13. *See also* Arrendatarios; Compañeros; Managers; Tenants; Yanaconas

Rutledge, Ian, 11, 172 n.2, 176 n.20

Salvucci, Richard, 12

San Jacinto, Hacienda, 22

Scarcity of labor, 13, 16, 34, 36–37, 39–41, 42, 50, 53, 75–76, 80, 86, 95, 99, 130–31, 162, 164

Scott, James C., xvi, 49–51, 59–62, 158, 166, 170 n.4, 171 n.9, 189 n.18

Scott, Rebecca J., 155

Scrip, 44–46

Sharecroppers, xvi, 50, 59, 169 n.4, 196 n.58, 199 n.15, 200 n.25. *See also* Arrendatarios; Campesinos; Compañeros; Peasants; Tenants; Yanaconas

Slavery, xiii, 16, 36, 172 n.2, 182 n.4

Smith (also Alderson-Smith), Gavin, 13, 116, 176 n.22, 187 n.5

Socialists. *See* Political protest

Sociedad Nacional Agraria. *See* National Agrarian Society

Soil exhaustion, 117–18

Stocks: on the plantations, xv, 156

Strikes (labor): in 1882–1883, 50

Subalterns, 11, 54–56, 189 n.18

Subdelegado de aguas, 24

Sub-rent. *See* Sub-yanaconas

Sub-yanaconas, 74–75, 107, 150–51, 201 n.29

Sugar-growing regions, 134

Sur chico, 16, 33–34, 136, 177 n.29

Tambo (plantation store), 26, 45, 118–20, 200 n.25, 201 n.28

Tangüis, Fermin, 22, 81, 185–86 n.40, 198–99 n.16

Tenant-planter dispute, 68–69, 78

Tenants, xiv, xvi, 30, 87–88, 96–97, 100, 102, 125, 143, 162–63; contracts, 187 n.5. *See also* Arrendatarios; Compañeros; Contracts; Fixed-rent Tenants; Yanaconas

Thompson, E. P., 9, 174 n.12

Thorp, Rosemary; and G. Bertram, 14, 134–35, 148

Thurner, Mark, 31, 32

Tractors, 112–14, 198 n.7

Treaty of Tientsin (1874), 37

Triangulation (theory of social dynamics), 84

Urrutia, Hacienda, 22

Van Young, Eric, 12
Velasco Alvarado, Juan, xii
Venn Vargas, 71

Wages, 10, 47–48, 50–51, 71, 161–66, 194 n.30. *See also* Jornaleros; Peasants; Rural labor; Tenants; Yanaconas
War of the Pacific: in Peru, xiii; in the Pisco valley, 25–27, 186 n.47
Water law of 1902, 32–33, 187 n.32

Williams, Raymond, 167
Wolf, Eric, 169 n.4, 171 n.8, 178 n.4
Women heads of household, 189 n.16
World War I, 94–95

Yanaconas (yanacón, yanaconaje), 82, 93, 101–2, 120, 123, 127, 128, 131, 132, 136, 138, 145, 152, 192 n.3, 196 n.2; compañeros and, 121–22; debts and flight, 124–26; family labor, 146, 147; resistance, 153, 164–66; types of, 110–12, 113; varied roles, 148–50; wage labor, 124, 149–51. *See also* Arrendatarios; Compañeros, Fixed-rent tenants; Peasants; Tenants

Vincent C. Peloso is Associate Professor in the Department
of History at Howard University. He is the editor (with
Barbara A. Tennebaum) of *Liberals, Politics, and Power:
State Formation in Nineteenth-Century Latin America.*

Library of Congress Cataloging-in-Publication Data

Peloso, Vincent C.
Peasants on plantations : subaltern strategies of labor
and resistance in the Pisco Valley, Peru / Vincent C.
Peloso.
p.   cm.
Includes bibliographical references and index.
ISBN 0-8223-2229-3 (cloth : alk. paper). —
ISBN 0-8223-2246-3 (paper : alk. paper)
1. Cotton plantation workers — Peru — Pisco River
Valley — History.   2. Peasantry — Peru — Pisco River
Valley — History.   3. Cotton trade — Peru — Pisco River
Valley — Personnel management — History.
4. Industrial relations — Peru — Pisco River Valley —
History.   I. Title.
HD8039.C662P416   1999
306.3'49 — dc21   98-27846